J.-K. Huysmans
Novelist, Poet, and Art Critic

Studies in the Fine Arts: Criticism, No. 19

Donald B. Kuspit, Series Editor

Professor of Art History
State University of New York at Stony Brook

Other Titles in This Series

No. 16   *Vermeer: Consciousness and the Chamber of Being*   Martin Pops

No. 17   *Modernism in the 1920s: Interpretations of Modern Art in New York from Expressionism to Constructivism*   Susan Noyes Platt

No. 18   *Aurier's Symbolist Art Criticism and Theory*   Patricia Townley Mathews

No. 20   *Cézanne and Formalism in Bloomsbury*   Beverly H. Twitchell

No. 21   *Matisse's "Notes of a Painter": Criticism, Theory, and Context, 1891–1908*   Roger Benjamin

No. 22   *Postminimalism into Maximalism: American Art, 1966–1986*   Robert Pincus-Witten

J.-K. Huysmans
Novelist, Poet, and Art Critic

by
Annette Kahn

U·M·I Research Press

Ann Arbor, Michigan

Produced and distributed by
UMI Research Press
an imprint of
University Microfilms, Inc.
Ann Arbor, Michigan 48106

Library of Congress Cataloging in Publication Data

Kahn, Annette, 1943-
J.-K. Huysmans: novelist, poet, and art critic.

(Studies in the fine arts. Criticism ; no. 19)
Revision of thesis (Ph.D.)—Columbia University,
1981.
Bibliography: p.
Includes index.
1. Huysmans, J.-K. (Joris-Karl), 1848-1907—
Criticism and interpretation.   2. Huysmans, J.-K.
(Joris-Karl), 1848-1907—Knowledge—Art.   3. Art in
literature.   4. Art and literature—France.   I. Title.
II. Series.
PQ2309.H4Z636   1987   843'.8   86-30752
ISBN 0-8357-1715-1 (alk. paper)

Contents

Introduction Art versus Reality: Dilemma and Solution   *1*
    The Relationship between Painting and Literature
    Organization and Methodology
    Structural Functions of Art Descriptions
    Criticism

1 The Aesthetic Development of a Novelist Art Critic   *11*

2 The Woman-Haters: Degas, Forain, Rops, and Moreau   *33*
    Manet, 1877
    Degas and Forain, 1879–81
    Degas, Forain, and Rops, 1889
    Moreau
    Chartres Cathedral
    Fra Angelico
    Anonymous Portrait of a Young Girl
    Virgin and Child by the Maître de Flémalle

3 L'Indicible Mélancolie: Raffaëlli and the Impressionists   *67*
    Impressionism
    Raffaëlli
    Le Drageoir aux épices, 1874
    Marthe, 1876
    Les Soeurs Vatard, 1879
    Croquis parisiens, 1880
    En Rade, 1887
    Là-Bas, 1891

4 Redon and the Terrifying World of the Subconscious   *103*
    Odilon Redon
    A Rebours, 1884
    "Cauchemar," 1886

"Damiens," 1886
En Rade, 1887
"Le Monstre," 1889

Conclusion   *133*

Notes   *137*

Select Bibliography   *151*

Index   *157*

Introduction

Art versus Reality: Dilemma and Solution

The Relationship between Painting and Literature

All nineteenth-century Naturalist writing contains detailed, visual descriptions. The distinctive nature of the work of J.-K. Huysmans (1848–1907) is that many of these descriptions can be traced specifically to his experience of the visual arts. Huysmans saw more pictures than even most cultured Parisians, for throughout his literary career he was also an art critic and he collected his most significant articles into three books of art criticism—*L'Art moderne*, 1883, *Certains*, 1889, and *Trois Primitifs*, 1905. This study of his art criticism, his fiction, his prose poems, and some of his extensive correspondence with major literary, artistic, and religious figures of his time illuminates the extent and the nature of the relationship between his knowledge of the visual arts and his literary works. My focus is the specific meeting points, the common ground between his art criticism and his novels and prose poems, which show that his passion for painting altered his perception of reality and that specific paintings provided for him a rich source of materials, especially at those times when he was not satisfied with the depiction of the life he found immediately around him.

The role the visual arts played in the life of Huysmans was encouraged by the artistic environment of the latter part of the nineteenth century, when the general consciousness of the relationship between the visual arts and literature, among writers, painters and critics, was particularly acute. Baudelaire, for instance, who, like Huysmans, wrote both poetry and art criticism, said in his article on Delacroix in 1863 that,

> It is, moreover, one of the significant characteristics of our century's spiritual state that the arts aspire, if not to stand in for one another, at least to mutually lend one another new forces.

> C'est, du reste, un des diagnostics de l'état spirituel de notre siècle que les arts aspirent, si-non à se suppléer l'un l'autre, du moins à se prêter réciproquement des forces nouvelles.[1]

And in 1884 Henry James wrote that "the analogy between the art of the painter and the art of the novelist is, so far as I am able to see, complete."[2] Such an artistic atmosphere, in which there was a general acceptance of the mutuality of interest between the two art forms, allowed for the specifically nineteenth-century phenomenon of novelist and poet art critics, of whom Huysmans was one. These novelists and poets had no inhibitions about writing and publishing art criticism, and the fact that they were esteemed writers added to their prestige as commentators on another art form.

This is not to say that there was a belief in the total equality of the art forms. Both writers and artists frequently made claims for the superiority of their own medium. Huysmans, for instance, in a letter he wrote in 1879 to Edmond de Goncourt to thank him for the "prestigieux *Gavarni*" which Edmond de Goncourt had sent him, writes:

> What a powerful argument to demonstrate the pen's superiority over the brush—when you, for instance, are the one who wields it!—For ultimately, however great they may be, painters in general, locked in as they are within a specialty, do not even try to reach beyond it, but rather keep fiercely to it.

> Quel fier argument pour démontrer la supériorité de la plume sur le pinceau—quand c'est manié par vous, par exemple!—Car enfin, si grands qu'ils soient, généralement les peintres, enfermés dans une spécialité, n'essaient même pas d'en sortir et s'y confinent avec acharnement.[3]

In the novel *En Ménage* Huysmans reiterates this belief that literature is a more effective medium than painting:

> Try, then, to render, with pencil or brush, the particular tone of a neighborhood! Such is not the business of painters, but of men of letters!

> Allez donc rendre, avec un crayon ou avec un pinceau, la note spéciale d'un quartier! Ce n'est pas l'affaire des peintres, c'est celle des hommes de lettres cela![4]

An interesting result of such an attitude is that the highest compliment paid to his favorite painters was that their art approached that of literature. Writing of Gustave Moreau, for instance, he praises "this art which crossed the frontiers of painting to borrow from the writer's art its most subtly evocative suggestions" ("cet art qui franchissait les limites de la peinture, empruntait à l'art d'écrire ses plus subtiles évocations") (*A Rebours,* VII, 90). Degas, on the other hand, wrote that "We say far more with a single stroke than a writer does in a volume" ("En un trait nous en disons plus long qu'un littérateur en un volume").[5]

There is, however, an interesting paradox in Huysmans' theory about the relative superiority of painting and literature. His love of the visual arts gives him an appreciation of the qualities which are peculiar to painting and in his definition of a prose poem, in *A Rebours,* des Esseintes claims that it is the pictorial quality of the poem that makes it the most perfect literary form:

By this means he [Mallarmé] managed to do away with the formal statement of a comparison that the reader's mind made by itself as soon as it had understood the symbol . . . producing, *as in the case of a picture,* a unique and comprehensive impression, an overall view.

Il [Mallarmé] parvenait ainsi, à abolir l'énoncé de la comparaison qui s'établissait . . . par l'analogie, dès qu'il avait pénétré le symbole . . . produisant, *comme pour un tableau par exemple,* un aspect unique et complet, un ensemble. (VII, 298) [my italics]

According to des Esseintes, a prose poem resembles a painting in its purity, conciseness, directness and its clear definition of reality, a reality which Huysmans largely perceived as chaotic, ugly, and frightening; it retains

the substance of a novel, while dispensing with the latter's long-winded analyses and superfluous descriptions . . . In short, the prose poem represented in Des Esseintes' eyes the dry juice, the osmazome of literature, the essential oil of art.

la puissance du roman dont elle supprimait les longueurs analytiques et les superfétations descriptives. . . . En un mot, le poème en prose représentait, pour des Esseintes, le suc concret, l'osmazone de la littérature, l'huile essentielle de l'art. (VII, 301–2).

Huysmans himself began his writing career in 1874 with the publication of a collection of prose poems called *Le Drageoir aux épices,* and it is here that he first tried to emulate painting and to integrate descriptions of paintings into his writing. After these early successes he experimented more frequently with the use of paintings, both in his fiction and in his more complex prose poems of 1880 and 1886. The underlying presumption of this moment in history that all the arts were in some way working towards a common goal was conducive to such integration of pictorial elements in novels and poetry.[6]

This practice of basing passages in his imaginative writing on paintings rather than reality is due partly to Huysmans' Decadent belief that art precedes or, at least, improves on nature. The immediate origins of this attitude can be found in Gautier, who regarded nature as a poor imitation of art, to the extent that

if painters create Nature, writers create morals and manners. . . . Raphael's Madonnas created the Italian women of the sixteenth century, and had it not been for Watteau and his school, the *Régence* would not have existed.

si les peintres font la nature les écrivains font les moeurs. . . . Les Madones de Raphael ont fait les Italiennes du XVI siècle et sans Watteau et son école, la Régence n'eût pas existé.[7]

The Goncourts, to whom Huysmans owes a great deal, were similarly aware of the impact of the visual arts on one's perception of reality and wrote the following as an explanation of artistic metaphors and similes:

It is very much a characteristic of our nature to see nothing in Nature that is not a reminder and a memory of art. No sooner do we see a horse in a stable than one of Géricault's studies takes shape in our minds.

Une chose bien caractéristique de notre nature, c'est de rien voir dans la nature qui ne soit un rappel et un souvenir de l'art. Voici un cheval dans une écurie, aussitôt une étude de Géricault se dessine dans notre cervelle.[8]

This tendency to see reality through art was part of Huysmans' philosophical heritage. Further, one of the characteristics of both Huysmans and his fictional characters was immobility. He hardly travelled beyond his own neighborhood and his protagonists suffered a kind of neurotic passivity which was conducive to daydreaming and looking at art as a means of gaining experience of the world. Huysmans himself was very conscious of the impact of the visual arts on his development, especially the extent to which it influenced his perception of reality and helped him formulate the aesthetic theories in his chosen field of literature.

Organization and Methodology

As a biographical background to the close textual studies which follow, the opening chapter traces Huysmans' development as a writer in the light of his interest in the visual arts.[9] It surveys his role as art critic and continues with an account of the explicit influence of art on his career as writer, starting with his initial inspiration to write on observing the seventeenth-century Dutch paintings in the Louvre, and ending with the formulation of his theory of "spiritual naturalism" ("naturalisme spiritualiste") on seeing a *Crucifixion* by Grünewald. It includes a discussion of Huysmans' concept of "modernity," his confusion of art and reality which led frequently to disillusionment with life, his "aesthetic" conversion to Catholicism, and his attempt to found an artistic monastery.

The next three chapters show the connections between Huysmans' writings on the visual arts and his imaginative writing. My aim is not to give a comprehensive account of Huysmans' art criticism but to discover relationships of content and style between his art criticism and literature. Each chapter focuses on one of the three topics which were of such pressing concern to Huysmans that they colored his outlook on everything—seductive women, melancholy landscape, and fantastic dreams. The chapter on women deals with Huysmans' treatment of Degas, Forain, Rops, Moreau, Chartres Cathedral, and some medieval paintings; it is in Raffaëlli and the Impressionists that Huysmans finds melancholy landscape; and the starting point for Huysmans' treatment of fantastic dreams is the work of Redon.

Huysmans' aesthetic tastes changed radically over the thirty years he wrote art criticism, but his attitudes towards women, nature, and the subconscious changed very little. They can be traced from his early Naturalist period to his late Catholic period and are evidence of a consistent pattern of thinking.

The thematic approach adopted in this study omits, by necessity, the discussion of many artists whom Huysmans admired and about whom he had interesting things to say, but the methodological model which is established in these chapters can be usefully applied to other artists whom he considered significant.

I first analyze the relationship between an existing painting and its description in Huysmans' art criticism. I am not looking at this relationship in order to judge his sensitivity as a critic but am interested in the aspects he chooses to comment on and the imagery he develops.

I then analyze the relationship between an existing painting and a specific text in one of Huysmans' novels or prose poems. Such a text can be an explicit description of an existing, named painting, such as Moreau's *Salomé* in *A Rebours* and Redon's lithographs in the prose poem "Cauchemar." Or it can be an implicit description of a painting in which no painting is alluded to by name, yet where there are textual indications that the description is indeed based on a painting. Intuitive, impressionistic comparisons of subject matter or style are not sufficient evidence and are mere speculations based on a reader's knowledge of art. I show that there are many cases where Huysmans gives signs within the text that he is about to introduce a description which is distinguishable from the rest of the narrative and frequently different in style. Ironically, these descriptions often contain more "action" than the narrative into which they are inserted. Moreover, we are constantly finding a coincidence of imagery between Huysmans' art criticism and his fiction, which to the informed critic, at least, proves a mutual influence of the way Huysmans perceives paintings when looking at them as a critic and his perception of reality which he expresses in his literature.

Structural Functions of Art Descriptions

I am not only interested in showing how Huysmans leaned heavily on his experience of paintings for his material in his imaginative writing. Huysmans' work contains fascinating variations on the different functions in literature of descriptions of art and, although a comprehensive study of such functions is beyond the scope of this study, I shall comment on those areas where such a discussion seems particularly relevant.

There are three broad categories of functions of descriptions of art. The first is to add veracity to a Realist text, since allusions to anything partaking of history place the novel or prose poem in a specific time and milieu. A description of a painting in fiction, especially when the artist and title are specified, is also a Naturalist detail which gives information about the taste and personality of the character who owns the work. In *Là-Bas,* 1891, for instance, Huysmans mentions that hanging in Durtal's room are reproductions of Botticelli's *Virgin and Child* and Breughel's *The Wise and Foolish Virgins.* The mixture of religious sentiment and sensuality found in these works reveals the inner conflict of Durtal himself.

Sometimes, a mere allusion to a particular style of painting can be an expression of an aesthetic ideal. In the novel *Marthe,* 1876, for instance, Huysmans describes the female fantasy of Marthe's lover Leo by alluding to Rembrandt:

> The mental stimulus he dreamed of, the peal of a gong that would awaken his dormant talent, was a monstrous fantasy of the poet and artist: a woman who loved him, a woman extravagantly arrayed, placed in odd instants of light, in singular attitudes of colors, an improbable woman, painted by Rembrandt, his God.
>
> Ce qu'il rêvait comme un excitant d'esprit, comme un coup de gong qui réveillerait son talent assoupi, c'était une fantaisie monstrueuse, de poète et d'artiste: une femme qui l'aimât, une femme vêtue de toilettes folles, placée dans de curieux arrêts de lumière, dans de singulières attitudes de couleurs, une femme invraisemblable, peinte par Rembrandt, son Dieu. (II, 50)

Ironically, while Leo is thus fantasizing about Marthe, she is looking at a Hogarth engraving of a brothel which he has hanging in his apartment. It represents the other, and maybe truer, aspect of his taste in women. The engraving also triggers memories in Marthe of when she was a prostitute and these references to opposed representations of women reflect the beginning of the couple's falling out.

In *A Rebours,* the description of certain paintings, especially those of Moreau, establishes a whole descriptive code which unifies the diverse elements of the novel—the character of des Esseintes, his art collection, his book collection, his turtle, his flowers, his nightmare, and the decoration of his rooms. Any discussion of *A Rebours* must, therefore, include the relationship of des Esseintes' paintings to other parts not explicitly connected to painting.

Michael Issacharoff, in his study of space in fiction, makes an interesting point about a written text evoking existing pictures. He implies that it is similar to the set in a theater.[10] This comparison fails to point out that the reader, unlike the theater-goer, does not *see* the pictures and may well not even be familiar with the picture in question. Moreover, the images in the description take precedence in the reader's perception over any previously gained knowledge of the picture.

The second function of a description of art is a basis for a general aesthetic discussion. The most notable example of this in Huysmans is in the opening chapter of *Là-Bas,* in which the Grünewald *Crucifixion* is taken as a model of "naturalisme spiritualiste," which was Huysmans' answer to the decline of Naturalism.

The third function is *transpositions d'art* used as dreams or flashbacks, as in the prose poem "Damiens." In these cases art is used like the madeleine in Proust, setting off a stream of involuntary memory. Art, dreams, and memory are then filters through which to see, understand, and perhaps change reality. As Huysmans says in *A Rebours,*

The main thing is to know how to set about it, to be able to concentrate your attention on a single detail, to forget yourself sufficiently to bring about the desired hallucination and so substitute the vision of a reality for the reality itself.

Le tout est de savoir s'y prendre, de savoir s'abstraire suffisamment pour amener l'hallucination et pouvoir substituer le rêve de la réalité à la réalité même. (VII, 34–35)

Since Huysmans always ends these descriptions with a clear reentry into reality, they allow for the reality/dream antithesis which is one of his work's distinctive features.

Criticism

Though the importance of Huysmans' relationship to painting has not been overlooked in the past, this study is the first attempt to investigate the subject systematically. Other critics have written about Huysmans' unusually developed sense of sight and about his painterly descriptions, and they have pointed to the similarities between the subject matter and style of his art criticism and his fictional writing. Zola, Huysmans' early mentor, praised him specifically for this quality:

He has one of the most highly colored imaginations I know. Life comes to him through his eyes: he translates everything into images, he is the ultimate poet of sensation.

C'est une des visions les plus colorées que je connaisse. La vie entre en lui par les yeux: il traduit tout en images, il est le poète excessif de la sensation.[11]

Helen Trudgian, in 1934, based her comprehensive study of Huysmans' aesthetic tastes and development on the premise that he had the instinct of a painter. The introductory paragraph typifies her approach:

J.-K. Huysmans numbers an entire race of painters on his father's side. From his Flemish and Dutch ancestors, he inherits a concern for precision, for cleanliness, even restraint, as well as the tendency to see boldly and in color. There is in him a touch of Rubens and Rembrandt.

J.-K. Huysmans compte dans son ascendance paternelle toute une lignée de peintres. De ses aïeux flamands et hollandais lui vient le souci de la précision, de la netteté, de la sobriété même; la tendance aussi, à voir large et coloré. Il y a, en lui, du Rubens et du Rembrandt.[12]

Fernande Zayed, in 1972, took the same approach. In her introduction she writes that

Huysmans is a born painter, as other writers are born poets, novelists, or playwrights. In his case, it is sight that is incontestably his most highly developed sense, and his taste for description, an irrepressible propensity. He received these through heredity, developed them through practice, maintained them by frequenting artists and visiting museums.

Huysmans est né peintre, comme d'autres écrivains naissent poètes, romanciers ou dramaturges. Chez lui, la vision est sans conteste le sens le plus développé, et son goût pour la description une tendance incoercible. Il les a reçus par l'hérédité, les a développés par l'exercice, les a entretenus par la fréquentation des artistes et par la visite des musées.[13]

This kind of vague, impressionistic, and intuitive study of the relationship and influences between the arts can only scratch the surface of this very fascinating issue. Detailed descriptions of people, rooms, neighborhoods, and landscapes are an integral part of the Naturalist aesthetic and so this alone does not set Huysmans apart from other writers of this period.

Frank Colucci's "Joris-Karl Huysmans' Art Criticism" (Diss. Cornell 1932) is a good account of Huysmans' three books of collected art criticism, but by limiting himself to this one body of work, Colucci has not even approached the relationship between Huysmans' tastes in art and the rest of his work.

The best study dealing critically with Huysmans' art criticism is Philip Ward-Jackson, "Huysmans" (*The Burlington Magazine,* November 1967). This short article has, however, only pointed to problems with which I deal in detail.

Many critics of Huysmans have tried to weigh the merits of his art criticism against his novels and prose poems. The American critic James Huneker, for instance, said that "One of the most notable of art critics in a city abundantly supplied with criticism was this same Huysmans. His critical achievement may outlive his fiction and his religious confessions."[14] Huysmans' contemporary G. R. Turquet-Milnes wrote that "Huysmans the critic is so much more interesting than Huysmans the pure novelist. The critic becomes absorbed from time to time in the masterpieces he observes, and a sincere note of enthusiasm will creep in; but the novelist has only one attitude—profoundest ennui."[15] She seems to be ignoring the role of Huysmans' enthusiasm for the visual arts in his novels. A. E. Carter, in a more recent study, took an opposite approach and interpreted Huysmans' Catholic novels as art criticism, saying that "his pious volumes are not spiritual odysseys but discussions of aesthetics."[16] Pie Duployé's *Huysmans* (Les Ecrivains devant Dieu. Paris: Desclée de Brouwer, 1968) is also useful in that it recognizes the complex interplay between Huysmans' spiritual development and his changing artistic tastes. Arthur Symons, the English critic and contemporary of Huysmans, recognized the fact that Huysmans' approach to art was integrally related to his life and literary work and that he therefore turned to artists who "have an interest beyond their mere skill as painters with various kinds of appeal to those who go to art for something which is certainly not the art of it."[17] Symons underestimated Huysmans' interest in and understanding of painting as an art form in its own right, but he did rightly point to the broader implications of Huysmans' choice of paintings. This broader approach is evident in Anita Brookner's study of six French art critics when she wrote that "for men of letters works of art provide an ideal vehicle for expressing truths about their experience not only of pictures but of life itself,"[18] and in Marc Eigeldinger's article, which says that

> For Huysmans, the plastic arts are often the pretext for an interpretative discourse whose vigor derives from the stamp of his poetic charge.
>
> L'oeuvre plastique est souvent pour Huysmans prétexte à un discours interprétatif, dont la vigueur tient à l'empreinte de la charge poétique.[19]

Ruth Antosh, in her brief article "The Role of Paintings in Three Novels by J.-K. Huysmans,"[20] has pursued a similar approach to mine and has done some work to link Huysmans the art critic to Huysmans the novelist. She looks at his perception of the relationship between literature and painting and illustrates, in three novels, the way in which Huysmans has been indebted to the plastic arts and looks to paintings for new creative concepts. My study develops fully ideas which Antosh and I were clearly contemplating simultaneously.

Whether one reads the work of Huysmans for what he has to say about painting, or about religion or life in Paris, this study will show that his use of painting in his literary works is complex and poses a stylistic challenge with which he battled throughout his life. If nothing else, I hope to show how incorrect Christopher Lehmann-Haupt is when he writes in a review in *The New York Times* that "there is nothing quite so tedious as reading a verbal description of what is ipso facto a visual experience."[21] It is these descriptions which constitute some of the most crucial and poignant moments in Huysmans' novels and prose poems.

1

The Aesthetic Development of a Novelist Art Critic

Huysmans wrote during a time of profound debate and fundamental changes in the arts. He experienced and influenced the end of Naturalism and saw the proliferation of many experimental groups of writers and painters. The lack of a confident direction which typified the arts in general at this time is reflected in Huysmans' perpetual search for the "true" aesthetic formula and his resultant changes of taste. Huysmans' unusually desperate attempt to understand the meaning and aim of art and literature stems largely from the fact that he was so dissatisfied with his own life that he turned to the world of the arts to fill a personal void.

Huysmans' literary works are uniformly depressing, revealing a pessimistic view of life, characterized by melancholy, disgust, and despair. He was irresistibly drawn to the sensual pleasures available in Paris, yet was always revolted by the experience; he had highly developed erotic tendencies yet feared and disdained women, seeing in them an embodiment of evil; he found little joy in nature and in travel; he respected very few people and showed contempt for the masses. Yet his works express, with great enthusiasm and an original, sardonic style, a passion for art which became both an escape and a guiding force for him.

Huysmans showed a love of painting from his earliest childhood. So it was natural for him to try his luck in art criticism for journals and newspapers to earn a little money while he began his more serious writing of fiction. Art criticism was a great source of pleasure to him and he approached it with less self-doubt than he did his literary writing. Moreover, it put him in touch with the work of many artists he would otherwise not have encountered and it gave him time to study certain paintings at length. This provided a rich source of material for his prose poems and novels, in which descriptions of art are frequently a focal point. Huysmans' criticism contains fine writing and original, perceptive views, and his collected articles lend valuable historical insight into the artistic debates of the eighties and nineties, in which Huysmans was a very active and influential participant. At present, however, his art criticism and its relationship to the rest of his writing are a much neglected aspect of his work.

In his own time Huysmans was known as a critic to be reckoned with and many of his contemporaries considered Huysmans to be an important figure in the development of artistic taste. Roger Marx, for instance, himself a distinguished critic, wrote in 1893:

> There is certainly no dearth, nowadays, of either erudite historians or of reporters on the lookout for news of the day . . . but J.-K. Huysmans' supremacy remains unchallenged. Whether or not it cares to admit it, very nearly all of today's criticism is descended from him. . . . Not since Thoré had one encountered so unerring an analysis, nor, since Baudelaire, the double gifts of intuition and expression, which make of their author at this time, not merely a judge among judges, but a unique personage, *the* critic of modern art.
>
> Certes, l'heure présente ne manque ni d'historiens érudits, ni de reporters à l'affût de l'actualité . . . mais la suprématie de J.-K. Huysmans demeure inattaquée. Qu'elle le veuille ou non confesser, la critique de maintenant descend de lui, à bien peu près, tout. . . . Il n'était pas arrivé de rencontrer depuis Thoré un diagnostic aussi peu faillible, depuis Baudelaire, le double don de la divination et de l'espression, qui fait de leur auteur, en ce temps, non point un juge parmi les juges, mais une personnalité unique, le critique le l'art moderne.[1]

The English critic Arthur Symons wrote, "No literary artist since Baudelaire has made so valuable a contribution to art criticism, and the *Curiosités esthétiques* are, after all, less exact in their actual study, less revolutionary, and less significant in their critical judgments than *L'Art moderne*."[2] Félix Fénéon, a critic of more lasting importance than Huysmans, after reading *Certains* wrote more flatteringly of his colleague that

> His two books of criticism are, by their sureness of judgment and their firm execution, the only ones to have been written on modern art.
>
> Ses deux livres de critique sont, pour leur sûreté de verdict et leur ferme exécution, les seuls qui aient été faits sur l'art moderne.[3]

Huysmans' criticism includes studies of individual artists, paintings, and exhibitions, and comprehensive accounts of the Paris Salons. He began his career as a writer on art in 1867 with a piece on contemporary landscape painting and he continued to submit art studies, in both French and Belgian newspapers and periodicals until 1904.

The articles can be divided roughly into four periods. The first, between 1867 and 1878, consists of sixteen articles, mainly on contemporary exhibitions, of which none were published in his collected works. They lack the originality, confidence, and stylistic excellence of his later articles. In "Le Salon de 1876: natures mortes" and "Notes sur le Salon de 1877: portraits et natures mortes," for instance, he even uses the identical text for the introduction and conclusion and simply changes the names of the pictures he is discussing. They are important, however, because they contain, in simple and tentative form, many of the ideas Huysmans developed in his mature work.

From 1879 to 1882, the second period, Huysmans wrote regular accounts of the Paris Salons for *Le Voltaire* and *La Réforme*. These articles were collected and published in 1883 in *L'Art moderne,* the book which established Huysmans as an important critic of contemporary art. It contains lengthy, sarcastic attacks on the Academic painters and enthusiastic praise for the Independents and the Impressionists.

The third period, from 1882 to 1889, is one of transition, corresponding to a similar phase in Huysmans' fiction, in which he turns from a confident Naturalism to a greater interest in human psychology. In art he becomes increasingly concerned with the emotional content of a work and less interested in its subject matter or its formal aspects. Huysmans collected the most important parts of these articles and published them, in 1889, together with some new essays, in *Certains,* which was his favorite among his books, not only because it deals with many of his favorite painters such as Degas, Moreau, Redon, Puvis de Chavannes, and Whistler, but because of its format—essays on individual artists. Huysmans was sceptical about schools of thought and general movements and was more interested in discussing individuals, a feeling expressed by des Esseintes in *A Rebours,* for whom "les écoles n'existaient point" (VII, 270).

The fourth and last period of Huysmans' criticism, 1889 to 1899, is devoted entirely to the study of religious art, both historical and contemporary. Most of these articles, all of which appeared first in *L'Echo de Paris,* were either published in *De Tout,* 1902, or used as material in *La Cathédrale.* After 1899 Huysmans wrote only one article, in 1904, on the Grünewalds in the Colmar Museum for *Le Mois Littéraire et Pittoresque.* Adding notes he took on a journey to Germany, Belgium and Switzerland in 1903, Huysmans developed this article into a larger study which he published in 1905 under the title *Trois Primitifs*.

Huysmans' aim in his art criticism was to give an honest account of what he saw at exhibitions. He was always very thorough and his honesty often resulted in angering and offending his more conservative readers. For Huysmans' tastes were always aggressively individualistic and he believed firmly, like Baudelaire, that a good critic must have strong, personal opinions—"unless one either loves passionately or hates passionately, one has no talent" ("l'on n'a pas de talent si l'on n'aime avec passion ou si l'on ne hait de même") (*Certains*, X, 12). He never held his tongue and as he proudly told Camille Lemonnier in a letter of August 1880, "because of my violent criticism of the people I hate, you can trust my sincerity in matters of art" ("Vous pouvez, étant donné la violence de ma critique contre les gens que je hais, au point de vue de l'art croire à ma sincérité").[4]

Huysmans did not have a well-developed general theory of art. He held strong views on particular issues such as Impressionism, Naturalism, and Catholic art and on particular artists such as Degas and Moreau, and he often provides perceptive analyses of the style and general direction of a work or movement. He certainly tried to evaluate paintings dispassionately and never lost sight of their objective qualities. He does not, however, claim to take an objective approach to aesthetic problems in general and throughout his criticism one finds the expression "my needs" ("mes besoins"); his is a self-centered kind of criticism. Despite a professional commitment to writing comprehensive accounts of the works on exhibit, Huysmans seems to be using his critical writings as a creative experiment, as a way of solving emotional and artistic problems of his own. This accounts for the large degree of interaction between his art criticism and his fiction. Huysmans himself was well aware that his tastes and his approach to art were very subjective and this consciousness is reflected by des Esseintes in *A Rebours:*

> Yet his literary opinions had started from a very simple point of view. For him, there were no such things as schools; the only thing that mattered to him was the writer's personality, and the only thing that interested him was the working of the writer's brain, no matter what subject he was tackling. Unfortunately this criterion of appreciation . . . was practically impossible to apply, for the simple reason that, however much a reader wants to rid himself of prejudice and refrain from passion, he naturally prefers those works which correspond most intimately with his own personality, and ends by relegating all the rest to limbo.

> En art, ses idées étaient pourtant parties d'un point de vue simple; pour lui, les écoles n'existaient point; seul le tempérament de sa cervelle intéressait quelque fût le sujet qu'il abordât. Malheureusement, cette vérité d'appréciation . . . était à peu près inapplicable, par ce simple motif que, tout en désirant se dégager des préjugés, s'abstenir de toute passion, chacun va de préférence aux oeuvres qui correspondent le plus intimement à son propre tempérament et finit par reléguer en arrière toutes les autres. (VII, 270)

Huysmans' career is characterized by remarkable changes in artistic taste. His devotion to Grünewald and Chartres Cathedral is far removed from his love of the Independent Parisian artists of the eighties, just as his novel *Sainte Lydwine de Schiedam,* the story of a saint, could hardly have been anticipated by *Marthe,* the story of a prostitute. In his later years Huysmans was embarrassed by his youthful enthusiasms and, in spite of the obvious passion and sincerity of his early writing, he often claimed that his opinions had not been serious. These changes in taste are not surprising, however, when one recognizes that Huysmans looked to art as a substitute for life. This attitude resulted in a fundamental confusion, in his mind, between art and reality, with ensuing disappointments and a constant reevaluation of his tastes.

The powerful influence which art exerted on Huysmans can be seen from the very inception of his literary career. As a law student he spent a great deal of time in the Louvre, often accompanied by his close friend Ludovic de

Francmesnil. He was attracted by the Dutch and Flemish masters of the seventeenth century and found in them an inspiration for his own writing. In a letter to Verhaeren of 1881 he wrote,

> The idea of writing no doubt came to me when, just out of school, I used to stroll through the Louvre; there, I ignored all the other rooms, to linger in those containing the Flemish and Dutch school.

> L'idée d'écrire m'est certainement venue, alors que sorti du collège, j'allais me promener au Louvre, où négligeant toutes les autres salles, je m'arrêtais devant celles renfermant l'école flamande et hollandaise.[5]

These paintings appealed to him because of the *joie de vivre* they seemed to portray, in painful contrast with Huysmans' own existence; and he tried to relive some of the experiences seen in the paintings through his first book of prose poems *Le Drageoir aux épices,* which appeared in 1874. Four of the eighteen poems are based on Dutch and Flemish works he had seen in the Louvre. They are the first examples of his experimentation with the integration of a visual experience into writing. He shows here a charming playfulness with the reader which he loses in his later works.

One of the poems based on works seen at the Louvre is "Le Hareng saur," a *transposition d'art* inspired by a Rembrandt still life. Foreshadowing his interpretation of Moreau, Huysmans uses mineral imagery to describe the herring:

> The patina of old bronze, the burnished gold of Cordovan leathers . . . one might say that your eyes were black nails driven into copper spheres.

> La patine du vieux cuivre, le ton d'or bruni des cuirs de Cordoue . . . l'on dirait de tes yeux des clous noirs plantés dans des cercles de cuivre. (I, 49)

In "Adrien Brauwer" Huysmans incorporates into a ten-page anecdote about the painter Brauwer a one-page *transposition d'art.* It is a description of a painting Brauwer paints to pay for his drinks. Huysmans breaks the fiction of the story by bringing the reader back to reality with "You know this canvas. It is in the Louvre" ("Ce tableau, vous le connaissez. Il est au Louvre") (I, 83). This poem also contains a discussion between Brauwer and his patron about his reasons for leaving Rubens' atelier to spend most of his time in brothels and cafés. Couched in a story about seventeenth-century Holland, this discussion is really about the contemporary debate between the Academics and the Independents, who believed that a studio portrait could never achieve the veracity of a painting executed with natural models in natural surroundings.

In "Claudine" Huysmans develops further this device of inserting a *transposition d'art* into a narrative. Incorporated into a story of sixteen pages about Les Halles, which was the topic of Zola's *Le Ventre de Paris,* is a half-page description of Rembrandt's *Flayed Ox* in the Louvre. In this poem Huysmans is not explicit about his source but the change from the banal, everyday vocabulary of the narrative to the dense physiological and plant vocabulary of the *transposition* clearly sets it apart from the rest of the prose poem. The type of vocabulary Huysmans uses here typifies his descriptions of Redon and certain nightmare episodes in *En Rade* and *A Rebours:*

> The carcass of a great ox exuded . . . the monstrous jewel box of his viscera. The head had been torn violently from the trunk and some of the nerve endings still twitched, convulsed . . . twisted. . . . The stomach . . . yawned horribly and disgorged from its large cavity pendants of red entrails. As though in some hothouse, a wondrous vegetation blossomed in that carcass.

> Le cadavre d'un grand boeuf étalait . . . le monstrueux écrin de ses viscères. La tête avait été violemment arrachée du tronc et des bouts de nerfs palpitaient encore, convulsés . . . tortillés. . . . L'estomac . . . baîllait atrocement et dégorgeait de sa large fosse des pendeloques d'entrailles rouges. Comme en une serre chaude, une végétation merveilleuse s'épanouissait dans ce cadavre. (I, 36)

Huysmans confirms the fact that the description of the ox is of a special nature by commenting that the butcher was amazed at the sight of the ox, a sight with which one would expect him to be familiar: "Le boucher semblait *émerveillé* par ce *spectacle*" [my italics].

"La Kermesse de Rubens" is a further example of a *transposition d'art* incorporated into a narrative. It begins with the words "The following evening, I was wandering through the streets of a small village . . ." ("Le lendemain soir, j'errais dans les rues d'un petit village . . .") (I, 25), as if the poem were a continuation of an episode. The description of the countryside is interrupted by the phrase "I noticed a faint glimmer gleaming red in the window of a barn" ("j'aperçus une faible lueur qui rougeoyait à la fenêtre d'une grange") (I, 26). This window acts as a frame for a painting Huysmans is describing. At the end of the description Huysmans gives a more explicit hint that he has just described a painting when he says, "It looked like one of Teniers' paintings" ("On eût dit un tableau de Teniers") (I, 27). The scene changes and Huysmans modifies his explanation—"It was no longer one of Teniers' village dances, it was Rubens' village fair" ("Ce n'était plus une danse villageoise de Teniers, c'était la kermesse de Rubens") (I, 28). These identifications bring the reader sharply back from the *rêverie* created by the *transposition* and prepare him for the important final paragraph which shows the extent to which the life described in these paintings afforded an escape for Huysmans:

> Well, I swear to you that it was good to see such joy; I swear to you that I was charmed by the naive simplicity of those fat sailors' wives and that I detested all the more those Paris dens where a crowd of sewer nymphs and ghastly boozers carry on frantically, as though lashed by hysteria's whip!

Eh bien! je vous jure que cette joie était bonne à voir, je vous jure que la naïve simplesse de ces grosses matelotes m'a ravi et que j'ai détesté plus encore des bauges de Paris où s'agitent, comme cinglés par le fouet de l'hystérie, un ramassis de naïades d'égout et de sinistres riboteurs! (I, 28)

That Huysmans had a naive view of Holland is seen again in a prose poem called "La Tulipe," written in 1875 but never published in his collected works. He sings the praises of the tulip as if addressing a lover and paints a conventional picture of Holland with cows, windmills, red houses, women in lace headdresses, all images gleaned from the paintings he saw in the Louvre. In the final paragraph, in which he recalls the smells and noises of the countryside, Huysmans writes: "I once again see Holland, land of village fairs and of great painters, of flowers and of skies . . ." ("Je revois la Hollande, pays des kermesses et des grandes peintres, des fleurs et des ciels . . .")[6].

Apart from short visits as a child to relatives in Breda, Tilburg, and Ginnik between 1850 and 1856, Huysmans as far as we know did not visit Holland or Belgium until 1876, when he had to go to Brussels for the publication of *Marthe*. He expected to find the way of life he had found so appealing in the Dutch and Flemish paintings in the Louvre and he was sadly disappointed. Contrary to his expectations, he found Holland to be a dull, puritanical country which did not live up to its rich and joyous past. He visited a great many museums, where his love for the Dutch and Flemish masters was confirmed. He wrote about some of these works, as of his personal disappointment, in an article called "En Hollande" which first appeared in the *Musée des Deux-Mondes* on February 15, 1877 and was reprinted in a longer version, in *La Revue Illustrée* ten years later.[7] Huysmans ends the article by dolefully bemoaning the future of Holland, which confirms his admiration for the art and his frustration with the fact that it is not an accurate representation of reality:

Yes, Holland is the land of the arts! but, oh, you artists, . . . soon the homeland of Rembrandt and Steen will no longer be Holland the joyous and the picturesque.

Ah, la Hollande est le pays des arts! oui, mais, vous les artistes . . . la patrie de Rembrandt et de Steen ne sera bientôt plus la joyeuse et la pittoresque Hollande.

Seven years later, in *A Rebours,* Huysmans makes use of this first experience of being deceived by art and expresses, in clearer and more explicit terms, the problem arising from the confusion of art and reality:

On the whole, this tour had proved a bitter disappointment to him. He had pictured to himself a Holland such as Teniers and Jan Steen, Rembrandt and Ostade had painted . . . he had to admit that the paintings of the Dutch School exhibited in the Louvre had led him astray. They had in fact served as a springboard from which he had soared into a dream world of false trails and impossible ambitions, for nowhere in this world had he found the fairyland of which he had dreamt.

Somme toute, il était résulté de cruelles désillusions de ce voyage. Il [des Esseintes] s'était figuré une Hollande, d'après les oeuvres de Teniers et de Steen, de Rembrandt et d'Ostade . . . en résumé, il devait le reconnaître, l'école hollandaise du Louvre l'avait égaré; elle avait simplement servi de tremplin à ses rêves; il s'était élancé, avait bondi sur une fausse piste et erré dans des visions inégalables, ne découvrant nullement sur la terre ce pays magique et réel qu'il espérait. (VII, 207–8)

Huysmans' love for the Dutch and Flemish paintings of the seventeenth century was based on their realism. Like Baudelaire, whom he greatly admired and sought to emulate in many ways, he believed in "la modernité," that in art "one must be of one's time" ("il faut être de son temps"). This meant a rejection of all ideas of classical, universal beauty, an acceptance of a variety of beauties peculiar to each age. New styles and new subject matter were essential elements of any important artistic movement. In keeping with this theory, Huysmans rejected any moralistic, didactic intention in art. In an 1875 article on *La Cruche cassée* by Greuze, for instance, he takes the opportunity to attack "this deplorable aesthetic whose spokesman Diderot had become; the regeneration of society by art" ("cette esthétique déplorable dont Diderot s'était fait le porte-voix; la régénération de la société par l'art").[8]

Huysmans' very first piece of art criticism was a simple exposé of this theory that one of the aims of good art is to express the spirit of the time, and in this he felt the Dutch seventeenth-century painters had been eminently successful:

Ruysdael, Berchem, Swanevelt van Artois, Hobbema and our immortal Claude Gelée understood landscape, just as Rembrandt did the dim interiors that he lit with dazzling rays, as Brauwer did the taverns, Van Goyen the sea in repose, Van de Velde the raging waves. . . .

Ruysdaël, Berchem, Swanevelt van Artois, Hobbéma et notre immortel Claude Gelée ont compris le paysage comme Rembrandt les intérieurs sombres, qu'il illuminait d'éblouissants rayons, comme Brauwer les tabagies, Van Goyen la mer en repos, Van de Velde les flots en courroux. . . .[9]

Huysmans' disappointment in Holland was shattering in that he did not find a place where he could feel at ease. At the same time, however, it was a valuable learning experience for him. It forced him to face the fact that life was not so different elsewhere and that he had to come to terms with his own immediate environment and, above all, himself. Fortunately, one of Huysmans' greatest qualities was an ability to "change gear" and to allow himself to be guided by his very receptive artistic sensibility. In the very year he went to Holland he discovered Degas, and this discovery radically changed his whole outlook on modern art and contemporary life.

Degas awakened Huysmans' interest in the Impressionists and they quickly replaced the Dutch and Flemish painters in his affections. As he wrote in *L'Art moderne,*

[they] bring with them a new technique, the scent of an art that is singular and true; [they] distill the essence of their time, as the Dutch Naturalists expressed the aroma of theirs.

[ils] apportent une méthode nouvelle, une senteur d'art singulière et vraie, [ils] distillent l'essence de leur temps comme les naturalistes hollandais exprimaient l'arôme du leur. (VI, 13–14)

The "essence" and "aroma," words typical of Huysmans' olfactory vocabulary, are none other than the spirit of the age to which Huysmans felt art should address itself. There is a certain irony, however, in the fact that Huysmans suddenly embraced an artistic movement which chose to depict aspects of Parisian life that he had been trying to escape. However, his appreciation of the Impressionists soon became very selective and he concentrated on those artists who seemed to him to express his own cynical and melancholy view of the world.

Huysmans was introduced to Degas the same year he published *Marthe,* his first Naturalist novel, and in his art criticism he emphasized the comparison between Impressionism and Naturalism. Huysmans was emotionally drawn to Baudelaire yet was a great admirer of Zola with his staunch defense of an objective reality. Huysmans contributed a story to *Les Soirées de Médan* and worked within the current theoretical framework of Naturalist doctrine.

In 1876 he wrote a lengthy article on Zola in *L'Actualité* which clarifies his general aesthetic views at this important junction in his career. He ignores the scientific premise of Zola's Naturalism and writes primarily of the type of subject matter he and his colleagues consider appropriate for literature, underlining the importance of accurate and detailed observation. Echoing his reasons for liking Degas and the Dutch and Flemish masters, and revealing his constant awareness of the art of painting, he writes that "a writer, just as much as any painter, must move with the times; we are artists thirsting for modernity" ("un écrivain aussi bien qu'un peintre doit être de son temps, nous sommes des artistes assoiffés de modernité").[10] He proudly claims that the Naturalist authors are comprehensive in their subject matter: "Society has two faces: we show these two faces" ("La société a deux faces: nous montrons ces deux faces") (II, 161). This statement typifies Huysmans' tendency to conceptualize in opposites or dualities and it is this approach which explains his subsequent rejection of the subject matter of the earthy Naturalist novels in favor of more spiritual topics. The one aspect of Naturalism to which Huysmans remained faithful, however, was honesty and truth of observation. As he writes in the 1876 article on Zola, "Naturalism is . . . the patient study of reality, the whole obtained by the observation of details" ("le naturalisme c'est . . . l'étude patiente de la réalité, l'ensemble obtenu par l'observation des détails") (II, 166). He frequently uses the words "vrai" and "vérité" such as in the expressions "to make it true is to make it moral" ("faire vrai, c'est faire moral") (II, 166) and "he achieves the artist's highest purpose: truth, life" ("il atteint le but suprême de l'artiste; la vérité, la vie") (II, 191). Similarly, in *L'Art moderne* Huysmans talks scathingly of academic painters for "not bringing to life and not making true" ("ne pas faire vivant et ne pas faire vrai") (VI, 8) and admires Degas for having painted "de vraies danseuses" (VI, 44).

Huysmans, like all defenders of realism, understood "true" ("vrai") not in opposition to "ideal" but to false. So whether he is talking here about the Naturalist novel, the Dutch and Flemish masters, the Impressionists, or, as he was to later, about Moreau, Redon, and the medieval Primitives, Huysmans is looking for art based on direct, precise, and detailed observation. At the same time, however, Huysmans, like Zola, was fully aware that if one took Naturalism, which aimed, as they both believed, at the objective rendering of contemporary life to its logical limits, art could be replaced by photography. They recognized the degree of personal vision in every work and they therefore introduced the concept of temperament so that a work of art was, as Zola put it, "a pocket of creation seen through a temperament" ("un coin de la création vu à travers un tempérament").[11] Huysmans follows Zola completely in his division between "the real element, which is Nature" ("l'élément réel, qui est la nature") and "the individual element, which is Man" ("l'élément individuel, qui est l'homme"),[12] so that, in *L'Art moderne,* he writes apropos of Dutch seventeenth-century paintings that

> although they are exact, almost photographic reproductions of Nature, they are yet marked by particular accents determined by each painter's temperament.
>
> tout en étant une reproduction exacte, presque photographique de la nature, elles sont néanmoins empreintes d'un accent particulier déterminé par le tempérament de chacun de ces peintres. (VI, 195–96)[3]

As a result, Huysmans became increasingly interested in the attitude of the artist towards his subject, preferring figure painters who portrayed the sordid aspects of women, such as provocative stances and vulgar clothes, and landscapists who conveyed the melancholy of the Parisian suburbs. He especially loved Degas, Forain, and Raffaëlli because their works reflected a pessimistic view of life similar to his own, but by the middle of the eighties he began to tire of the type of art which portrayed contemporary Paris, where he found only manifestations of man's limitations. He was bored by the Post-Impressionists such as the Pointillists and the Synthetists because they were more concerned with form than with subject matter. He began to express a general lack of faith in the future of painting.

He needed an escape and turned more and more to artists such as Moreau and Redon to satisfy his growing need for the fantastic, the mystical, and the occult. Zola's aesthetics had at first been very appealing to Huysmans because of their involvement with the contemporary, but Zola's writing lacked a metaphysical dimension and Huysmans began, by the late eighties, to express an overwhelming "need for the supernatural" ("besoin de surnaturel") (*Là-Bas,*

XII, 13). Huysmans was reflecting a general shift of emphasis from the realist to the imaginative type of art, described as follows by Marcel Schwob:

> We had ended up in an extraordinary time: the novelists had shown us every aspect of human life and all the undersides of thought. We were tired of many feelings before experiencing them; many had allowed themselves to be drawn toward a chasm of mystical and unknown shadows; others were possessed by a passion for the strange, by the search for the quintessence of new sensations; and still others melted away into a vast compassion that swept across everything. . . .

> Nous étions arrivés dans un temps extraordinaire où les romanciers nous avaient montré toutes les faces de la vie humaine et tous les dessous des pensées. On était lassé de bien des sentiments avant de les avoir éprouvés; plusieurs se laissaient attirer vers un gouffre d'ombres mystiques et inconnues; d'autres étaient possédés par la passion de l'étrange, par la recherche du quintessencié de sensations nouvelles; d'autres enfin, se fondaient dans une large pitié qui s'étendait sur toute chose. . . .[14]

A Rebours, 1884, marked Huysmans' first step away from Naturalist topics by entering into a whole new world of unusual sensations and unorthodox tastes, but his first attempt to broaden the psychological scope of his novels was *En Rade,* 1887, in which the soul was given as much importance as the body. He did this by incorporating substantial dream chapters into the realistic narrative. He felt, however, that the novel was unsuccessful and he lost faith in his own ability as a writer and became increasingly convinced that literature, especially the novel, had reached a total impasse.

Huysmans' first lucid explanation of his dissatisfaction with Naturalism is in the opening of *Là-Bas:*

> I do not really care how the naturalists maltreat language, but I do strenuously object to the earthiness of their ideas. . . . Filth and the flesh are their domain. They deny wonder, reject the extrasensual, and don't even understand that artistic curiosity begins at the very point where the senses leave off!

> ce que je reproche au naturalisme, ce n'est pas le lourd badigeon de son gros style, c'est l'immondice de ses idées. . . . Vouloir se confiner dans les buanderies de la chair, rejeter le suprasensible, dénier le rêve, ne pas même comprendre que la curiosité de l'art commence là où les sens cessent de servir! (XII, 1)

In spite of his instinct that art begins where the senses end, Huysmans was still committed to the values of realist description and thus conceived of a modern novel in the following way:

> We must [thought Durtal] retain the documentary veracity, the precision of detail, the compact and sinewy language of realism, but we must also dig down into the soul and cease trying to explain mystery in terms of our sick senses. If possible the novel ought to be compounded of two elements, that of the soul and that of the body, and these ought to be inextricably bound together as in life. Their interreactions, their conflicts, their reconciliation, ought to furnish the dramatic interest. In a word, we must follow the road laid out once and

for all by Zola, but at the same time we must trace a parallel route in the air by which we may go above and beyond, and create, in a word, *a spiritual naturalism!* It must be complete, powerful, daring in a different way from anything that is being attempted at present.

Il faudrait, se disait [Durtal], garder la véracité du document, la précision du détail, la langue étoffée et nerveuse du réalisme, mais il faudrait aussi se faire puisatier d'âme et ne pas vouloir expliquer le mystère par les maladies des sens; le roman, si cela se pouvait, devrait se diviser de lui-même en deux parts, néanmoins soudées ou plutôt confondues, comme elles le sont dans la vie, celle de l'âme, celle du corps, et s'occuper de leurs réactifs, de leurs conflits, de leur entente. Il faudrait, en un mot, suivre la grande voie si profondément creusée par Zola, mais il serait nécessaire aussi de tracer en l'air un chemin parallèle, une autre route, d'atteindre les en deçà et les après, de faire, en un mot, un *naturalisme spiritualiste;* ce serait autrement fier, autrement complet, autrement fort! (XII, 10–11) [my italics]

Just as Huysmans had originally been inspired to write when he saw the seventeenth-century Dutch paintings in the Louvre, it was painting, once again, which helped him out of the impasse he believed literature to be in, by showing him the possibilities of his new aesthetic of spiritual naturalism:

[He began to think that Des Hermies] was right. In the present disorganized state of letters there was but one tendency which seemed to promise better things: the need for the supernatural. . . . Now his thoughts carried him away from his dissatisfaction with literature to the satisfaction he had found in another art, in painting.

C'était vrai, il n'y avait plus rien debout dans les lettres en désarroi; rien, sinon un besoin de surnaturel. . . . En s'acculant ainsi à ces pensées, il finissait, pour se rapprocher de cet idéal qu'il voulait quand même joindre, par louvoyer, par bifurquer et s'arrêter à un autre art, à la peinture. (XII, 12–13)

In the summer of 1888 Huysmans' doctor had recommended a trip to help his "dreadful nervous complaint."[15] Prompted by Verhaeren's article on the German Primitives in *Société Nouvelle,* August 15, 1886, Huysmans finally decided to accept a long-standing invitation from Arij Prins to visit him in Hamburg and continue with him to visit several museums throughout Germany. Their trip took them to Cologne, Berlin, Weimar, Lübeck, Gotha, and Cassel. It was in the Cassel museum that Huysmans saw the *Crucifixion* by Grünewald, which was a revelation to him on two levels. It led him one step closer to the Catholic faith, towards which he had gradually been groping, and also to a solution of his aesthetic problems. As he wrote to Jules Destrée on December 12, 1890,

All art was within them, the Supernaturalism that is the only truthful and great art. The only and true formula, so sought after, is in Roger van der Weyden, Metsys, Grünewald—absolute Realism with spurts of soul, what material Naturalism has not understood . . . and thereby collapsed!—despite all the services it rendered.

Tout l'art était en eux, le surnaturalisme qui est le seul art véridique et grand. La seule et vraie formule tant cherchée est dans Roger van der Weyden, Metsys, Grünewald—le réalisme absolu avec des jets d'âme; ce que le naturalisme matérialiste n'a pas compris . . . et il en est crevé[1]!—malgré tous les services qu'il a rendus.[16]

Huysmans' impressions of Cologne, Hamburg, Lübeck, Berlin, and Gotha were introduced, years later, into *La Cathédrale* and *De Tout*. But the impact of the Grünewald *Crucifixion* was so enormous that it was given a place of honor in the opening chapter of *Là-Bas,* in which Durtal and Des Hermies discuss the problem of contemporary literature. The painting is introduced into the novel as part of Durtal's personal experience: "Durtal's introduction to this naturalism had come as a revelation the year before" ("La révélation de ce naturalisme, Durtal l'avait eue, l'an passé") (XII, 13). In order to create the impression that he is in the presence of the painting, as des Esseintes is in the presence of Moreau's *Salomé,* Durtal closes his eyes and relives the experience:

> He shuddered in his armchair and closed his eyes as if in pain. With extraordinary lucidity he saw the picture again, there, in front of him, as he evoked it.

> Et il frissonna dans son fauteuil et ferma presque douloureusement les yeux. Avec une extraordinaire lucidité, il revoyait ce tableau, là, devant lui, maintenant qu'il l'évoquait. (XII, 14)

He even repeats the scream he let out when he first saw the painting in the museum: "He screamed again, mentally, as here, in his study, the Christ rose before him, formidable, on his cross" ("Il le hurlait mentalement encore, alors que, dans sa chambre, le Christ se dressait, formidable, sur sa croix") (XII, 14).

The description reveals that Durtal is at first totally absorbed by the realism and the physicality of the Christ figure. Indeed there is a marked similarity between the portrayal of Christ and the *Flayed Ox* which forms part of the prose poem "Claudine," and Huysmans' viewpoint is still clearly guided by Zola's tenets of Naturalism which demand a faithful, honest, detailed rendering of external appearances. He uses a mixture of plant, kitchen, and medical terminology which typifies much of his writing:

> The trembling chest was greasy with sweat. . . . the flesh swollen, blue, mottled with flea-bites, specked as with pin-pricks by spines broken off from the rods of the scourging and now festering beneath the skin where they had penetrated.
> Purulence was at hand. The fluvial wound in the side . . . inundated the thigh with blood that was like congealing blackberry juice . . . the flesh tumefied. . . .

> Les pectoraux tremblaient, beurrés par les sueurs . . . les chair gonflaient, salpêtrées et bleuies, persillées de morsures de puces, mouchetées comme de coups d'aiguilles par les pointes des verges qui, brisées sous la peau, la lardaient encore, çà et là, d'échardes.
> L'heure des sanies était venue; la plaie fluviale du flanc . . . inondait la hanche d'un sang pareil au jus foncé des mûres . . . la chair bourgeonnait. . . . (XII, 14–15)

The power of Grünewald's descriptive ability overwhelms Durtal and he judges that "Grünewald was the most daring of realists" ("Grünewald était le plus forcené des réalistes") (XII, 18). Yet he quickly modifies that comment and explains that the earthly figures in the painting all exude a spiritual quality:

"Thief, pauper, and peasant had vanished and given place to supraterrestrial creatures in the presence of their God" ("Il n'y avait plus de brigand, plus de pauvresse, plus de rustre, mais des êtres supraterrestres auprès d'un Dieu") (XII, 19). To complete his description of Grünewald as a great realist he adds the seemingly antithetical judgment that

> Grünewald was the most daring of idealists. Never had an artist known such magnificent exaltation, nor so resolutely jumped from the heights of the soul to the rapt orb of heaven.
>
> Grünewald était le plus forcené des idéalistes. Jamais peintre n'avait si magnifiquement exalté l'altitude et si résolument bondi de la cime de l'âme dans l'orbe éperdu du ciel. (XII, 19)

Grünewald thus fulfills the two requirements of Huysmans' "naturalisme spiritualiste."

Huysmans' admiration for Grünewald, based on the dichotomy of matter and spirit, led him to do further research into the life of the painter, and he published a study of the Grünewalds in the Colmar museum in *Trois Primitifs* in 1905, two years before his death. Unlike the dramatic description in *Là-Bas,* this study is a less emotional and more objective work of art criticism. Huysmans is primarily concerned with the history of the painter, the problems of identification and the analysis of picture space and color. Not that Huysmans was less impressed by the Isenheim Crucifixion than the one in Cassel, for "It looms up fiercely, as soon as one enters, and it overwhelms you instantly with the dreadful nightmare of a Calvary" ("Il surgit, dès qu'on entre, farouche, et il vous abasourdit aussitôt avec l'effroyable cauchemar d'un Calvaire") (*Trois Primitifs,* XI, 271). And it was the unique contradictions in Grünewald's work, the mixture of naturalism and spiritualism, which continued to fascinate Huysmans. He seemed to find in Grünewald the combination of contrasts to which he himself aspired:

> He is, in fact, all paradoxes, all contrasts; this furious Orlando of painting leaps without respite from one extravagance to another, but this demoniac is, when the occasion requires, a very skilled painter, a master of every trick of the trade. Though he may go mad for the dazzling clash of colors, he also possesses, on his good days, a very refined sense of hue— his *Resurrection* proves it—and he can join the most hostile colors by coaxing them, by drawing them together little by little, by adroitly negotiating the tints.
>
> He is at the same time Naturalist and mystic, savage and civilized, frank and devious.
>
> Il est, en effet, tout en antinomies, tout en contrastes; ce Roland furieux de la peinture bondit sans cesse d'une outrance dans une autre, mais l'énergumène est, quand il le faut, un peintre fort habile et connaissant à fond les ruses du métier. S'il raffole du fracas éblouissant des tons, il possède aussi, dans ses bons jours, le sens très affiné des nuances—sa *Résurrection* l'atteste—et il sait unir les couleurs les plus hostiles, en les sollicitant, en les rapprochant peu à peu par d'adroites diplomaties de teintes.
>
> Il est à la fois naturaliste et mystique, sauvage et civilisé, franc et retors. (XI, 305)

As Huysmans explains in the opening chapter of *Là-Bas,* he had been searching for a formula which would resolve the contradiction between his respect for the documentary method of the Naturalists, and his dislike for their crude, materialistic subject matter. Having found the answer in medieval painting, Huysmans naturally turned to the Middle Ages as a source for his contemporary novel which would put into practice his new theory. In contradiction to the nineteenth century which Huysmans now regarded as mediocre and materialistic, he viewed the reign of Charles VII as an age of high villainy and high virtue, in which rich and poor seemed to dedicate themselves wholeheartedly to God or to Satan. It was also natural that Huysmans chose as his hero Gilles de Rais, the antithesis of the nineteenth-century Naturalist protagonist, who had touched the extremes of human experience, from satanic vice to Christian fervor.

Reflected in the story of Gilles de Rais and in Durtal's study of contemporary satanism is Huysmans' own spiritual anguish. Huysmans was spending part of his free time in the company of prostitutes and petty criminals and at the same time was beginning to attend Church and to find, to his surprise, that it held increasing fascination and consolation for him. The discovery of Grünewald and other medieval mystical artists had first awakened in him the possibilities of a return to a Catholic faith:

"But then," said Durtal to himself, awakening from his reverie, "if I am consistent, I shall end up at the Catholicism of the Middle Ages, to mystical naturalism. Ah, no I will not— and yet perhaps I may!"

Mais alors . . . se dit Durtal, qui s'éveillait de sa songerie, mais alors, si je suis logique, j'aboutis au catholicisme du Moyen Age, au naturalisme mystique; ah non, par exemple, et si pourtant! (XII, 20)

and the peace and serenity he found when attending Church services persuaded him to seek help from a priest. On May 28, 1891 he met for the first time with the Abbé Mugnier and his conversion was completed by 1892. This reversion to organized religion ended Huysmans' trend away from contemporary art and he turned wholeheartedly now to a comprehensive study of medieval art.

Huysmans' conversion to Catholicism has been the subject of much debate, both at the time and after, many people arguing that it represented a genuine return to the religion of his childhood, others that it was merely an escape from the literary life of Paris. Some people see in it a mere fascination with the occultism practiced at that time by some Catholic sects; others explain it purely by Huysmans' love of Catholic art and liturgy.

Huysmans himself was troubled by doubts and confusion about his conversion and recognized that he was being pulled in many directions. In *En Route,* 1895, the account of his conversion, as told through Durtal, he certainly puts art first in the list of motives leading him to the Church:

his love of art, his heritage, his weariness of living. . . . It was art that brought Durtal back to religion. More than his disgust for life itself, art was the irresistible lover that had drawn him toward God.

l'amour de l'art, l'hérédité, l'ennui de vivre. . . . Durtal avait été ramené à la religion par l'art. Plus que son dégoût de la vie même, l'art avait été l'irresistible aimant qui l'avait attiré vers Dieu. (XIII, 1, 33 and 43)

Durtal recalls, for instance, how

he used to take refuge—during his idle days, after coming out of the Louvre, where he had drifted for a long time in front of the canvases of the Primitives—in the old Church of Saint Séverin, tucked away in a corner of the poor section of Paris. He brought there with him the visions of the canvases that he had admired in the Louvre and he contemplated them anew in those surroundings, where they were truly at home. Then he knew moments of delight.

il se réfugiait, les jours de flâne, en sortant du Louvre où il s'était longuement évagué devant les toiles des Primitifs, dans la vieille Eglise de Saint Séverin, enfouie en un coin du Paris pauvre. Il y apportait les visions des toiles qu'il avait admirées au Louvre et il les contemplait à nouveau dans ce milieu où elles se trouvaient vraiment chez elles. Puis c'étaient des moments délicieux. (XIII, 1, 44)

His greatest fear remained, however, that his love for medieval art was a substitute for true faith:

He wore himself out in arguments, to the point that he doubted the sincerity of his conversion, telling himself, when all is said and done, I'm only interested in the Church for its art; I only go to see or hear, not to pray; I'm not seeking the Lord, but my own pleasure.

Il s'usait en disputes, en arrivant à douter de la sincérité de sa conversion, se disait, en fin de compte, je ne me suis emballé à l'église que par l'art; je n'y vais que pour voir ou pour entendre et non pour prier; je ne cherche pas le Seigneur, mais mon plaisir. (XIII, 1, 58–59)

Whatever the role of art in Huysmans' conversion and his post-conversion years, his return to faith cannot be dismissed as a dilettantish flirtation with Catholicism. The life he chose to lead as a result of his beliefs was by no means an easy one and the faith he displayed during the years he suffered from his own illness and endless misfortunes among his friends is ample proof of a genuine commitment to Catholicism. It is too easy to accuse Huysmans derogatively of "aesthetic Catholicism,"[17] implying that love of Catholic art precluded genuine beliefs. As T. S. Eliot writes in a study of Pater:

When religion is in a flourishing state, when the whole mind of society is moderately healthy and in order, there is an easy and natural association between religion and art. Only when religion has been partly retired and confined, when an Arnold can sternly remind us that Culture is wider than Religion, do we get "religious art" and in due course "aesthetic religion". Pater undoubtedly had from childhood a religious bent naturally to all that was liturgical and ceremonious. Certainly this is a real and important part of religion and Pater cannot thereby be accused of insincerity and "aestheticism".[18]

Marcel Proust, in the introduction to his translation of John Ruskin, shows great sensitivity about the process whereby works of religious art awaken a latent faith:

> He [Ruskin] will be able to speak of the years in which the Gothic appeared to him with the same gravity, the same emotional remembrance, the same serenity with which a Christian speaks of the day the truth was revealed to him. The events of his life are intellectual and the important periods are those in which he understands a new art form. . . . Just so did his religious feeling guide his aesthetic feeling. . . . That divine something that Ruskin felt at the heart of the feeling that works of art inspired in him was precisely what, in that feeling, was profound and original and thrust itself upon his taste without possibility of modification. And the religious respect that he brought to the expression of that feeling, his fear that translating it would subject it to the least deformation, prevented him—contrary to what has often been believed—from ever adulterating his responses to works of art with any alien tricks of reason. Thus, those who see in him a moralist and an apostle who loved in art what was not of art, are as mistaken as those who, ignoring the deepest essence of his aesthetic feeling, confuse it with a sensual dilettantism.

> Il [Ruskin] pourra parler des années où le gothique lui apparut avec la même gravité, le même retour ému, la même sérénité qu'un chrétien parle du jour où la vérité lui fut révélée. Les événements de sa vie sont intellectuels et les dates importantes sont celles où il pénètre une nouvelle forme d'art. . . . C'est ainsi que son sentiment religieux a dirigé son sentiment esthétique. . . . Ce quelque chose de divin que Ruskin sentait au fond du sentiment que lui inspiraient les oeuvres d'art, c'était précisément ce que ce sentiment avait de profond, d'original et qui s'imposait à son goût sans être susceptible d'être modifié. Et le respect religieux qu'il apportait à l'expression de ce sentiment, sa peur de lui faire subir en la traduisant la moindre déformation, l'empêcha, au contraire de ce qu'on a souvent pensé, de mêler jamais à ses impressions devant les oeuvres d'art aucun artifice de raisonnement qui leur fût étranger. De sorte que ceux qui voient en lui un moraliste et un apôtre aimant dans l'art ce qui n'est pas l'art, se trompent à l'égal de ceux qui, négligeant l'essence profonde de son sentiment esthétique, le confondent avec un dilettantisme voluptueux.[19]

Whereas Huysmans' initial appreciation of medieval art had been emotional in this way, and in his art criticism he analyzes works from an aesthetic viewpoint, his interest became increasingly ethical. In *La Cathédrale,* 1898, he defines Christian symbolism in art as "The allegorical representation of a Christian principle, in a perceptible form" ("La représentation allégorique d'un principe chrétien, sous une forme sensible") (XIV, 157), and in this novel he was intent on comprehending and explaining this symbolism. For he believed that the Gothic period marked the height of truth and that all periods since then were morally inferior and their art less significant. Already in 1879 he had written that

> Religious painting has been floundering in its rut for centuries. Aside from the murals executed by Delacroix at Saint-Sulpice, we find only a precise formula scrupulously respected by all the chrism-mongers.

> La peinture religieuse patauge dans l'ornière depuis des siècles. Ecartons les peintures murales exécutées par Delacroix, à Saint-Sulpice, et nous ne trouvons qu'une précise formule scrupuleusement respectée par tous les batteurs de saint-chrême. (VI, 28)

And in *La Cathédrale* he confirms that

> after Rembrandt. . . . There follows the irreparable decay of religious impression in art. . . . As for the eighteenth century, there wasn't even any to speak of; that century was an age of belly and bidet, and whenever it sought to approach worship, it turned a holy-water font into a wash basin.

> après Rembrandt. . . . C'est l'irrémédiable déchéance de l'impression religieuse dans l'art. . . . Quant au dix-huitième siècle, il n'y avait même pas à s'en occuper; ce siècle fut une époque de bedon et de bidet et, dès qu'il voulut toucher au culte, il fit d'un bénitier une cuvette. (XIV, 2, 148–49)

Huysmans thus became committed to the idea, expressed later by the sculptor Rodin in his book on the French Cathedrals, that "if we could manage to understand Gothic art, we would be irresistibly brought back to the truth" ("si nous parvenions à comprendre l'art gothique, nous serions irrésistiblement ramenés à la vérité").[20]

Unfortunately, Huysmans' Catholic novels, sincere as they are in their attempt to investigate Church art, make for tedious reading. They are lengthy and didactic and lack the humor and imaginative treatment of his earlier novels and prose poems. It is indeed ironical and pathetic that after Huysmans felt he had discovered a new aesthetic formula to spur him on to new creative endeavors, he felt less confident than ever in his work. On April 3, 1893, for instance, he wrote to Arij Prins:

> I am working in disgust—and I have strong urges to toss every damn thing into the fire, for what I am writing at the moment seems to me mediocre indeed. I have lived for art—and—now that I am forty-five years old, I realize its emptiness

> Je travaille avec dégoût—et j'ai de fortes envies de tout foutre au feu, car ça me paraît bien médiocre, ce que j'écris pour l'instant. J'ai vécu pour l'art—et—aujourd'hui que j'ai quarante-cinq ans, j'aperçois son néant[21]

and after the publication of *La Cathédrale* he wrote despondently to Abbé Ferret on March 7, 1897:

> It's a pot of erudition, a concentrated bouillon of Church art, but it seems to have been pasted together with albumin; these enumerations and these quotations are not really springboards for writing, packed as though by a hydraulic press, compressed into chapters. Well, anyway. That completes *En Route*.

> C'est un réceptacle d'érudition, un bouillon consommé de l'art de l'Eglise, mais ça a l'air d'être écrit avec de l'albumine; ce ne sont vraiment pas des tremplins à phrases que ces énumérations et ces citations, tassées comme à la presse hydraulique, comprimées dans des chapitres. Enfin! Cela complète *En Route*.[22]

Huysmans' realization of his own creative problems are all the more painful when one remembers the criticism he levelled at his own mentor Zola years earlier. Attacking Zola's systematic method of writing a certain number of pages each day, he wrote that "his novels are not works of art, but works of ideas" ("ses romans ne sont pas des oeuvres d'art, mais des oeuvres d'idées").[23]

Aware of artistic failure in himself yet still determined to recreate the moral and spiritual character of medieval art, Huysmans began to work towards the founding of an artistic monastery where talented Catholic artists, himself included, could live together according to Christian principles. He had first felt this strong need to escape bureaucratic life in 1893 and, as he expresses it in *La Cathédrale,*

> he envisioned himself a monk in an accommodating monastery inhabited by a lenient order, one that loved the liturgies and was enamored of art.
>
> il se voyait moine dans un couvent débonnaire, desservi par un ordre clément, amoureux de liturgies et épris d'art. (XIV, 1, 298)

In *L'Oblat,* 1903, the novel in which Huysmans attempts to present an accurate account of life in a French religious community at the beginning of the century, he lays great stress on the role of art in maintaining true religious practice:

> One has, moreover, to be ignorant indeed to deny the power of art, even if only from the standpoint of practicality. It was the surest aid to mysticism and liturgy during the Middle Ages. . . . If the Benedictine rule has an objective, it is precisely to create it anew and to promote it.
>
> Il faut être bien ignorant, du reste, pour nier, en ne se plaçant même qu'au point de vue pratique, la puissance de l'art. Il a été l'auxiliaire le plus sûr de la mystique et de la liturgie, pendant le Moyen Age. . . . Si l'oblature Bénédictine a une raison d'être, c'est précisément de le créer à nouveau et de l'élever. (XVII, 2, 149–51)

Huysmans was not alone in his ideas of setting up a religious artistic community. He knew that there were similar attempts being made all over Europe, notably by the Rosicrucians and by Lenz and his followers at Beuron, Germany. In England, the writer Rolfe, whose life is described by A. J. A. Symons in his novel *The Quest for Corvo,* was asked by a friend whether he was interested in taking part in such a plan: "This ambitious project was the founding of a secular semi-monastic order which, by joint studies, should, in a spirit of disinterestedness, add to the learning of the world."[24] It was Rolfe's belief, as it was also Huysmans' that "it is desirable to revive the virtues of that period of the World's history commonly called the Middle Ages, and to practice them, in the hope that we may thereby the better pursue wisdom."[25]

The overwhelming problem which faced Huysmans, however, was the lack of what he considered gifted and genuine Catholic artists. As he wrote in *La Cathédrale,*

> There is no point in seeking among modern artists either; painters like Overbeck, Ingres, and Flandrin were wan old nags harnessed to commissioned works of piety; in the church of

> Saint-Sulpice, Delacroix crushes all the daubers around him, but his feeling for Catholic art is nonexistent. And the same is true of our contemporary artists.

> Dans le moderne, il n'y a non plus à chercher; les Overbeck, les Ingres, les Flandrin furent de blèmes haridelles attelées à des sujets de commande pieux; dans l'église Saint-Sulpice, Delacroix écrase tous les peinturleurs qui l'entourent, mais son sentiment de l'art catholique est nul. Et il est de même de ceux de nos artistes contemporains. (XIV, 2, 149)

In spite of the fact that Huysmans' aesthetic aims seemed to correspond to the ideas of the Rosicrucians, as set out in Péladan's *Comment on devient artiste,* 1874, Huysmans dismisses that group as fake mystics. He is no kinder towards the artists at Beuron and describes some of their work as follows:

> Those frescos refer back to the imagery of Assyria and Egypt. . . . Beuron's ideal had become a mixture of French art of the First Empire and modern English art.

> Ces fresques reportaient à l'imagerie de l'Assyrie et de l'Egypte. . . . L'idéal de Beuron était alors devenu un alliage de l'art français du Premier Empire et de l'art anglais moderne. (XIV, 2, 152–53)

In contrast, many of the Synthetists, such as Emile Bernard, Paul Sérusier and Maurice Denis, were in close contact with Beuron and were much inspired by its art. Sérusier even translated Lenz's book into French and Denis wrote an introduction to it, mentioning what he considered the unfounded judgment of Huysmans in *La Cathédrale.* Huysmans' lack of sympathy with these artists was, of course, grounded in his belief that realism was still a fundamental part of symbolism and that true-to-nature description was still the starting point of all art. He could therefore understand and support the theoretical thrust of the Synthetists and the Rosicrucians, among others, but totally rejected their style. As he writes in *La Cathédrale:*

> To stop working from nature, to impose an unvarying ritual of colors and line . . . indicated an absolute incomprehension of art in anyone who took such a chance. This system was destined to end in the ossification, the paralysis of painting, and indeed these were the results achieved.

> Supprimer l'étude d'après nature, exiger un rituel uniforme de couleurs et de lignes . . . dénotait chez celui qui risqua cet effort, une incompréhension absolue de l'art. Ce système devait aboutir à l'ankylose, à la paralysie de la peinture et tels furent, en effet, les résultats atteints. (XIV, 2, 154)

Since Huysmans did not feel at ease with any of the existing artistic communities but was more and more determined to leave Paris for a sheltered existence in the country, he made attempts to set up his own artistic monastery, where he could write better in the presence of religious artists. His first hopes were raised in 1894 when he was introduced to a certain Dom Besse, who had similar ideas about an artistic retreat and told Huysmans of his plans to restore the Benedictine Abbey of Saint-Wandrille. When Huysmans heard that Dom

Besse had been sent to Spain and had to drop any thought of Saint-Wandrille, he fell into despair.

His hopes were raised again in 1895 when Antoinette Donavie, a seventy-year-old nun, wrote him about setting up an artistic cloister in the convent of Fiancey near Valence. On May 29 Huysmans wrote about it to Abbé Moeller:

> The joy—in an abbey where there would be nothing but plainsong and clean things—of being able to work in peace on a life of the good Lydwine! This attempt to renew religious art in truly propitious surroundings would be so beautiful.

> La joie, dans une abbaye où il n'y aurait que du plain-chant et des objets propres, de pouvoir travailler en paix à une vie de la bonne Lydwine! Ce serait si beau cette tentative de rénover l'art religieux dans un milieu réellement propice.[26]

However, when Huysmans visited the nun at Fiancey, he realized that the plans would never materialize because Mother Célestine, as she was known, was more concerned with her hydrotherapy clinic than with artistic projects.

Huysmans' third hope of joining an artist's community was also frustrated. Knowing of his desire of retreating to a monastery, Abbé Mugnier suggested to Huysmans that he should spend some time at the Abbey of Saint-Maur de Glanfeuil, in Anjou. On visiting he decided that he was probably unsuited to the life of the cloister and he accepted the advice that he would be happier as an oblate. On July 8 he wrote his close friend Léon Leclaire, with whom he had hoped to set up an artistic community: "Cloisters are fine in dreams, but dreadful in reality; and one certainly finds one's salvation less there than in the world" ("Les cloîtres, c'est beau en rêve, mais affreux en réalité; et l'on y fait certainement moins son salut que dans le monde").[27]

The idea of oblature became more attractive in August of that year, when Huysmans spent a very happy time at Ligugé near Poitiers and even found a perfect plot of land for building a house. He incited the Leclaires with the same enthusiasm and after some negotiation they decided to build a shared house at Ligugé in which they could be joined by other oblates with similar tastes and aims. Huysmans did not intend to have much connection with the monks, because he had a very low opinion of most clergymen's aesthetic judgment and believed they would only interfere with his plans. Huysmans greatly hoped that he could persuade Marie-Charles Dulac to join this community. Dulac was a young painter whom he had singled out in *La Cathédrale* as the most talented of all contemporary Catholic artists. Dulac approached Huysmans in January 1898 to thank him for the favorable criticism of his work in *La Cathédrale* and to discuss the possibilities of setting up an artistic community. At no time had Huysmans been more optimistic, but then, one by one, the prospective members of the project backed out. The plans were given their final blow when Dulac, the cornerstone of it all, died after Christmas 1898. After this failure to set up his community, Huysmans never mustered the courage again. He isolated himself for two years at Ligugé to write *Sainte Lydwine de Schiedam*, but gradually the unpleasant atmosphere created by impending government legislation directed against Catholic associations, combined with his ill health, made life unbearable. In 1901 he left Ligugé and returned to his lonely and miserable life in Paris.

Huysmans never saw the revival of Catholic art but, in spite of great suffering, he died in peace in 1907. In the painting, architecture, sculpture, and music of the Middle Ages he had found an expression of spiritualism, anguish, and faith which gave meaning to his life. Inspired by the beliefs expressed in these works, he was able to dedicate the last years of his life to the account of his own conversion, the explanation of Church symbolism and the story of a saint who personified the suffering Huysmans had first seen in the Grünewald *Crucifixion* and who could now inspire him with the faith he needed to endure his own painful illness.

We have seen how Huysmans had difficulty dealing with reality and therefore looked to art as a substitute. He often found it easier to find inspiration in paintings than in people or nature and sublimated many of his deepest feelings in art, often mistaking art for reality. This accounts, to a large degree, for the impact of the visual arts on his aesthetic development and the influence of specific paintings on his literary imagination and language.

2

The Woman-Haters:
Degas, Forain, Rops, and Moreau

Listen, infamous wench, I hate you, I despise you . . . and I love you!

Entends-tu, ribaude infâme, je te hais, je te méprise—et je t'aime!

"Déclaration d'amour," *Le Drageoir aux épices*

Throughout his work Huysmans demonstrated an ambivalence towards women which was never resolved. Both in his art criticism and in his novels and prose poems women are depicted as sensual and attractive, sometimes consoling, and yet ultimately evil and cunningly sophisticated in their quest to initiate men into love and and then destroy them. Only occasionally does Huysmans show compassion for woman's lot. This explains why he was sympathetic to artists who painted prostitutes, actresses, dancers, loose working women, and enchantresses and why he depicted the same types in his novels and prose poems. Many of Huysmans' works do not contain a female character of any consequence; this very omission reinforces the fact that Huysmans was scared of women, was disgusted by what he considered their stupidity, often despised them for the power they exerted over him, experienced trouble relating to them, and tried hard to live without them.

The views and images developed in Huysmans' articles on Degas and Forain, and one on Manet's *Nana,* written in 1877 for *L'Artiste,*[1] are found in his early Naturalist novels, *Marthe,* 1876, *Les Soeurs Vatard,* 1879, and *En Ménage,* 1881, and in the collection of prose poems *Croquis parisiens,* 1880. In these works he depicts the urban working girl, the actress, and the prostitute. These are all common themes in the Naturalist literature but underlying Huysmans' treatment of them is a fundamentally decadent attitude, shared by many other writers of the eighties. In spite of the fact that Huysmans' choice of Parisian middle- and lower-class subjects indicated an adherence to the Naturalist aesthetic of Zola, his treatment of these subjects showed that he had a strong urge towards something more exciting, more unusual, less tied to the trivialities of everyday life. All the men in Huysmans' works are unhealthy, neurotic, and passive and they often look to women to provide the stimulation lacking in their own daily lives. Huysmans' taste for the artificial in dress, makeup, and demeanor, found in the prostitute and the actress, was a stand against the natural which had come to mean banal, totally devoid of the heroic qualities seen by Rousseau. As A. E. Carter writes in his analysis of decadence, "The abnormal becomes a proof of man's superiority to natural law, a demonstration of free will, an artificiality, which, although more lurid than face-paint or dyed hair, is of the same order. This is the main idea behind the cult of artificiality, and, for that matter, behind the whole theory of decadence."[2]

The works of Moreau and Rops treat the perversely erotic woman and thus respond even more closely to Huysmans' decadent sensibility than those of Degas and Forain. In *A Rebours,* 1884, the Moreau pictures of Salome are the embodiment of des Esseintes' sexual inclinations. It will be shown that the images developed in the description of these Moreau works became not only an important part of the whole descriptive code of *A Rebours* but also influence the descriptive code of parts of *En Rade,* 1887, and *Là-Bas,* 1891. In *En Rade,* the Salome image, combined with some images developed in the description of a Degas work, is integrated into a disturbing dream sequence. In *Là-Bas* the images of sexual perversity seen in Moreau and Rops are found both in the trial scene and in the characterization of the satanist Madame Chantelouve, who is the manifestation of the evil woman, the temptress, and the seducer who initiates innocent men into the more perverse aspects of love.

After his conversion to Catholicism, Huysmans' obsession with women is less openly expressed. His sexual urges are frequently sublimated in his enthusiasm for certain religious works of art and his ambivalence towards women continues to be a tension in his work. As indications of Huysmans' views on women in his post-conversion period, I shall briefly discuss the identification Huysmans perceives between Chartres Cathedral and woman. Huysmans develops the theme of initiation at the time when he is tempted to enter the Church. The beauty of its art and architecture attract him, he looks to it for consolation and yet finds it intimidating and frightening when it comes to a total commitment. Further examples of Huysmans' ambivalent feelings towards women at that time are the descriptions of Fra Angelico's *Le Couronnement de la Vierge* in *La Cathédrale,* 1898, of an anonymous Renaissance portrait of a young girl, and of a *Virgin and Child* by the Maître de Flémalle in *Trois Primitifs,* 1905.

Manet, 1877

The essay Huysmans wrote on Manet's *Nana* in 1877 was never included in his collected works, probably because he had such strong reservations about the painting technique of Manet.[3] It is an important text, however, because it con-

tains the fundamental elements of all Huysmans' descriptions of the prostitute—her animal characteristics, her aggressive nature, and her malicious intent to overpower men. Huysmans begins the article with a description of what
he considers to be one of the major achievements of the Impressionists, among
whom he includes Manet:

> To render the provocative attitude of swinging hips, to render the lewdness of swimming
> glances, to make one smell the odor of flesh moving beneath cambric, to render the street-
> walkers' irritations, their joyous animal sensuality or their resignedness.

> Rendre l'attitude irritante des hanches qui se tortillent, rendre la polissonnerie des regards
> noyés, faire sentir l'odeur de la chair qui bouge sous la batiste, rendre les énervements, la
> bestialité joyeuse ou la resignation des filles.[4]

Here Huysmans talks not only of the prostitute's animal sensuality—her walk,
her provocative look, her odor, and her extravagant clothes—but recognizes
the misery of her existence. He also talks, however, of her "complicated and
skillful depravity" ("vice compliqué et savant"), a first allusion to the idea
Huysmans develops in the discussions of Moreau's *Salomé* and in *Là-Bas,* that
a woman, far from being the innocent and passive lover, is usually consciously
involved in a science of initiation and castration. His sympathy is thus tem-
pered by a certain disgust, mingled with fear.

This disgust is expressed by the use of animal vocabulary, in this case a
horse, which demeans the woman described. When Huysmans says of Nana
that "her hindquarters swell beneath the white skirt, her legs encased in gray
silk stockings" ("la croupe renfle sous le jupon blanc, les jambes serrées dans
des bas en soie grise"), we picture the animal beneath the sophisticated clothing. In the description of Nana, as of women in so many later texts, the emphasis shifts specifically from women/animals as embodiments of sensuality to
women/animals as aggressive fighters. Huysmans talks of Nana as harnessing
herself and describes her beautiful clothes as "battle dress" ("ses toilettes de
bataille"). This image of a woman clothed in equine battle dress reappears in
Là-Bas in a rather amusing, ironic scene. Durtal is planning the seduction of
Madame Chantelouve and is worried about the logistics of the situation:

> But then there is that damned question of the skirts! I admire those novelists who can get
> a virgin *unharnessed* from her dresses, *ungirthed* from her corsets and deflowered with a
> quick kiss and in the winking of an eye—as if this were possible!

> Mais, il y a cette damnée question des jupes! j'admire les romanciers qui font déflorer des
> vierges *harnachées* dans des robes, *sanglées* dans des corsets, et cela, naturellement, en un
> tour de baiser, en un clin d'oeil, comme si c'était possible! (XII, 1, 241) [my italics]

Degas and Forain, 1879–81

The vocabulary which Huysmans first developed in the *Nana* article is found
again in the discussions of Degas and of Huysmans' other favorite Impres-

sionist, Forain. In "Le Salon de 1879" in *L'Art moderne* Huysmans describes the women in Degas' paintings as "those exquisite Parisian women with their lusterless complexions, their rouged lips, their lewd hips that move in clinging armor of satin and silk" ("ces exquises Parisiennes au teint mat, aux lèvres far-dées, aux hanches polissonnes, qui bougent dans de moulantes armures de satin et de soie") (VI, 13). In addition to the provocative hips and the seductive armor there is here the other recurrent theme of makeup worn both by the women in the street and on the theater stage. Huysmans is fascinated by the mask or clownlike effect created by the contrast between the pale, powdered skin and the bright lips, emphasized in many of Degas' paintings by the play of artificial light on these faces. The emphasis on makeup is another way of de-humanizing and depersonalizing women, and the expression "sickly splendor" ("maladif éclat") (VI, 12), used to describe the made-up faces seen from a dis-tance, is a contradiction in terms which expresses the ambivalence Huysmans feels towards these women. It is this very sickliness which sometimes appeals to him and he frequently mentions in his art criticism that he has no interest in the smooth, unnatural skin of the academic paintings. In spite of his attraction to these women, however, his negative feelings are indicated by the words "bray" ("brailler") (VI, 12) to describe the singers and "gambol" ("s'ébattre") (VI, 12) to describe the dancers.

In "L'Exposition des Indépendants en 1880" there are further examples of horse vocabulary to describe women. Huysmans talks, for example, of three ballerinas who are "steady on their hips" ("campées sur les hanches") (VI, 130). He is here quoting from the article he claims to have written in 1876 for *La Gazette des Amateurs,* in which he expresses the excitement he experienced that year on discovering the works of Degas, who fulfilled his "needs for reality and everyday life" ("besoins de réalité et de vie intime") (VI, 130), a satisfac-tion Huysmans had previously found only in seventeenth-century Dutch paint-ings.

In this article of 1880 Huysmans shifts his focus somewhat from the phys-ical appearance of the dancers to their emotions. Like Degas himself, who was impressed by the difficulty and the exhaustion involved in dance, Huysmans develops an imagery of pain, immobility, and automation. He talks of

> the tedium of painful, mechanical work . . . the indifference of their fellows to weariness familiar to them . . . a statue of irritation and fatigue.

> l'ennui d'un travail mécanique pénible. . . , l'indifférence des camarades pour des lassitudes qu'elles connaissent . . . une statue de l'embêtement et de la fatigue. (VI, 132)

The idea of dancers doing mechanical, mindless work is emphasized by the fact that "les jambes," "les mains," and "la pointe des souliers" (VI, 133), rather than the dancers themselves, are the subject of the sentence, and by the fact that Huysmans uses a mixture of animal and machine vocabulary. When the dancers return to the floor after their rest they "resume their clownlike dislocations" ("reprennent leurs dislocations de clowns") (VI, 132–33) and "the lips smile automatically" ("les lèvres sourient automatiques") (VI, 133). Huysmans describes the poor dancers as "the giraffes that could not break, the elephants whose hinges refused to bend" ("les girafes qui ne pouvaient se rompre, les éléphants dont les charnières refusaient de plier") (VI, 133) and he completely dehumanizes them when he writes of

> the wiry girls, whose muscles stand out beneath their tights, real baby goats built for jumping, real dancers, steel-sprung, iron-legged.

> les filles nerveuses, sèches, dont les muscles saillent sous le maillot, de vraies biquettes construites pour sauter, de vraies danseuses, aux ressorts d'acier, aux jarrets de fer. (VI, 134)

The machine vocabulary employed by Huysmans to describe Degas' dancers denotes a certain detachment on his part: a fascination with the unnatural stances of their bodies but no attraction to them as women. An interesting change takes place between this article and *A Rebours,* in which machine vocabulary is used positively to describe Miss Urania, one of des Esseintes' mistresses: "an American girl with a supple figure, sinewy legs, muscles of steel, and arms of iron" ("une Américaine, au corps bien découplé, aux jambes nerveuses, aux muscles d'acier, aux bras de fonte") (VII, 156). Machine metaphors are found again in the article Huysmans wrote in 1887, using notes he made on his visit to Holland in 1876. Impressed by the physical strength of the Dutch women, he describes them as "beautiful machines, solid and broad-backed, equipped with steel biceps and iron hams" ("belles machines, solides et râblées, munies de biceps en acier et de jarrets de fonte").[5] In *Là-Bas* the relationship between women and machines is developed more explicitly, not to say crudely, when Des Hermies lectures Durtal about the naturalness of sex:

> The heart, which is supposed to be the noble part of man, has the same form as the penis, which is the so-called ignoble part of man. There's symbolism in that similarity, because every love which is of the heart soon extends to the organ resembling it. The moment the human imagination tries to create artificially animated beings, it involuntarily reproduces in them the movements of animals propogating. Look at machines, the action of pistons in cylinders: Romeos of steel and Juliets of cast iron. Human expression does not differ at all from the back-and-forth motion of our machines.

> Le coeur qui est réputé la partie noble de l'homme a la même forme que le pénis qui en est, soi-disant, la partie vile; c'est très symbolique, car tout amour de coeur finit par l'organe qui lui ressemble. L'imagination humaine, lorsqu'elle se mêle d'animer des êtres d'artifice, en est réduite à reproduire les mouvements des animaux qui se propagent. Vois les machines, le jeu des pistons dans les cylindres; ce sont dans des Juliette en fonte des Roméo d'acier; les expressions humaines ne diffèrent pas du tout du va-et-vient de nos machines. (XII, 56)

The most notable stylistic feature of most of Huysmans' essays on art which we have seen so far is an extensive use of simile and metaphor which is associated with imaginative writing rather than art criticism. It is this treatment which allows Huysmans to integrate parts of his art criticism so naturally into his novels and prose poems. In the 1880 essay on Degas we find the first example of another of Huysmans' stylistic characteristics—the introduction of a narrative into a description of a painting. He develops the account of a ballet scene by Degas by the use of a series of verbs which introduce a time sequence: "But here they come now," "Their rest is over," "the limbs' torture begins again," "the exercises speed up," and "Then, the metamorphosis is complete" ("Mais les voici maintenant," "Le repos est fini," "la torture des membres recommence," "les exercices s'accélèrent," "Puis, la métamorphose s'est accomplie") (VI, 133). Huysmans even goes so far as to describe the sounds "painted" by the artist. So we read that "the music starts its scratching once more" ("la musique regrince") and that

> The illusion becomes so complete . . . that they all come to life and pant, that one seems to hear the cries of the dancing mistress piercing the shrill din of the kit violin: "Heels forward, hips in, wrists up, bend."

> L'illusion devient si complète . . . que toutes s'animent et pantellent, que les cris de la maîtresse semblent s'entendre, perçant l'aigre vacarme de la pochette: "Avancez les talons, rentrez les hanches, soutenez les poignets, cassez-vous." (VI, 133)

This tendency of Huysmans to bring a painting to life by describing it as if it were a play, or even a slice of reality, is preparation for the integration of paintings into his fiction.

Many of the animal and warfare images in Huysmans' discussion of Degas in "L'Exposition des Indépendants en 1880" are found again in the main essay on Forain in the same article. Further, there are close parallels between this description of Forain and the third of the series of prose poems which constitute "Les Folies Bergère en 1879" in *Croquis parisiens,* 1880. When discussing Forain's painting of the Folies-Bergère Huysmans alludes to "The alluring rot, all that dissolute charm" ("L'attirante pourriture, toute l'élégance libertine") (VI, 123), an expression echoed in the prose poem's "powerful aroma of their underarms and the very subtle perfume of a dying flower at their bodice" ("puissant arome de leurs dessous de bras et le très fin parfum d'une fleur en train d'expirer à leur corsage").[6] In one of Forain's portraits of a prostitute he writes:

> . . . her impudent laughter, her provocative eyes and her wicked manner; no one has better understood the pleasing vagaries of her styles, the enormous thrusting breasts, the arms as thin as matchsticks, the pinched-in waist, her bust splitting from the strain of the armor that compresses and diminishes the flesh in one place, to distend and increase it in another.

> . . . son rire impudent, ses yeux provocants et son air rosse; nul n'a mieux compris les plaisants caprices de ses modes, les seins énormes, jetés en avant, les bras grêles comme des allumettes, la taille amenuisée, le buste craquant sous l'effort de l'armure comprimant et diminuant la chair, d'un côté, pour la distendre et l'augmenter, d'un autre. (VI, 125)

In the prose poem we find the same proud, armored women with their provocative makeup and emphasized bust:

> They are outrageous and they are splendid, when, in the hemi-cycle around the room, they walk two by two, powdered and painted, eyes swimming in pale blue smudges, lips encircled in a startling red, breasts thrusting forward over tight hips.

> Elles sont inouïes et elles sont splendides, lorsque dans l'hémicycle longeant la salle, elles marchent deux à deux, poudrées et fardées, l'oeil noyé dans une estompe de bleu pâle, les lèvres cerclées d'un rouge fracassant, les seins projetés en avances sur des reins sanglés. . . . (VIII, 11)

In "L'Exposition des Indépendants en 1881," in which Huysmans describes a series of paintings of down-and-outs, including prostitutes, we find again the image of the clown and his mask. Huysmans modifies the image, however, with an incipient moralistic interpretation: "they are the masks, worn out but almost purified by vice's victories" ("ce sont les masques, usés mais comme sublimés, par les triomphes du vice" (VI, 270). In this same article of 1881, Huysmans writes also of Degas' sculpture of the fourteen-year-old dancer, the first sculpture which Degas ever exhibited. All critics were shocked, many outraged. Only Huysmans seemed fully to comprehend the importance of the work and admired it without reservation. All the critics saw in the sculpture a combination of a realistic technique and a disturbing content, pointing to the girl's ugliness and her expression of vice.[7] Huysmans focuses on the girl's decadent characteristics, perceiving in her the sickly yet aggressive female he finds in both Degas' and Forain's paintings of singers and ballerinas. He feels that she has "a sickly and swarthy face" ("la face maladive et bise"), that she is "haggard and old before her time" ("tirée et vieille avant l'âge"), that she is "ready for the struggle" ("en place pour la lutte"), and that her legs are "sinewy and gnarled" ("nerveuses et tordues") (VI, 249). It is the image of this young ballerina which reappears in the first dream sequence in *En Rade*, to be discussed later in this chapter.

In *Marthe*, 1876, there are numerous passages which use the same imagery as that found in the texts on Degas and Forain in *L'Art moderne* and clearly express the same feelings about women. The art criticism and the fiction complement each other to an unusual degree. Indeed, as an innocent girl who becomes a cabaret singer and progresses to prostitution, Marthe is like a composite picture of all the types portrayed in the paintings of Degas and Forain, and Huysmans expresses about her the same combination of attraction, disgust, and pity and uses the same imagery of rich luxury mixed with that of animals and warfare. So on the one hand Marthe

> looked charming in her outfit which she herself had cut out of various silks bought on sale. A pink *cuirass,* studded with artificial pearls, a *cuirass* of exquisite pink, that fading, faint pink of oriental fabrics, hugged her hips, which were barely contained in their silken prison;

with her *helmet* of opulent red hair, with her titillating, wet, voracious red lips, she was enchanting and irresistibly seductive!

était charmante avec son costume qu'elle avait elle-même découpé dans des moires et des soies à forfait. Une *cuirasse* rose, couturée de fausses perles, une *cuirasse* d'un rose exquis, de ce rose faiblissant et comme expiré des étoffes du Levant, serrait ses hanches mal contenues dans leur prison de soie; avec son *casque* de cheveux opulemment roux, ses lèvres qui titillaient, humides, voraces, rouges, elle enchantait, irrésistiblement séduisante! (II, 16) [my italics]

On the other hand Marthe finds it hard to resign herself to "this surrendering of her own body" ("cette abdication d'elle-même") (II, 33), and this disgust is expressed in a moment of self-awareness as she looks, as if for the first time, at a group of fellow prostitutes:

she looked with dazed wonder at the strange poses of her friends, banal and vulgar beauties . . . crouched *like dogs* on a stool . . . hair piled up in every which way: . . . black or blond *manes,* either with pomade or whitened with powder.

elle regardait avec hébètement les poses étranges de ses camarades, des beautés falotes et vulgaires . . . accroupies *comme des chiennes,* sur un tabouret . . . les cheveux édifiés de toutes sortes: . . . *crinières* noires ou blondes, pommadées ou poudrées d'une neige de riz. (II, 35) [my italics]

This passage in *Marthe* is notable for two reasons. Firstly, Huysmans uses in it many of the same animal similes and metaphors as in his articles on Degas and Forain. Secondly, it is an excellent example of Huysmans' stylistic treatment in which he creates the illusion that the passage is a *transposition d'art.* He introduces the passage with a verb of seeing or looking, in this case "regarder"; he then describes the space in which the subject poses, talks of the colors and the shapes of the subject, and finally ends the description by a clear return to reality, prompted very commonly by a noise, which awakens the viewer from his "looking" or "dreaming." In this case it is a bell, followed by a silence which falls over the tired prostitutes. Given the similarity of subject matter and images, certain critics have been tempted to read this passage as either a description of a specific Degas painting or to believe it had an influence on the painter.[8] From the point of view of this study, however, the significance of the relationship lies not so much in the specific influence between author and painter but in the fact that Huysmans, by integrating a prose style developed in his art criticism and using certain stylistic devices, creates the illusion of a painting within his narrative. Such descriptions provide breaks in the narrative and create moments of great intensity and plasticity.

As *Marthe* progresses, the heroine becomes more entrenched in her aggressive attitudes, claiming that "people reproach us for looting fortunes! but war is war, after all! You ravage, you pillage!" ("l'on nous reproche de saccager des fortunes! mais c'est la guerre après tout! L'on ravage et l'on pille!")

(II, 117). The novel ends, however, on a positive note as far as women are concerned, and in a letter from Marthe's lover Léo to a friend we find the kind of moralistic interpretation of vice which Huysmans began to express in his later articles on Degas and Rops: "girls like her are good in that they make men love women who are unlike them; they serve as a foil to decency" ("les filles comme elle ont cela de bon qu'elles font aimer celles qui ne leur ressemblent pas; elles servent de repoussoir à l'honnêteté") (II, 140).

Les Soeurs Vatard, 1879, is the other Naturalist novel in which the treatment of women corresponds closely to Huysmans' discussions of Degas' and Forain's paintings in *L'Art moderne*. The scanty plot of the novel is based on the parallel development of two sisters as they deal with their work in the bindery and with their lovers. Désirée is the innocent, kind, and consoling one who looks after her father and is bashful of men and Céline is the harder, more attractive and more aggressive type. They are the embodiments of two aspects of woman described in an article called "La Cruche cassée d'après Greuze," which Huysmans wrote in 1875 for the *Musée des Deux-Mondes*. In it he describes the woman in Greuze's painting as "this mixture of frank artlessness and striking sensuality" ("ce mélange de candide simplesse et de piquante volupté").[9] The most successful aspect of the novel, however, is the series of descriptions of scenes typical of the Impressionist painters Huysmans loved—the streets of Paris, cabarets, railway sidings, a fair ground, and, above all, working women.

In the opening chapter there are two descriptions of workshops which are reminiscent of articles on Degas and Forain. The first contains images of women as loud instruments and unruly animals:

> The paperfolders hit the tables, the liter-bottles passed from one mouth to the next, dripping saliva and wine; a worker, standing, was trying to get back to her seat, her companions pushed their chairbacks into her stomach. A girl blew her nose, *as if blowing a trumpet;* a bottle broke its neck on the edge of a table, light red wine poured over dresses, two women vomited abuse on one another, *they were restrained by the napes of their necks and their rags, but they twisted and barked, chins forward, teeth bared, drooling, kicking, arms in air, armpits exposed beneath the split seams of their shirts.*
>
> There was another break in the tumult, and only the muffled tapping of the collators in the other room was heard.
>
> The stitchers had voices like broken *kazoos; they growled.*

> Les plioirs frappaient les tables, les litres passaient d'une bouche à l'autre, suintant la salive et le vin;—une ouvrière, debout, voulait regagner sa place, ses compagnes lui écrasèrent le ventre avec les dossier de leurs chaises.—Une fille se moucha, *sonnant comme d'une trompette;*—une bouteille se brisa le bec au rebord d'une table, le petit bleu coula sur les robes, deux femmes vomirent, l'une contre l'autre, des injures de poissardes, *on les retint par leurs chignons et par leurs loques, mais elles se tordaient et aboyaient, le menton en avant et les dents sorties, bavant, se ruant, les bras en l'air, la fosse des aisselles à jour sous la chemise craquée.*
>
> Il y eut encore un moment de répit et l'on n'entendit plus que le tapotement sourd des assembleurs dans l'autre pièce.
>
> Les brocheuses avaient des voix de *mirlitons* crevés; *elles râlaient.* (III, 9–10) [My italics]

The second description, by including the women in a list of odors given off by the coal, gas, food, cats, latrines, paper, and glue, puts them on a level of machines and other inanimate objects:

> A heavy vapor hung over the room; an unbearable odor of coal and gas, of the sweat of women with dirty underthings, a stench of goats dying in the sun, mixed with the putrid smells of sausages and wine, with the acrid piss of the tomcat, with the coarse stink of the privies, with the sickly scent of the wet paper and the tubs of glue.
>
> The forewoman put back *the chairs thrown any which way, on their sides, on their backs, their legs in the air, their golden-strawed entrails coming out in corkscrews or escaping in strings by the holes in their bellies.* She piled *the crowd* of high stools onto trestles.

> Une buée lourde planait au-dessus de la salle; une insupportable odeur de houille et de gaz, de sueur de femmes dont les dessous sont sales, une senteur forte de chèvres qui auraient gigoté au soleil, se mêlaient aux émanations putrides de la charcuterie et du vin, à l'âcre pissat du chat, à la puanteur rude des latrines, à la fadeur des papiers mouillés et des baquets de colle.
>
> La contremaître rangea *les chaises jetées au hasard, sur le flanc, sur le dos, les jambes en l'air, leurs tripes de paille blonde se dressant en tire-bouchon ou fuyant en mèches par le trou du ventre.* Elle empila sur des tréteaux *la cohue* des tabourets. (III, 14) [my italics]

The second paragraph is a description of chairs but is a prime example of Huysmans' inverted use of female imagery, where the impression given to the reader is truly sexual. In this case the effect is especially forceful because, in spite of the fact that it is separated from the first text by four pages, it echoes its account of one of the women being pushed in the stomach by the other workers leaning back in their chairs: "ses compagnes lui écrasèrent le ventre avec les dossiers de leurs chaises" (III, 10).

Céline's lover Cyprien Tibaille is a painter, in character and taste an embryonic version of des Esseintes. Through him Huysmans expresses his views on contemporary art, especially the portrayal of women:

> he needed, for a painting, a common, *broad-backed, solid* girl, a lewd tart, the kind that fires your senses with every stride. . . . The Venus de Milo, to use his expression, looked half-witted to him . . . he needed, according to him, to capture her, to paint her unawares, and when, with unaffected movements, she dragged herself along or skipped with the sadness or the joy of an animal unleashed and unwatched! Basically, the girl, young and played out, *her complexion already faded* by the long evenings, *breasts still pliant* but sagging and beginning to fall, *her face—tempting and evil, depraved and painted—*attracted him.

> il avait besoin pour un tableau d'une fille populacière, *râblée, solide,* d'une goton lubrique, propre à vous tisonner les sens à chaque enjambée. . . . La Vénus de Médicis, pour se servir de son expression, lui semblait imbécile . . . il fallait, selon lui, la saisir, la peindre, alors qu'elle ne s'y attendait pas, et quand, sans emphase apprêtée de gestes, elle se traînait ou sautillait avec la tristesse ou la joie d'une bête lachée sans qu'on la surveille! Au fond, la fille, jeune et vannée, *au teint déjà défraîchi* par les soirées longues, *les seins encore élastiques,* mais mollissant et commençant à tomber, *la figure alléchante et mauvaise, polissonne et fardée,* l'attirait. (III, 161) [my italics]

Many of these expressions echo the articles written at the same time, on which we have already commented, and the phrase "râblée, solide" reappears in the 1887 article "En Hollande," in which Huysmans describes the Dutch "belles machines, solides et râblées, munies de biceps en acier et de jarrets de fonte," emphasizing again his association of women and machines. The phrase "biceps en acier et de jarrets de fonte" has already been noted in the 1880 article on Degas in *L'Art moderne,* in which Huysmans describes "de vraies danseuses, aux ressorts d'acier, aux jarrets de fer" (VI, 134).

In *Marthe* we noted a description of a brothel which reads like a *transposition d'art* because Huysmans introduces the description by a verb of seeing and ends it clearly with a sudden change of atmosphere and also describes the prostitutes, not as people so much as objects of color, light, and shape. In *Les Soeurs Vatard* there is another example of this type of *transposition d'art*—a description of a singer at the Folies-Bobino to which Auguste takes Désirée.[10] Again, the illusion that they are in front of a painting is created by a verb of looking: "Désirée was wrenching her neck trying to look up" ("Désirée se démanchait le cou à tenter de regarder en l'air") (III, 137) and the singer shares many characteristics with the subjects of Degas' and Forain's paintings—she is doll- or clownlike as she collapses "comme une marionnette" (III, 138), and "She was wrapped in a very low-cut pink dress, and her arms—bare and still red—were whitened with powder" ("Elle était enveloppée d'une robe rose très décolletée, et ses bras nus et encore rouges étaient blanchis par de la poudre") (III, 138). Reminiscent of the verb "brailler" which Huysmans uses to describe the singer of one of Degas' paintings of 1879, he here talks of "her gullet's raucous noise" ("le graillement de son gosier") (III, 138). The description contains many phrases referring to light, shadow, and spatial organization which are normally found in art criticism:

> Her chin cast a shadow onto the base of her neck. Her gullet's raucous noise was accompanied by four gestures: one hand on her heart and the other pressed along her thigh; her right arm extended straight out, the left one, behind; the same movement performed in reverse; lastly, both hands reaching out together toward the audience.

> Son menton projetait une ombre sur le bas de son cou. Elle accompagnait le graillement de son gosier avec quatre gestes: une main sur le coeur et l'autre collée de long de la jambe,— le bras droit en avant, le gauche en arrière,—le même mouvement effectué en sens inverse,—les deux mains enfin se tendant ensemble vers le public (III, 138–39)

and it ends with a return to reality, with Auguste and Désirée observing the scene from the perspective of the imaginary artist:

> From afar, from where Desirée and Auguste were seated, her wide-open mouth, as she bawled out the last line of the refrain, gaped like a black hole.

> De loin, de la place où Désirée et Auguste étaient assis, sa bouche grande ouverte, quand elle hurlait le dernier vers du refrain, béait comme un trou noir. (III, 139)

The female imagery which Huysmans developed in the articles in *L'Art moderne* was not only used to describe the women in his prose poems and his novels but was carried over to describe, for instance, machines and landscape. This shows the extent to which his preoccupation with women affected his whole descriptive code. To take but a few of the most flagrant examples, we must look at the description of the two trains in both *Les Soeurs Vatard* and *A Rebours*, in which Huysmans could exploit the identification between women and machines, women and wild animals. In the first we have

> One of the locomotives proceeded slowly, *belching* showers of sparks from her smokestack, *pissing* in little spurts, letting cinders fall, drop by drop, from her open *underbelly*. . . .
> She *roared,* and grumbled as she breathed harder, her belly rounded and *sweating,* and in the grumbling of her *flanks,* the clicking of the shovel against her iron *mouth* rang more clearly. The other machine . . . slowed down, shooting jets of white steam, *swaying*—on the zigzag of a track that linked two lines—the *skirt* of her tender, studded with a bleeding ruby.

> L'une [locomotive] se promenait lentement, éructant par son tuyau des gerbes de flammèches, *pissant* à petits coups, laissant tomber, de son *bas-ventre* ouvert, des braises, gouttes à gouttes. . . .
> Elle *rugissait,* et grondait soufflant plus fort, la panse arrondie et *suante,* et, dans le grommèlement de *ses flancs,* le cliquetis de la pelle sur le fer de *sa bouche* sonnait plus clair. L'autre machine . . . ralentissait sa marche, dardant des jets de vapeur blanche, faisant *onduler* sur le zigzag d'un rail qui reliait deux voies, *la jupe* de son tender, piquée d'un rubis saignant. (III, 120–21) [my italics]

The description of the train in *A Rebours* is more provocative and one is reminded of the American acrobat in the same novel with her steel muscles and her armorlike clothing:

> One of these, bearing the name of Crampton, is *an adorable blonde* with a shrill voice, *a long slender body* imprisoned in a shiny brass *corset,* and supple *catlike movements; a* smart golden *blonde* whose extraordinary grace can be quite terrifying when she stiffens her muscles of steel, sends the sweat pouring down her steaming flanks, sets her elegant wheels spinning in their wide circles, and hurtles away, full of life, at the head of an express or a boat-train.
> The other, Engerth by name, is *a strapping saturnine brunette* given to uttering raucous, guttural cries, with a thick-set figure encased in armour-plating of cast-iron; a monstrous creature with *her dishevelled mane* of black smoke and her six wheels coupled together low down, she gives an indication of her fantastic strength when, with an effort that shakes the very earth, she slowly and deliberately drags along her heavy train of goods-wagons.

> L'une [locomotive], la Crampton, *une adorable blonde,* à la voix aigüe, à *la grande taille frêle, emprisonnée dans un étincelant corset* de cuivre, au souple et nerveux *allongement de chatte, une blonde* pimpante et dorée, dont l'extraordinaire grâce épouvante lorsque, raidissant ses muscles d'acier, actibranle l'immense rosace de sa fine roue et s'élance toute vivante, en tête des rapides et des marées!
> L'autre, L'Engerth, *une monumentale et sombre brune* aux cris sourds et rauques, aux *reins* trapus, étranglés dans *une cuirasse en fonte,* une monstrueuse bête, à *la crinière échevelée* de fumée noire, aux six roues basses et accouplées: quelle écrasante puissance lorsque, faisant trembler la terre, elle remorque pesamment, lentement, *la lourde queue* de ses marchandises! (VII, 36–37) [my italics]

There are two landscape descriptions in *A Rebours* which also develop the female imagery of Huysmans' earlier criticism. Huysmans usually preferred melancholy countryside but in *A Rebours* all of des Esseintes' tastes are consistent and it is the artificial aspect of some landscapes which appeals to him. They remind one of Huysmans' descriptions of prostitutes and actresses portrayed by Degas and Forain. We thus read of a landscape where,

> The plain, lying partly in the shadow of the hills, appeared to have shrunk in size; and in the middle it seemed as if it were sprinkled with face-powder and smeared with cold-cream. . . . On account of its artificial, made-up appearance, des Esseintes found this landscape not unattractive. . . .

> Rétrécie par l'ombre tombée des collines, la plaine paraissait, à son milieu, poudrée de farine d'amidon et enduite de blanc cold-cream. . . . En raison de son maquillage et de son air factice, ce paysage ne déplaisait pas à des Esseintes. . . . (VII, 38)

We read of another where

> Once he had roughed out this background in its main outlines, so that it stretched away into the distance behind closed eyelids, he sprayed the room with a light rain of essences that were half-human, half-feline, smacking of the petticoat, indicating the presence of woman in her paint and powder . . . to give the factitious, cosmetic, indoor life they evoked the natural appearance of laughing, sweating, rollicking pleasures out in the sun.

> Ce décor posé en quelques grandes lignes, fuyant à perte de vue sous ses yeux fermés, il insuffla une légère pluie d'essences humaines et quasi félines, sentant la jupe, annonçant la femme poudrée et fardée . . . afin de donner dans la vie factice du maquillage qu'ils dégageaient, un fleur naturel de rires en sueur, de joies qui se démènent au plein soleil. (VII, 178)

Degas, Forain, and Rops, 1889

Between the publication of *L'Art moderne,* 1883, and the publication of *Certains,* 1889, an enormous change took place in Huysmans' attitude to life. The distaste for certain aspects of contemporary society which one perceived in his earlier articles and novels developed into a true hatred and Huysmans' own desire to escape is given literary expression in *A Rebours,* written in 1884. A comparison of the articles on Degas in *L'Art moderne* and *Certains* illustrates well the kind of change which takes place in that one decade. The reserved, ambivalent, but nonetheless real attraction to women which is expressed in *L'Art moderne* vanishes completely. In *Certains* there is only the kind of perverted attraction to women which is found in the highly sexual scenes of black magic and satanism in *Là-Bas.*

Certains contains fewer descriptions of actual paintings and more discussion of Degas' aims. The language is more passionate, the analogies more outrageous. The interpretation of Degas as an exposer of the animal and the fighter in woman is taken much further. Huysmans perceives Degas' paintings of 1886 purely as an expression of disgust towards women:

Mr. Degas, who, in certain wonderful paintings of dancers, had already rendered so implacably the degeneration of the professional stupefied by mechanical frolics and monotonous leaps, this time brought us, in his studies of nudes, a searching cruelty, a patient hatred.

M. Degas qui, dans d'admirables tableaux de danseuses, avait déjà si implacablement rendu la déchéance de la mercenaire abêtie par de mécaniques ébats et de monotones sauts, apportait, cette fois, avec ses études de nus, une attentive cruauté, une patiente haine. (X, 21–22)

He believes Degas chose bathing women as his subject matter because it showed them at their most debased and was thus a way to "throw the most offensive excess in his century's face" ("jeter à la face de son siècle le plus excessif outrage") (X, 22).

This hatred towards contemporary society is mitigated though, by a growing sense of moral outrage and a quasi-religious belief, developed fully in *Là-Bas,* that one can attain virtue through evil. In "L'Exposition des Indépendants en 1880" Huysmans had called Degas "this man of so subtle a temperament, such vibrant nervousness." ("cet homme d'un tempérament si fin, d'un nervosisme si vibrant") (VI, 131) and had admired his works for their realism. Now he adds to this neurotic sensitivity and clear, precise realism an element of mystery which is an early version of Huysmans' spiritual naturalism. This dualism is expressed by phrases which contain contradictory elements, such as "a lucid and bridled passion" ("une fougue lucide et maîtrisée"), "a cold fever" ("une fièvre froide"), "the burning and muted color" ("la couleur ardente et sourde"), "the precise strangeness" ("l'étrange exact"), and "the so correct unseen" ("l'invu si juste"), where one part describes something exciting and mysterious and the other something controlled, precise, and down-to-earth. And when he talks of

an art that expresses either an expansive or an abbreviated surge of the soul, in living bodies, in perfect harmony with their surroundings

un art exprimant une surgie expansive ou abrégée d'âme, dans des corps vivants, en parfait accord avec leurs alentours (X, 23–25)

we have that combination of spiritualism expressed in a naturalist milieu which Huysmans later admired in the Grünewald *Crucifixion.* Indeed, Huysmans feels that Degas' paintings are not only spiritual but, in their call to chastity, are truly religious in the manner of medieval art:

if any works were ever fully, decisively chaste, with no dilatory precautions and no tricks, they are these!—They even glorify the disdain for the flesh, as no artist had dared to do since the Middle Ages!

si jamais oeuvres furent, sans précautions dilatoires et sans ruses, pleinement, décisivement chastes, ce sont bien celles-ci!—Elles glorifient même le dédain de la chair, comme jamais depuis le Moyen Age, artiste ne l'avait osé! (X, 24–25)

Huysmans' enthusiasm for Forain, on the other hand, was somewhat diminished by 1889, when he published *Certains*. He admits to having very little to add to his articles in *L'Art moderne*. He talks of the unique quality of Forain's style, his way of depicting people with "a certain ironic rigidity" ("une certaine roideur ironique") (X, 41). Under the influence of Degas Forain lost this naïve quality and produced the spiced watercolors which so influenced Huysmans' writing. His importance lies in his studies of women, for

> Thus armed, Mr. Forain sought to do what Guys, as Baudelaire showed, had done for his age: paint Woman wherever she is present, in the place where she works.
>
> Ainsi armé, M. Forain a voulu faire ce que le Guys, révélé par Baudelaire, avait fait pour son époque: peindre la femme où qu'elle s'affirme, dans les lieux où elle travaille. (X, 42)

Repeating exactly the words that he had written in "L'Exposition des Indépendants en 1881" in *L'Art moderne* (VI, 270), Huysmans sums up with a description of the prostitute's ambivalent mixture of suffering, aggression, and feminine charms:

> no one, finally, has more accurately expressed the delightful horror of her lewd mask, the charms that avenge the deprivations she has suffered, the hard times veiled beneath her gay flounces and her brilliant paints.
>
> personne, enfin, n'a plus justement exprimé la délicieuse horreur de son masque rosse, ses élégances vengeresses de famines subies, ses dèches voilées sous la gaieté des falbalas et l'éclat des fards. (X, 43)

In *Certains* Huysmans does not talk of any work executed by Forain after 1881, although he had written about it in the "Salon officiel de 1884" for *La Revue Indépendante* of June 1884. Unlike other parts of this article, however, the part on Forain was never printed in his collected works. The following extract sheds some light on Forain's change of style and the writer's diminished interest:

> Some parts of this canvas are lively: all of the background, for example, but—I don't know how to explain this—the painting is nevertheless gloomy. . . . I confess that, for myself, I prefer the old Forain to the new.
>
> Il y a, dans cette toile, des coins fringants, tout le fond, par exemple, mais, je ne sais comment expliquer cela, ce tableau est quand même morne. . . . J'avoue, pour ma part, préférer l'ancien Forain au nouveau.

In spite of the fact that the two men remained friends and were converted at the same time, Huysmans never wrote about Forain's later works—neither the harsh Christian art nor his illustrations for the antisemitic paper *Psst!*

In the article on *Les Sataniques* of Félicien Rops in *Certains* Huysmans expresses a medieval contempt for the flesh which is developed into a belief of woman as *instrumentum diaboli*. He claims that even if one refuted the theory that woman was actually possessed by the devil, she, at the very least, was the great initiator of vice and crime. Huysmans traces the history of erotic art and attempts a partly psychological, partly religious analysis of the licentious mind. He dismisses as crude and obscene all earlier attempts in painting to portray erotic subjects, including those of Rembrandt and Rowlandson. The article covers many of the theoretical ideas which Huysmans was to develop in *Là-Bas,* especially one he had already used in the prose poem "L'Ouverture de Tannhaeuser," 1886:—the relationship between good and evil. On the one hand woman and the devil are one, for

> She is, in short, the great vessel of iniquities and crimes, the charnel-house of afflictions and shame, the veritable mistress of ceremonies of the embassies assigned to our souls by all the vices.
>
> Elle est, en somme, le grand vase des iniquités et des crimes, le charnier des misères et des hontes, la véritable introductrice des ambassades déléguées dans nos âmes par tous les vices. (X, 88).

These "ambassades," when taken to their literal extreme, become the succubae of Madame Chantelouve. On the other hand purity and wickedness can both be expressions of the same mystical aspirations and man can find salvation through sin just as Rops can advocate chastity through the portrayal of erotic acts. Satanism, after all, implies faith. Huysmans finds in Rops, as he does in Degas, a spiritual Satanism on the level of the great religious painters of the Middle Ages; his works attempt to "spiritualize filth" ("spiritualiser l'ordure") (X, 72), and he calls Rops "the soul of an inverted Primitive" ("une âme de Primitif à rebours") (X, 82). In *Là-Bas,* when talking of the relationship between Jeanne d'Arc and Gilles de Rais, Huysmans explains that "from lofty Mysticism to base Satanism there is but one step. In the Beyond all things touch" ("du Mysticisme exalté au Satanisme exaspéré, il n'y a qu'un pas. Dans l'au-delà, tout se touche") (XII, 82). Huysmans goes so far, in fact, as to claim that "only the chaste are truly obscene" ("il n'y a de réellement obscènes que les gens chastes") (X, 70), which foreshadows des Hermies' justification to Durtal of sex being the only natural instinct.

Huysmans' interest in Degas and Forain, especially in *L'Art moderne,* was due in large part to the realism of their works. With Rops he gives up all demands of realism and is concerned only with the symbolic content of his work. Huysmans' interest relates more to his incipient religious yearnings and his bad conscience than to aesthetic appreciation. As he says,

> whenever he allegorizes or synthesizes Woman, whenever he abstracts her from a real milieu, he instantly becomes inimitable.
>
> dès qu'il allégorise et synthétise la femme, dès qu'il la distrait d'un milieu réel, il devient tout de suite inimitable. (X, 86)

After *Là-Bas* there was no way out and, turning his back completely on women and contemporary society, he embarked on a study of medieval art and symbolism which was to lead him back to the Catholic faith.

In *En Route*, 1895, which relates the story of Huysmans' conversion through the fictional character Durtal, there is no longer any sexual conflict. As far as he is concerned,

> no matter which way one turns with Woman, one suffers, for she is the most powerful instrument of sorrow that God has given Man!

> de quelque côté que l'on se tourne avec la femme, on souffre car elle est le plus puissant engin de douleur que Dieu ait donné à l'homme! (XIII, 1, 126)

and Durtal rejects all contact with women. It is in this work that Huysmans begins to develop the doctrine of mystical substitution, culminating in his study of Sainte Lydwine de Schiedam. It is a theory, inspired by the suffering of Christ, whereby certain women take the suffering and temptations of the world upon themselves and, in so doing, protect those who live in sin. This gave Huysmans personal strength as he observed the illnesses and deaths of many of his close friends and in his own painful death. It also put woman into a new and ideal role so that she could become an inspiration to him, rather than a threat.

Moreau

By comparing descriptions of certain paintings to descriptions or discussions of the same subject matter in his fiction, we have seen how Huysmans' experience of Degas, Forain, and Rops influenced or reinforced his vision of women and helped develop a literary imagery. The influence of Gustave Moreau on Huysmans' fiction is more apparent because he chose to use two of the painter's works—*Salomé* and *L'Apparition*—as centerpieces of des Esseintes' art collection. Inversely, the descriptions of these paintings in *A Rebours* were instrumental in spreading Moreau's reputation, ascribing certain characteristics to his work which it may not have had, were it not for its association with des Esseintes. For *A Rebours* was a very influential book among the Symbolists and Valéry expressed the feelings of many of his contemporaries when he wrote,

> I am always rereading *A Rebours;* it is my Bible and my bedside book. Nothing stronger has been written in the last twenty years.

> J'en suis toujours à relire *A Rebours,* c'est ma Bible et mon livre de chevet. Rien n'a été écrit de plus fort ces derniers vingt ans.[11]

Very few books or articles on Moreau, even today, fail to quote from Huysmans, who has clearly become part and parcel of the Moreau mystique and in some way can be said to have recreated the paintings. Julius Kaplan, for instance, accuses Huysmans of hyperbole in that he "paid undue attention to Salome's physical appeal and when he described her, she became much more physically tempting than she actually is in the painting."[12] This opinion was already expressed by Valéry, who had to admit that the impression left by *A Rebours* did not correspond to the real paintings:

> I remember the great disappointment that I felt when, very heated by Huysmans' mad and raging descriptions in *A Rebours,* I finally saw some of Moreau's works. I could not resist telling Huysmans that "they were as gray and dull as a sidewalk."
> Huysmans defended himself very limply. He alleged that the paints Moreau used were of poor quality, that the brilliance that had astonished him had died, etc.
>
> Il me souvient de la grande déception que j'aie eue quand, très échauffé par les folles et furieuses descriptions d'Huysmans dans *A Rebours,* je vis enfin quelques oeuvres de Moreau. Je ne pus me tenir de dire à Huysmans que "c'était gris et terne comme un trottoir."
> Huysmans se défendit fort mollement. Il allégua que les couleurs dont Moreau se servait étaient de mauvaise qualité, que l'éclat qui l'avait émerveillé avait péri, etc.[13]

This anecdote serves as an excellent reminder that Huysmans' fiction should not be read as art criticism but that the descriptions of art serve a literary function. They are metaphors of a general attitude and must be seen as just one part of a descriptive code which forms the basic structure of his writing. This will become clearer when we relate the descriptions of Moreau's paintings to other episodes in *A Rebours* and also to passages in other works.

At first sight it would appear that Huysmans' admiration for Moreau, coexisting as it did with his love for Degas and Forain, was a strange aberration in taste. On the one hand he chose painters of very contemporary subjects with new techniques which allowed for a great deal of movement and life, and on the other hand Moreau, who painted historical themes in a stylized, architectonic manner which emphasized detail and symbol over movement and expression. Huysmans was usually very critical of Academic painters, so why did he choose as the centerpiece of des Esseintes' art collection the paintings of an artist stylistically so far removed from the Impressionists he loved?

The answer lies partly in the fact that Huysmans, like so many other writers, did not apply the same standards to Moreau as to other contemporary painters. According to Huysmans in *L'Art moderne,*

> his paintings seem no longer to partake of painting in the usual sense. . . . The one analogy that might obtain between these works and those hitherto created would only exist in literature. Indeed, one experiences before these paintings a sensation almost identical with the one that one feels when one reads certain bizarre and charming poems by Charles Baudelaire, such as *Rêve* dedicated, in *Les Fleurs du mal,* to Constantin Guys.
>
> ses toiles ne semblent plus appartenir à la peinture proprement dite. . . . La seule analogie qu'il pourrait y avoir entre ces oeuvres et celles qui ont été créées jusqu'à ce jour n'existerait vraiment qu'en littérature. L'on éprouve, en effet, devant ces tableaux, une sensation presque

égale à celle que l'on ressent lorsqu'on lit certains poèmes bizarres et charmants, tels que le *Rêve* dédié, dans les *Fleurs du Mal*, à Constantin Guys, par Charles Baudelaire. (VI, 153)

Valéry, when analyzing his disappointment on actually seeing the paintings, came to the conclusion that

One cannot deny that he aimed very high. He sought poetry; but, like many in those days, he sought it in details. It was not given him, moreover, to be profoundly a painter.

On ne peut lui refuser d'avoir visé très haut. Il a cherché la poésie; mais, comme plus d'un de ce temps-là, il l'a cherchée dans l'accessoire. Il lui a manqué, d'ailleurs, d'être profondément peintre.[14]

It was the "poésie" which attracted the attention of the Symbolists, among them Mallarmé and De Wyzewa, and made Moreau, according to André Breton, the precursor of the Surrealists:

It was inevitable that G. Moreau's attitude, which clung to all those crossroads at which one turns one's back on life (let us be clear: the entirely superficial life on which others feed), earned him, from most of the painters of the *tangible,* a hostility that still endures, but which will be compensated, to a great extent, by the dilection of poets.

Il était fatal que l'attitude de G. Moreau s'accrochant à toutes les croisées d'où l'on tourne l'épaule à la vie (entendons: la vie toute extérieure dont se repaissent les autres) lui valût de la plupart des peintres du *tangible* une hostilité qui dure encore mais que compensera, dans une large mesure, la dilection des poètes.[15]

The affinity which writers in general felt for Moreau's symbolism explains in part Huysmans' admiration for him. Partly also Moreau and Degas were emotionally not as far apart as one might at first think. Huysmans was drawn to their personalities, their temperaments, and their ideas, always more important to him than style or technique. Degas was considered somewhat of an outsider by the Impressionists, partly because he still preferred interiors to outdoor scenes, working with artificial light, and partly because he had a difficult character which led to constant quarrels with his colleagues. Moreau was also a recluse, both socially and artistically, and Huysmans shared these antisocial feelings. Above all he sympathized with their interpretation of women, for in both men's work we find the ambivalence represented by the two Vatard sisters and found throughout Huysmans' writing. We have noted how Huysmans sees Degas' ballet dancer as a somewhat virginal creature, a tool in the hands of a ballet master, a machine which can be taught to make beautiful patterns. In the theater and the brothel Huysmans and Degas find a theme where the natural and truthful (sex) are mingled with the artificial and disguised (makeup, alluring clothes, anonymity), and in the prostitute a representation of the woman who initiates and ultimately castrates men.

In Moreau there is the same combination—the stylized, rigid, sexless woman who is, at the same time, temptress, enchantress, castrator, and destroyer of men. In the figures of Salome, Herodias, and Helen, Moreau finds the symbols of evil and death incarnate in female beauty. In spite of their apparent differences in style, Huysmans sensed the compatibility of these two artists to such a degree that he based the first dream in *En Rade* on a combination of their works.

Most of the brief article on Moreau in *L'Art moderne* is given to the *Hélène* of 1880—"resembling a maleficent, poisonous goddess" ("semblable à une divinité malfaisante qui empoisonne") (VI, 154),—and to *Galatée*, in which he is most impressed by the "strange mineral flora" ("flore minérale étrange") (VI, 155); there is no mention of the *Salomé* or *L'Apparition* which feature in *A Rebours*. Huysmans does write briefly about the *Salomé* exhibited at the Paris World's Fair of 1878, but there is little in the tone, enthusiasm, or style of the article which indicates the role Moreau's paintings would play a few years later in the life of des Esseintes, except maybe the introductory passage in "Le Salon officiel de 1880," in which Huysmans uses mystical and religious vocabulary untypical of *L'Art moderne* but basic to his later works:

> Monsieur Gustave Moreau is an extraordinary, unique artist. He is a cloistered mystic in the middle of Paris. . . . Engulfed by ecstasy, he sees enchanted visions shine, bloody apotheoses from past ages.
>
> Monsieur Gustave Moreau est un artiste extraordinaire, unique. C'est un mystique enfermé, en plein Paris. . . . Abîmé dans l'extase, il voit resplendir les féeriques visions, les sanglantes apothéoses des autres âges. (VI, 152)

Indeed, this passage is incorporated, with only slight modifications, in *A Rebours*, where Huysmans discusses

> the antecedents of this great artist, this mystical pagan, this illuminee who could shut out the modern world so completely as to behold, in the heart of present-day Paris, the awful visions and magical apotheoses of other ages.
>
> les origines de ce grand artiste, de ce païen mystique, de cet illuminé qui pouvait s'abstraire assez du monde pour voir, en plein Paris, resplendir les cruelles visions, les féeriques apothéoses des autres âges. (VII, 89)

There has been much discussion about the model for the character of des Esseintes; among others the Comte Robert de Montesquiou and Francis Poictevin have been mentioned. All critics point out also that the lifestyle of des Esseintes is a natural development of the characters in Huysmans' earlier novels, particularly Fromentin in *A Vau-l'eau*. None have mentioned, however, the correspondence between des Esseintes and the descriptions, quoted above, of Moreau. In the "Notice" of *A Rebours*, when introducing his protagonist in a kind of Naturalist justification, Huysmans talks of des Esseintes' desire to live in isolation:

Already he had begun dreaming of a refined Thebaid, a desert hermitage equipped with all modern conveniences, a snugly heated ark on dry land in which he might take refuge from the incessant deluge of human stupidity.

Déjà il rêvait à une thébaïde raffinée, à un désert confortable, à une arche immobile et tiède où il se réfugierait loin de l'incessant déluge de la sottise humaine. (VII, 10)

His dream is fulfilled

in a lonely spot close to the Fort and far from all neighbors . . . in this district which had so far remained unspoilt by rampaging Parisians, he would be safe from molestation. . . . Thinking of the new existence he was going to fashion for himself, he felt a glow of pleasure at the idea that here he would be too far out for the tidal wave of Parisian life to reach him.

dans un endroit écarté, sans voisins, près du fort . . . dans ce pays peu ravagé par les Parisiens, il était certain d'être à l'abri. . . . En songeant à la nouvelle existence qu'il voulait organiser, il éprouvait une allégresse d'autant plus vive qu'il se voyait retiré assez loin déjà, sur la berge, pour que le flot de Paris ne l'atteignît plus. (VII, 13)

This correspondence between Moreau and des Esseintes is crucial in understanding the metaphorical role of the Moreau paintings in *A Rebours*. They are metaphors of des Esseintes' feelings, which explains why there is a high degree of subjectivity in Huysmans' descriptions of the paintings and why they contain elements which relate them to other parts of the novel not concerned with paintings.

Paintings are one of the many different subjects treated in *A Rebours* but they are, in fact, all variations on a theme of decadence of which the evil woman threatening men is one of the main aspects. Hence the apt characterization of *A Rebours* as a prose poem, in which the lack of what Philippe Hamon calls "une prévisibilité logique" is replaced by "une prévisibilité lexicale."[16] There is no linear temporal development in the traditional sense that there is a necessary sequence of events or that meaning depends on temporal relationships; the novel has an internal structure which depends on the repetition of the same theme in different guises, and change in time and space is brought about by dreams, periods of memory, and descriptions of objects, in this case art.

The relative unimportance of the development of des Esseintes' character can be seen by the rare number of times he is actually mentioned in the part of chapter 5 which describes Moreau's paintings—sixteen times in twelve pages. The references to des Esseintes consist, moreover, of very neutral words which express minimal activity—they serve primarily as introductory phrases for the paintings, as justifications for their discussion. That at the beginning of the chapter these are all words of desire underlines the fact that the Moreau paintings are a fulfillment of a personal vision, part of the world des Esseintes was trying to create at Fontenay. So we have "*the desire* to escape from a hateful period of sordid degradation," *"he had resolved* to allow nothing to enter his hermitage which might breed repugnance or regret," *"he had set his heart* on finding a few pictures of subtle, exquisite refinement," *"He had bought* Moreau's two masterpieces," *"he would stand dreaming* in front of one of them," "Des Esseintes *saw realized* at long last the weird and superhuman Salome of *his dreams"* (*"son désir* de se soustraire à une haïssable époque d'indignes muflements," *"il avait résolu* de ne pas introduire dans sa cellule des larves de répugnances ou de regrets," *"avait-il voulu* une peinture subtile, exquise," *"Il avait acquis* ses deux chefs-d'oeuvre," *"il rêvait* devant l'un d'eux," "des Esseintes *voyait enfin réalisée* cette Salomé, surhumaine et étrange qu'*il avait rêvée"*) (VII, 79–83) [my italics].

In stark contrast to the lack of development and character on the part of des Esseintes, the descriptions of Moreau's *Salomé* and *L'Apparition* are full of life and are the focal point of the chapter. They are positively theatrical, reminiscent of the 1880 descriptions of Degas in *L'Art moderne* in which Huysmans discusses the scene as if watching a play, tracing the development of the action and even describing the accompanying noises. The organization and tone of the *Salomé* description are also very similar to those of the trial of Gilles de Rais in *Là-Bas,* pointing yet again to the fact that Huysmans integrates descriptions of art into his general descriptive code in which the work practically loses its status as pure art to become a point of departure for storytelling, a means of setting an atmosphere.

The *Salomé* description begins with the architectural setting, in which one can detect Huysmans' growing religious orientation:

> This painting showed a throne like the high alter of a cathedral standing beneath a vaulted ceiling—a ceiling crossed by countless arches springing from thick-set, almost Romanesque columns, encased in polychromic brickwork, encrusted with mosaics, set with lapis lazuli and sardonyx—in a palace which resembled a basilica built in both the Moslem and Byzantine styles.

> Un trône se dressait, pareil au maître-autel d'une cathédrale, sous d'innombrables voûtes jaillissant de colonnes trapues ainsi que des piliers romans, émaillées de briques polychromes, serties de mosaïques, incrustées de lapis et de sardoines, dans un palais semblable à une basilique d'une architecture tout à la fois musulmane et byzantine. (VII, 80)

The trial scene in *Là-Bas* begins with a description of the crowds thronging to see

> the memorable beast whose very name, before his capture, had served to close the doors those evenings when in universal trembling the women dared not weep aloud

> le mémorable fauve dont le nom seul faisait, avant sa capture, clore les portes dans les tremblantes veillées où pleuraient, tout bas, les femmes (XII, 137)

reminding one of the "érudites hystéries" provoked in des Esseintes by the mythological figures in Moreau's pictures. The description continues with an architectural setting similar to that of *Salomé:*

> The courtroom, massive, obscure, upheld by heavy Roman pillars, had been rejuvenated. The wall, ogival, threw to cathedral height the arches of its vaulted ceiling, which were joined together, like the sides of an abbatial mitre, in a point.

> La salle, massive, obscure, soutenue par de lourds piliers romans, se rajeunissait à mi-corps, s'effilait en ogive, élançait à des hauteurs de cathédrale les arceaux de sa voûte qui se re-joignaient ainsi que les côtes des mitres abbatiales, en une pointe. (XII, 137)

The images Huysmans created for *Salomé* are thus carried over into a later novel, in quite another context. Further on in *Là-Bas* Huysmans is quite explicit in his reference to Moreau when he describes Notre-Dame de Fourvière in Lyons as

> the most extraordinary jumble of Assyrian, Roman, Gothic. . . . It's Asiatic and barbarous, and reminds one of the architecture shown in Gustave Moreau's Hérodiades.

> le plus extraordinaire mélange d'Assyrien, de Roman, de Gothique. . . . C'est asiatique et barbare; cela rappelle les architectures que Gustave Moreau élance, autour de ses Hérodiades, dans son oeuvre. (XII, 201–2)

The *Salomé* description starts very statically with this detailed account of the architecture and the rendering of Herod as "this immobile, statuesque figure, frozen like some Hindu god in a hieratic pose" ("cette statue, immobile, figée dans une pose hiératique de dieu Hindou"). It continues with an account of the smells and atmosphere of the scene, using vocabulary not usually associated with paintings: "incense was burning, sending up clouds of vapor. . . . Amid the heady odor of these perfumes, in the overheated atmosphere of the basilica . . ." ("des parfums brûlaient, dégorgeant des nuées de vapeurs. . . . Dans l'odeur perverse des parfums, dans l'atmosphère surchauffée de cette église . . .") (VII, 81). The description moves on to the slow, deliberate entry of Salome, who maintains "a withdrawn, solemn, almost august expression on her face" ("La face recueillie, solennelle, presque auguste") (VII, 81), and then the pace quickens dramatically when "she begins the lascivious dance" ("elle commence la lubrique danse") (VII, 81). Whereas Huysmans used predominantly nouns before, he now emphasizes the verbs of movement, so that even where he is describing jewelry and clothes, the overall impression is one of dramatic activity:

> her breasts *rise and fall*, the nipples hardening at the touch of her *whirling* necklaces; the strings of diamonds *glitter* against her moist flesh; her bracelets, her belts, her rings all *spit out* fiery sparks . . . the jewelled cuirass . . . *seems to be ablaze* with little snakes of fire, *swarming* over the mat flesh. . . .

> ses seins *ondulent* et, au frottement de ses colliers, qui *tourbillonnent,* leurs bouts se dressent; sur la moiteur de sa peau les diamants, attachées, *scintillent;* ses bracelets, ses cein-

tures, ses bagues, *crachent* des étincelles . . . la cuirasse des orfèvreries . . .*entre en combustion,* croise des serpenteaux de feu . . . *grouille* sur la chair mate. . . . (VII, 81–82) [my italics]

This frenzy ends just as suddenly as it began with Salome as "fixed in the concentrated gaze of a sleepwalker" ("concentrée, les yeux fixes, semblable à une somnambule") and totally unaware of "the Tetrarch, who sits there quivering" ("le Tétrarque qui frémit") (VII, 82), like Degas' dancers, who are also characterized as unemotional machines, exciting their onlookers.[17]

The development of this scene, beginning with the architectural setting, the description of static Herod, the slow entrance of Salome, the dance, the return to immobility, contrasted with the devastating effect she has on her audience, is exactly paralleled in *Là-Bas.*

The scene is set. Here the tribunal seat (comparable to the throne in *Salomé*) is surrounded by motionless, rigid priests. Gilles enters: "he began the recital of his crimes" ("il commença le récit de ses crimes") (XII, 139). He recounts in detail some of the horrendous crimes he perpetrated against children and, in spite of the "few short cries . . . fainting women, mad with horror" ("cris brefs . . . des femmes évanouïes, folles d'horreur") (XII, 140), he seems to remain unmoved: "And with the eyes of a somnambulist. . . . He seemed to see nothing, to hear nothing" ("Et d'un oeil de somnambule. . . . Lui, semblait ne rien entendre, ne rien voir") (XII, 139–40).

By stressing the indifference on the part of Salome and Gilles, Huysmans emphasizes the absolute strength of the evil embodied in these two characters. As he writes in *A Rebours,*

Des Esseintes saw realized at long last the weird and superhuman Salome of his dreams. Here she was no longer just the dancing-girl who extorts a cry of lust and lechery from an old man by the lascivious movements of her loins . . . she had become, as it were, the symbolic incarnation of undying Lust, the Goddess of immortal Hysteria, the accursed Beauty . . . the monstrous Beast, indifferent, irresponsible, insensible, poisoning. . . .

Des Esseintes voyait enfin réalisée cette Salomé, surhumaine et étrange qu'il avait rêvée. Elle n'était plus seulement la baladine qui arrache à un vieillard, par une torsion corrompue de ses reins, un cri de désir et de rut . . . elle devenait, en quelque sorte, la déité symbolique de l'indestructible Luxure, la déesse de l'immortelle Hystérie, la Beauté maudite . . . la Bête monstrueuse, indifférente, irresponsable, insensible, empoisonnante. . . . (VII, 83–84)

She is the ultimate example of the sadistic character Huysmans perceived in Degas' prostitutes, in Madame Chantelouve, and in Rops' women.

A very similar description of Evil embodied in a beautiful woman is found in the prose poem "L'Ouverture de Tannhaeuser," 1886, from the collection *Croquis parisiens.* Huysmans was not very interested in music and this prose poem is the result of an article he had been asked to write by Dujardin for his *Revue Wagnérienne.* Huysmans went to the concert on April 3, 1885 and sat next to Mallarmé, who loved it so much that he began to attend the Lamoureux concerts regularly. Huysmans never went again but the overture afforded an occasion for him to develop his ideas on women. After a sensuous description of the music in which "the volutes of the great clouds take on the rearing shapes of hips and quiver with the elastic billowings of bosoms" ("les volutes des nuées prennent des formes cabrées de hanches et palpitent avec d'élastiques gonflements de gorges") (VIII, 167), Huysmans expounds the symbolism of the Venus figure, using the same images as in *A Rebours:*

> Indeed, this is no longer the unfading Beauty appointed only to earthly joys, to artistic and sensual excitations, as the salacious sculpture of Greece understood her; this is the incarnation of the Spirit of evil, the effigy of omnipotent Lust, the image of the irresistible and magnificent She-Satan who, ceaselessly hunting Christian souls, aims her delightful and maleficent weapons.

> Ce n'est plus, en effet, l'immarcescible Beauté seulement préposée aux joies terrestres, aux excitations artistiques et sensuelles telle que la salacité plastique de la Grèce la comprit; c'est l'incarnation de l'Esprit du mal, l'effigie de l'omnipotente Luxure, l'image de l'irrésistible et magnifique Satane qui braque, sans cesse aux aguets des âmes chrétiennes, ses délicieuses et maléfiques armes. (VIII, 167–68)

The description of the *Salomé* in *A Rebours* has its parallels also in the first dream sequence of *En Rade,* 1887, in which a king observes, then rapes, a young, innocent girl. The palace setting is

> a gigantic hall . . . paved with porphyry, supported by vast pillars, their capitals flowering with bronze colocynths and golden lilies.

> une gigantesque salle . . . pavée de porphyre, supportée par de vastes piliers aux chapiteaux fleuronnés de coloquintes de bronze et de lys d'or. (IX, 29)

Whereas in *Salomé* it is the clothes and skin which are alive with jewels, in *En Rade* it is the columns which are intertwined by "a vineyard of jewels" ("un vignoble de pierreries") (IX, 30). The king, like Herod, is a statuelike figure, threatening to the young girl—"the King appeared, immobile in his purple robe" ("le Roi parut, immobile dans sa robe de pourpre") (IX, 31). The characterization of the girl herself is very close to that of Degas' fourteen-year-old dancer, discussed in "L'Exposition des Indépendants en 1881." Both of them have boyish figures, pale, sickly faces, and an arrogant, provocative stance. Degas's dancer had

> a painted head, slightly thrown back, the chin tilted up, half-opening the mouth in the sickly, dark face . . . the hands brought together behind the back, a flat chest.

> la tête peinte, un peu renversée, le menton en l'air, entr'ouvrant la bouche dans la face maladive et bise . . . les mains ramenées derrière le dos et jointes, la gorge plate. (VI, 249)

In *En Rade* the young girl was

almost boyish . . . her painted lips crackled in a superhuman pallor. . . . Standing thus in her dress dotted with blue flames, seeped in emanations, her arms brought behind her back, her head thrown back slightly on her taut neck, she remained immobile. . . .

presque garçonnière . . . ses lèvres fardées crépitaient dans une pâleur surhumaine. . . . Ainsi debout dans sa robe égrenée de flammes bleues, imbibée d'effluves, les bras ramenés derrière le dos, la nuque un peu renversée sur le cou tendu, elle demeurait immobile. . . . (IX, 33–34)

The nightmare ends with Huysmans' classical return to reality: "A great cry broke the silence, reverberated under the vaults" ("Un grand cri rompit le silence, se répercuta sous les voûtes") (IX, 36). Indeed the whole structure of the dream sequence is very similar to his *transpositions d'art*.

There is nothing in the description of *L'Apparition* as sensuous or erotic as the dance in *Salomé*, for in spite of the fact that the Salome in *L'Apparition* is practically nude, Huysmans concentrates on the jewelry which forms an intricate pattern over her body. One loses sight of the woman herself as "every facet of every jewel catches fire; the stones burn brightly, outlining the woman's figure in flaming colors" ("toutes les facettes des joailleries s'embrassent; les pierres s'animent, dessinent le corps de la femme en traits incandescents" (VII, 87). Des Esseintes is more moved by this watercolor than by *Salomé:*

Like the old King, Des Esseintes invariably felt overwhelmed, subjugated, stunned when he looked at this dancing-girl, who was less majestic, less haughty, but more seductive than the Salome of the oil-painting.

Tel que le vieux roi, des Esseintes demeurait écrasé, anéanti, pris de vertige, devant cette danseuse, moins majestueuse, moins hautaine, mais plus troublante que la Salomé du tableau à l'huile. (VII, 88)

In this one expression—"Tel que le vieux roi"—there is total identification between des Esseintes and the observer of Salome in the painting, emphasizing the extent to which des Esseintes' art collection is part of his overall emotional experience.

Huysmans brings des Esseintes and the reader quite abruptly back to earth by pointing out that

these two pictures of Salome . . . lived constantly before his eyes, hung as they were on the walls of his study, on panels reserved for them between the bookcases.

ces deux images de la Salomé . . . vivaient, sous ses yeux, pendues aux murailles de son cabinet de travail, sur des panneaux réservés entre les rayons des livres. (VII, 90)

The presence of the paintings in the study between the bookshelves not only reminds us that they are, after all, only paintings but also establishes the link between des Esseintes' collection of paintings and his literature. It is this kind of link which provides the only continuity and progression in *A Rebours* and makes some sense out of des Esseintes' very eclectic collections.

The very specific connection between the *Salomé* watercolor and literature is the fragment of Mallarmé's *Hérodiade* ("O mirror! Cold water frozen by boredom in your frame. . . . I have known the nakedness of my scattered dream!" ["O miroir! Eau froide par l'ennui dans ton cadre gelée. . . . J'ai de mon rêve épars connu la nudité!"]) which des Esseintes recites while looking at the Moreau. Huysmans prepares the reader for the nudity, the severity, and the whiteness of Mallarmé's poem by completely changing the images of the Moreau watercolor. Whereas in the chapter on art he stresses the bright colors and the brilliance of the jewels, the work is now in shadow and des Esseintes can only see

the vague shape of a white statue in the midst of a feebly glowing brazier of jewels.
The darkness hid the blood, dimmed the bright colors and gleaming gold, enveloped the far corners of the temple in gloom, concealed the minor actors in the criminal drama where they stood wrapped in their dark garments, and, sparking only the white patches in the water-color, drew the woman from the scabbard of her jewels and emphasized her nakedness.

une confuse statue, encore blanche, dans un brasier éteint de pierres!
L'obscurité cachait le sang, endormait les reflets et les ors, enténébrait les lointains du temple, noyait les comparses du crime ensevelis dans leurs couleurs mortes, et n'épargnant que les blancheurs de l'aquarelle, sortait la femme du fourreau de ses joailleries et la rendait plus nue. (VII, 296)

Just as there is this connection between the Salome pictures and the Mallarmé poem, there is also a connection drawn between the pictures, the poem, and a seemingly unrelated subject—the turtle in chapter four of *A Rebours*. Des Esseintes, in fact, creates a work of art out of the turtle's shell by covering it in gold and then encrusting it with precious stones in the pattern of a bouquet of flowers. The vocabulary used to describe the shining jewels is very similar to the description of the bejeweled Salome. In the Moreau paintings there is a combination of this sparkling beauty and perversion, of realistic detail and mystery. All these elements are also found in the earlier description of the turtle. Des Esseintes, considering how to decorate the shell,

finally made a selection of real and artificial stones which in combination would result in a fascinating and disconcerting harmony. . . . three stones which all sparkled with mysterious, deceptive flashes, painfully drawn from the icy depths of their turbid water.

finit par trier une série de pierres réelles et factices dont le mélange devait produire une harmonie fascinante et déconcertante. . . . Ces trois pierres dardaient en effet des scintillements mystérieux et pervers, douloureusement arrachés du fond glacé de leur eau trouble. (VII, 66, 67)

These last images of cold, troubled water are clearly related to the mirror image in *Hérodiade,* thus connecting more intricately still the different elements of the novel:

> O mirror! Cold water frozen by boredom in your frame, how many times and for hours, grieved by dreams and seeking my memories which are like leaves beneath your ice and its deep gulf. . . .

O miroir!
Eau froide par l'ennui dans ton cadre gelée
Que de fois, et pendant les heures, désolée
Des songes et cherchant mes souvenirs qui sont
Comme des feuilles sous ta glace au trou profond. . . .

(VII, 297)

Chartres Cathedral

It is in *La Cathédrale,* 1898, the second of Huysmans' post-conversion novels, that we find the total integration of his religious and sexual instincts. All physical urges have been sublimated into a love of the Virgin Mary, who finally fulfills the quest for an ideal woman. This love of the Virgin Mary is manifest in two ways—in the adoration of Chartres Cathedral itself, which Huysmans describes in female terms, and in the lengthy analysis of *Le Couronnement de la Vierge* by Fra Angelico.

> In short, with the color of its stones and windows, Notre-Dame de Chartres was a blue-eyed blonde. She became transmuted into a sort of pale fairy, a slender and elongated Virgin, her large azure eyes open between the transparent lids of her roses.

> En somme, avec la teinte de ses pierres et de ses vitres, Notre-Dame de Chartres était une blonde aux yeux bleus. Elle se personnifiait en une sorte de fée pâle, en une Vierge mince et longue, aux grands yeux d'azur ouverts dans les paupières en clarté de ses roses. (XIV, 218)

Such descriptions of the cathedral lead Ruth Antosh to write that "The cathedral represents a blending of the various ideals of all Huysmans' protagonists. . . . Des Esseintes and other protagonists had pursued the image of an ideal woman, whether a painting or a product of the hero's own imagination; the cathedral is for Durtal the embodiment of that ultimate ideal woman, the Virgin Mary."[18]

As much as Huysmans loved the Church and as much as he admired the life of the priest, he was still too frightened by a life of total commitment to religion. He became an oblate in the same spirit that he had had love affairs. For he could never enter a religious order for good, just as he had never been able to make a lifelong commitment to a woman in marriage.

Fra Angelico

As part of Huysmans' comprehensive study of medieval symbolism which forms the meager structure of *La Cathédrale,* he chose to include Fra Angelico as the painter most representative of the spirit he was trying to elucidate. As a device for including an area of study which is not contained in Chartres itself, Huysmans has Durtal write an article on Fra Angelico's *Le Couronnement de la Vierge* in the Louvre. He quotes this article in its entirety, a rather uninspired way of including subject matter which does not fit in naturally.

Part of Huysmans' enormous admiration for Fra Angelico, a monk who spent his life detached from the "realities" of life which Huysmans was trying to escape, was due to the fact that Huysmans himself was emotionally unable to retire into a monastery. The second reason for his choice is Fra Angelico's symbolic use of color and the way he depicts the Virgin Mary herself. Huysmans feels that Fra Angelico has expressed, as far as humanly possible, the mysticism and the spiritualism of the Middle Ages. Using terminology reminiscent of his criticism of Moreau, Huysmans writes that Angelico is "the soul of a mystic who has attained the contemplative life and pours it out, as in a pure mirror, onto a canvas" ("l'âme d'un mystique arrivé à la vie contemplative et l'effusant, ainsi qu'en un pur miroir, sur une toile") (XIV, 243). He compares him to Metsys, Memling, Thierry Bouts, Gérard David, and Roger van der Weyden, all of whom he admires greatly and considers "more observant and more profound, more learned and more skillful, even more of a painter than Angelico" ("plus observateurs et plus profonds, plus savants et plus habiles, plus peintres même que l'Angelico") (XIV, 244) but whom he finds too involved in the worldly life. Huysmans' position that they "frequently could not help endowing their virgins with the bearing of elegant ladies, were obsessed by worldly memories" ("ne pouvaient bien souvent s'empêcher de laisser à leurs vierges des allures d'élégantes dames, étaient obsédés par des souvenirs de la terre") (XIV, 244), is a far reach from his earlier calls for realism and simple descriptive honesty above all. This rejection of the portrayal of realistic women is a temporary phase as Durtal grapples with his desire to embrace Catholicism in its entirety.

The conflict between lust, sexuality, and evil on the one hand and purety, chastity, and virtue on the other, which has run through all his work up to this point, is resolved unequivocally for Huysmans in the image of Mary in *Le Couronnement de la Vierge.* In this painting which is "l'hymne de la chasteté" (XIV, 237) Fra Angelico has excluded all the colors which "désignent les qualités des vices" (XIV, 239). It is above all the Virgin Mary herself who is the incarnation of agelessness, sexlessness, and purity:

> She is ageless; She is not a woman and She is no longer a child. And one cannot even tell
> if She is an adolescent, barely nubile, a little girl, so sublimated is She, above humanity,

beyond the world, exquisite in purity, forever chaste! . . . The other Madonnas are vulgar compared with her; they are, in any case, women.

Elle est sans âge; ce n'est pas une femme et ce n'est déjà plus une enfant. Et l'on ne sait même si Elle est une adolescente, à peine nubile, une fillette, tant Elle est sublimée, au-dessus de l'humanité, hors le monde, exquise de pureté, à jamais chaste! . . . Les autres Madones, sont, en face d'Elle, vulgaires; elles sont, en tout cas, femmes. (XIV, 247–48)

Just as Ruth Antosh sees the embodiment of Huysmans' ideal woman in the cathedral itself, Helen Trudgian sees in Fra Angelico's Virgin

she whom Huysmans seeks, dimly, in *Salon de poésie, Marthe,* and *Les Soeurs Vatard,* in the accumulation of canvases by Degas, Forain, Raffaëlli, Chéret, Whistler and Rops, the eternally modern Child-Mother.

elle que Huysmans cherche, obscurément, dans le *Salon de Poésie, Marthe* et *Les Soeurs Vatard,* à travers l'amoncellement de toiles de Degas, Forain, Raffaëlli, Chéret, Whistler et Rops, la Fille-Mère éternellement moderne.[19]

In spite of the fact that after a lifetime of disappointments and frustration, the simplicity of chastity seemed to Huysmans to be a solution, I think both these critics underestimate the extent of his real appreciation of the physical and earthly aspects of women in his early years.

La Cathédrale was Huysmans' most ambitious and comprehensive study of medieval art and architecture and, although he was not satisfied with its result from the artistic point of view, it fulfilled his need to investigate the medieval soul in its most tangible form. As he says in *En Route,* "Ah! the real proof of Catholicism was the art that it founded, that art that no one has yet surpassed" ("Ah! la vraie preuve du catholicisme, c'était cet art qu'il avait fondé, cet art que nul n'a surpassé encore") (XIII, 1, 10).

An essential part of his view of medieval Catholic belief was chastity, as we have seen in the interpretation of Fra Angelico's *Le Couronnement de la Vierge.* His flirtations with the other more worldly side of women were not totally suppressed, however, as we learn when we read his study *Trois Primitifs,* 1905. This short book of art criticism, his last, was the result of a trip Huysmans took to Germany and Belgium in September 1903, accompanied by l'Abbé Mugnier. Besides the second of his important studies on Grünewald, it contains a description of an anonymous fifteenth-century portrait of a young girl and of a *Virgin and Child* by the Maître de Flémalle, both in Frankfurt. These two portraits represent the two extremes of the woman dichotomy which plagued Huysmans from his earliest prose poems till his death, and in these discussions we find many of the views expressed in his articles on Degas, Forain, Rops, and Moreau.

Anonymous Portrait of a Young Girl

Huysmans finds the young girl in the anonymous portrait both alluring and menacing. Even her clothing is "delightful and wicked" ("délicieuse et méchante"),[20] and disturbing in its combination of a very substantial and intricate head covering and a minimal, diaphanous blouse. The description of her hair continues to employ the warfare and horse vocabulary indicated in so many of the articles on Degas:

> from this strange hairstyle fall long strands braided with gold; they curl and twist, giving the illusion of a *coat of mail* unmeshing, and this flashing *mane* is so singular that one draws nearer to assure oneself that this astonishing hair is just that.

> de cette étrange coiffure tombent de longs cheveux tressés d'or; ils ondulent et se tordent, donnent l'illusion d'une *cotte d'armes* qui se démaillent et cette *crinière* fulgurante est si singulière que l'on s'approche pour s'assurer que ces cheveux étonnants en sont. (XI, 323) [my italics]

The fact that she is so young, like Salome and the young girl in Jacques Marles' dream, makes the girl's apparent innocence all the more intriguing to Huysmans. She is full of contradictions:

> What is this enigmatic being, this implacable, pretty hermaphrodite, so astonishingly composed when she provokes? She is impure but she plays fair; she excites but she gives warning; she tempts but she is reserved; she is the purity of impurity: "puritas impuritatis," to use Justus Lipsus's phrase, she is at once the instigatrix of lust and the messenger of the atonement of sensual pleasures.

> Qu'est-ce que cet être énigmatique, cette androgyne implacable et jolie, si étonnamment de sang-froid quand elle provoque? elle est impure mais elle joue franc jeu; elle stimule mais elle avertit; elle est tentante mais réservée; elle est la pûreté de l'impûreté "puritas impuritatis", selon l'expression de Juste Lipse, elle est en même temps l'instigatrice de la luxure et l'annonciatrice de l'expiation des joies des sens. (XI, 325)

Like the women in Rops' paintings, like Gilles de Rais and Madame Chantelouve, she treads that narrow path between Lust and Purity, between Sin and Virtue. Indeed Huysmans' description of the Italian Renaissance, the period of this painting, could be an apt introduction to his own *Là-Bas*. The country was "the trough of all lusts, the reservoir of all crimes" ("l'auge de toutes les luxures, le réservoir de tous les crimes") (XI, 331). As for love, it

> seemed insipid if it remained natural and did not transgress against the permitted degrees of consanguinity; and even then one was obliged, in order to heighten the flavor, to let it steep in a brine of poisons, in a sauce of blood.

> paraissait fade s'il restait naturel et ne franchissait pas le degré permis des parentés; et encore fallait-il, pour en relever le goût, le faire macérer dans une saumure de poisons, dans une sauce de sang. (XI, 332)

Huysmans pays some serious attention to the art-critical problems of the painting's source but is, as usual, less interested in this aspect of the work than in its effect on him. He classifies this painting among the few other great works of art which he has discovered during his life as having that magical mixture of naturalism and spiritualism which places the work beyond the normal limits of pictorial art:

> the greatest portrait painters of all times embraced nature no more closely nor rendered better the discreet life of the derm's blood system; above all, no one better reproduced the soul of a gaze . . . the Museum's most beautiful works seem merely paintings, in the strict sense of the word, compared to that one which goes further, which is something other, which penetrates, in a word, into the territory of that blameworthy world beyond. . . .

> les plus grands portraitistes de tous les âges n'ont pas serré la nature de plus près et mieux rendu la vie discrète du sang dans les réseaux du derme; nul surtout n'a mieux reproduit l'âme d'un regard . . . les plus belles oeuvres du Musée ne paraissent que des peintures, au sens strict du mot, en comparaison de celle-là qui va plus loin, qui est autre chose, qui pénètre, pour tout dire, dans le territoire de cet au-delà blâmable. . . . (XI, 325–26)

Huysmans also discusses various hypotheses on the painting's symbolism, in an attempt to understand whom the work portrays. Pausing briefly to consider the possibility of a young witch or a prophetess, Huysmans returns to his first love: "the Frankfurt hermaphrodite has in her even more of the princess and the courtesan" ("l'androgyne de Francfort tient encore plus de la princesse de théâtre et de la courtisane") (XI, 330), and with this he has come full circle, in spite of his conversion and his new faith in the Virgin Mary and the female Saints.

Huysmans himself is amazingly clear in his own mind that the painting of the young Renaissance girl and the *Virgin and Child* by the Maître de Flémalle represent two very real aspects of his own character. He makes this point very strongly by introducing the latter with great enthusiasm right after the other in the same paragraph.

Virgin and Child by the Maître de Flémalle

Again Huysmans has done some thorough research into the sources of this painting, comparing it to other works by its purported painter and to works by Roger van der Weyden and Robert Campin. His main interest, however, is in the fact that the work stands out as

> an exceptional case, when compared to a work that goes further than painting per se and that, unlike the little Florentine She-Satan, transports us to that divine beyond that so few painters knew. Art criticism is almost irrelevant; the Virgin answers above all to the domain of liturgy and mysticism.

> un cas exceptionnel, en face d'une oeuvre qui va plus loin que la peinture proprement dite et qui, au rebours de la petite satane florentine, nous transporte dans cet au-delà divin que

si peu de peintres connurent. La critique d'art n'a presque plus rien à voir, avec elle; la Vierge relève surtout du domaine de la liturgie et de la mystique. (XI, 340)

It even stands apart from another *Madonna and Child* by the same artist in the Somzée Gallery in its combination of realism and spirituality:

Until now, indeed, his Virgins had looked to me like ostentatious bourgeoises of Flanders . . . it was painting of charming affectations, a frail and mannered art, but it was only, after all, painting. . . . All the divine part that cannot be learned . . . the outpouring of prayer, the projection of the purified soul . . . surge suddenly in the isolated volet of Frankfurt.

Jusqu'ici, en effet, ses Vierges m'étaient apparues, ainsi que de fastueuses bourgeoises des Flandres . . . c'était de la peinture à simagrées charmantes, de l'art frêle et maniéré, mais ce n'était, au demeurant, que de la peinture. . . . Toute cette partie divine qui ne s'apprend pas . . . cette effluence de la prière, cette projection de l'âme épurée . . . jaillissent soudain dans le volet isolé de Francfort. (XI, 347–48)

In this one masterpiece Huysmans feels of the artist that

While remaining a most precise Realist, he has nevertheless succeeded in painting a woman who can be none other than the Virgin Mother, the Coredemptress of a God.

Tout en demeurant le réaliste le plus exact, il n'en a pas moins réussi à peindre une femme qui . . . ne peut être une autre que la Vierge Mère, que la Corédemptrice d'un Dieu. (XI, 351)

Returning to the theme of mystical substitution discussed in *En Route,* Huysmans sees the Virgin here as the suffering mother, the consoler, the ideal woman. The article ends with a description of Huysmans' difficulty in leaving the presence of the Virgin, to walk out again into the streets of Frankfurt which he hated. His solution is to make a stopover at a church, where the spirit of the painting can remain intact, before making his way to the station. For as he writes in a paragraph full of self-awareness,

And now, as I contemplate them in turn, I am like a man whom temptation spurs. The eyes of the pseudo-Giulia [mistress of Alexander Borgia, possible model of the young girl in the anonymous painting] inflame in me the inextinguished embers of my old vices, yet despite everything, how I prefer to stay near the Virgin.

Et voici qu'à les contempler tour à tour, je suis tel qu'un homme que la tentation lamine. Les yeux de la pseudo Giulia attisent en moi les brandons inéteints de mes vieux vices, mais combien, malgré tout, je préfère rester près de la Vierge. (XI, 356)

This attraction accompanied by fear which Huysmans felt of women is one of the most powerful emotions in his writing. He portrays women as entrancing, cunning, evil, and destructive, not only in his novels and prose poems but also in his choice of paintings. In the work of Forain, Degas, Moreau, and

Rops he found the type of woman to whose sensuous manner he was attracted yet in whom he clearly found a threat to his own virility. The *transpositions* which Huysmans makes of some of these works are poignant and important parts of his fiction.

The little solace Huysmans found in women is translated in his post-conversion period into a love of the Church and the Virgin Mary. Before turning wholeheartedly to Catholicism, however, he did express strong views about nature, to which generations of poets, writers, and artists have turned to find beauty or consolation. Indeed, he was a prominent defender of the Impressionists and, although he veers from a standard interpretation of their work, he found pleasure in many of their paintings and incorporated his views on landscape painting into his portrayal of nature in his novels and prose poems.

3

L'Indicible Mélancolie:
Raffaëlli and the Impressionists

Huysmans discovered Degas as late as 1876, but as a result he turned his artistic interests away from seventeenth-century Dutch painters and began to look very seriously at the work of contemporary painters. His journalistic work, in which he reported on the official and independent Salons, threw him into the midst of the artistic debates of the seventies, the heyday of Impressionism, and after only two years of exposure to the independent painters, he asks rhetorically about Degas: "When will they understand that this artist is the greatest that we possess in France today?" ("Quand comprendra-t-on que cet artiste est le plus grand que nous possédions aujourd'hui en France?") (VI, 139). His admiration for Degas, whom he considered the major Impressionist, stems largely from his attitude towards women, although he certainly was very appreciative of Degas' achievements in painting subjects in strong artificial light and at unusual angles.

The position of Degas among the Impressionists remains a topic of debate. Since he always exhibited with them and was supportive of their aims, he is usually included in any study of Impressionism. Yet his social background, his emphasis on drawing which stemmed from his classical training, and his indifference to landscape and preference for urban figures place him in a special category.

Raffaëlli was one of Huysmans' favorite painters of this period and hailed by him as the quintessential Impressionist landscape painter. Raffaëlli was considered a minor artist even at that time; in fact, his inclusion in some of the Impressionist exhibitions, at the instigation of Degas, was the cause of some friction among the painters. Huysmans' views on Raffaëlli, their relationship to Impressionism in general, and the way they are reflected in his fiction are analyzed in this chapter.

Impressionism

Huysmans' contemporary Félix Fénéon points out that Degas, Forain, and Raffaëlli did not truly belong to the Impressionist group because they were more interested in anecdote and character than the treatment of color in natural light, one of the cornerstones of Impressionism.[1] Yet this same critic did not fault Huysmans for including them in his somewhat elastic definition of Impressionism and hailed him as the most important critic of contemporary art. Literary critics and biographers, such as Helen Trudgian and Robert Baldick, tend to exaggerate Huysmans' artistic insights and the impact of his criticism on his own writing style.[2] On the other hand, art historians tend to point out the weaker aspects of Huysmans' criticism, faulting him for showing lapses in taste and for not making fine distinctions.[3]

My aim is not to evaluate Huysmans' critical judgments, not to do a stylistic analysis of literary Impressionism or "l'écriture artiste" in the work of Huysmans. I am interested in discovering why he was dissatisfied with the Impressionists, why he was drawn to Raffaëlli, and how his concept of nature which he developed in his criticism is reflected and developed further in his fiction.

From the very first independent exhibition in 1874 there was a broad spectrum of styles represented, but the artists were united by a hostility towards the noble, didactic subject matter of the Academic painters and the lack of "realism" in their style. With the exception of Degas, they were all passionately interested in the problems of painting outdoors. By the time Huysmans was writing his articles on contemporary art between 1879 and 1881, the individual painters who constituted the Impressionist group were each confronting personal crises and were being forced to reconsider the direction of their work. On political and pragmatic grounds most of them continued to exhibit together till the last Impressionist exhibition of 1886. By 1883, however, the year that Huysmans' *L'Art moderne* was published, most of the painters had moved away from Paris and no longer took part in the exchange of aesthetic ideas which had characterized their early years together. It seems unreasonable, therefore, to fault Huysmans, living as he did in the midst of a very complicated and changing artistic scene, for lack of perspective and understanding. Moreover, he himself made no pretensions to give hard and fast definitions of artistic schools and movements and was always proud of his personal and eclectic tastes. He even stated from the outset:

And so I have indiscriminately designated them by the current, comprehensible, familiar epithets: Impressionists, Intransigeants, or Independents. This bias alone could allow me to limit myself to the little framework that I had marked out for myself: simply to show the parallel progress, over the last few years, of the Impressionist salons and the official salons, and to point out the consequences that resulted from this, in terms of art.

Aussi, les ai-je indifféremment désignés par les épithètes, usitées, compréhensibles, connues, d'impressionnistes, d'intransigeants ou d'indépendants. Ce parti pris me permettait seul de me confiner dans le petit cadre que je m'étais tracé; montrer simplement la marche parallèle, pendant ces dernières années, des salons indépendants et des salons officiels, et mettre au jour les conséquences qui ont pu en résulter, au point de vue de l'art. (VI, 11)

It is to his credit that he studies all exhibits with an open mind and does not try to get involved in the limiting game of labelling. As a writer, he could afford to include artists of various approaches, whereas the artists themselves, fighting for identities and recognition, were forced to spend a great deal of energy on defining the limits of their exhibitions. This is not to say that in the course of these articles Huysmans does not try to define Impressionism but, on the whole, he is more successful when discussing individual painters and broad tendencies.

His concerns, typical of a writer, were divided radically into subject matter and technique. This, in spite of the fact that in "Le Salon de 1879" in *L'Art moderne* he claims that he is primarily concerned with method and not subject matter: "As if the distinction derived, not from the way in which a subject is treated, but from the subject itself" ("Comme si la distinction ne venait point de la manière dont on traite un sujet et non du sujet lui-même") (VI, 8). Pissarro, the least quarrelsome of all the Impressionists and basically very grateful that Huysmans wrote well of his work, complained nevertheless to his son,

> You will see, alas, that like all critics, under the pretext of *naturalism,* he judges as a man of letters, and most of the time sees only the subject matter. He places Caillebotte above Monet.
>
> Tu verras, hélas, que comme tous les critiques, sous prétexte de *naturalisme,* il juge en littérateur, et ne voit la plupart du temps que le sujet. Il met Caillebotte au-dessus de Monet.[4]

For Degas, on the other hand, the choice of subjects was of greater intellectual significance than for the majority of the Impressionists. It was the fact that he expressed an attitude towards his subjects, one that largely corresponded to Huysmans' own, that allowed the strong empathy on the part of the writer towards the painter. Valéry, from a distance of some fifty years, analyzes the situation very clearly, providing insight into the growing split between the Impressionists who were concerned with form and were the precursors of modern abstract art, and those who, like Degas, demanded significance and meaning from a work:

> Degas finds himself caught between Mr. Ingres' commandments and Delacroix's strange charms; while he hesitates, the art of his time decides to study the spectacle of modern life. Compositions and the grand manner are aging visibly in the public opinion. Landscape is invading the citadel that the Greeks, the Turks, the Knights, and the Cupids are abandoning. He destroys the notion of *subject* matter, reduces, within a few years, all of the intellectual side of art to a handful of debates on *material* and the color of shadows. The brain became pure retina. . . .
>
> Degas se trouve pris entre les commandements de Monsieur Ingres et les charmes étranges de Delacroix; tandis qu'il hésite, l'art de son temps se résout à exploiter le spectacle de la vie moderne. Les compositions et le grand style vieillissent à vue d'oeil dans l'opinion. Le paysage envahit les murs qu'abandonnent les Grecs, les Turcs, les Chevaliers et les Amours. Il ruine la notion du *sujet,* réduit en peu d'années toute la part intellectuelle de l'art à quelque débats sur la *matière* et la couleur des ombres. Le cerveau se fit rétine pure. . . .[5]

The correlation established by Valéry between the interest in nature shown by the Impressionists and the lack of intellectual content is at the basis of Huysmans' ultimate dissatisfaction with Impressionism.

As Valéry rightly points out, the Impressionists were mainly interested in method and selected their subjects as vehicles for these methods. Their choice of subjects, influenced to a large extent by their middle- and lower-class backgrounds in which they felt comfortable, included street scenes in Paris, scenes of social outdoor activities in the suburbs and countryside, such as picnics and boating, landscapes, and seascapes. They were interested in observing and recording the actual, the here and now. For the Impressionists, nature was interesting in itself and was something which could be observed and described objectively. Above all they were experimenting with the effect of natural light on colors and shapes at different times of the day, so these ordinary bourgeois activities were perfect subjects for their studies. The people in their paintings are often no more than dots of movement and the artists express no personal attitude towards them. The overall tone of the Impressionist works, due to the very social subject matter and to the dominance of the sun, is positive, joyful, relaxed.

Clearly, this general tone of Impressionist art is far from Huysmans' attitude towards life. He himself sought solitude and did not love the sunny, open countryside. He preferred to remain indoors, either at home, in art galleries, in book stores, and, later on, in churches, where he could pursue his very cerebral life of dream and fantasy. These tastes are reflected throughout his fiction, since he writes about people who spend their time indoors, such as actresses; writers; prostitutes; des Esseintes, whose one venture beyond his own doorstep took him no further than an English pub in Paris; Jacques Marles, who travels through the multiple floors of a castle; and Durtal, who spends his time investigating the different aspects of Church life. All of his major characters are neurotically depressed, and, in contrast to the positive joy which is expressed by the Impressionist paintings, his fiction is characterized by a bleak, dark view of life. The few moments of happiness derive from intellectual pursuit, not from any sense of communion with society or nature. Whereas the Impressionists were eager to record the beauty of the present moment, Huysmans' characters only express dissatisfaction with the present and a desire to find some escape from it, both physically and psychologically. This feeling is expressed dramatically in "L'Obsession," one of the prose poems Huysmans added to the 1886 edition of *Croquis parisiens,* in which the writer describes his fears at having to return to Paris after a brief vacation: "Oh! to think that there will always be a Before and an After and never an enduring Now!" ("Ah! dire qu'il y aura toujours un Avant et un Après et jamais un Maintenant qui dure!") (VIII, 142).

Given that Huysmans' temperament was so different from that of the Impressionists and the tone of his fiction so contrary to that of the Impressionist paintings, one must ask why he identified himself so closely with their cause and committed himself so wholeheartedly to their defense. For, in spite of the fact that he perceived, as did Degas, many intrinsic problems and did not fully approve of the final results of the Impressionist experiment, he certainly was genuinely supportive of all the artists involved.

His enthusiasm for their endeavors sprung mainly from the fact that they rejected the noble subjects and traditional painting techniques of their Academic colleagues and painted instead specifically contemporary subjects in their natural surroundings and reevaluated color quality under the impact of natural sunlight. Independence of spirit and experimentation were valuable to Huysmans in and of themselves and values which he himself pursued rigorously in his own writing—"new days, new ways. It is a simple matter of common sense" ("à temps nouveaux, procédés neufs. C'est simple affaire de bon sens") (VI, 14). It is true that he criticized a large number of the Impressionists' works, especially the landscapes, and his sense of their failure, as we shall see, stems from the very techniques which he claims to have admired. He had faith, however, that they were working in the right direction and so, in spite of his honest criticisms, he writes in the Salon of 1879 that

> Until a man of genius, uniting all the curious elements of Impressionism, rises up and storms the fortress, I can only applaud the Independents' endeavors.

> En attendant qu'un homme de génie, réunissant tous les curieux éléments de la peinture impressionniste, surgisse et enlève d'assaut la place, je ne puis trop applaudir aux tentatives des indépendants. (VI, 13)

What *is* Huysmans' understanding of Impressionism and of the direction modern art should take? He tries to establish a direct relationship between trends in literature and in painting. A fervent Naturalist at the time of writing his salon accounts, he looks in the work of the independent artists for a treatment of reality corresponding to the novels of Zola and his followers. Already in "Notes sur le Salon de 1877: portraits et natures mortes," published in *L'Actualité,* he regrets

> That one cannot find, with the exception of one or two Impressionists, seven or eight talented painters at least, who attempt in their art what we attempt in ours.

> Qu'il ne se trouve pas, à l'exception d'un ou deux impressionnistes, sept ou huit peintres de talent au moins qui tentent, dans leur art, ce que nous tentons dans le nôtre.

His faith in the Impressionists grows, for he says in the "Salon de 1879" in *L'Art moderne* that the Naturalist movement in literature is "defined in painting by the Impressionists and by Manet" ("déterminé en peinture par les impressionnistes et par Manet") (VI, 12). He is not making stylistic analogies; he is talking purely of subject matter, for what he is looking for in art at this point is "a real concern for contemporary life" ("un réel souci de la vie contemporaine") (VI, 12), that is, modernity. He praises Pissarro, Sisley, Cassatt, Caillebotte, Raffaëlli, Morisot, Renoir, Degas, and Forain for having begun to portray the kind of people he considered the right material for contemporary art, but who in 1880 he felt were still lagging behind the writers. In the salon account of that year he writes:

> All of modern life has yet to be studied; barely a few of its manifold faces have been observed and recorded. Everything is still to be done: the official galas, the salons, the balls, the bits of family life, of the lives of artisans and bourgeois, the stores, the markets, the restaurants, the cafés, the bars, in short, all of humanity, whatever class of society they may belong to and whatever function they serve, at home, in the hospitals, in the dance-halls, at the theater, in the public squares, in the poor streets or on the vast boulevards whose American looks are the necessary framework for the needs of our age.

> Toute la vie moderne est à étudier encore; c'est à peine si quelques-unes de ses multiples faces ont été aperçues et notées. Toute est à faire: les galas officiels, les salons, les bals, les coins de la vie familière, de la vie artisane et bourgeoise, les magasins, les marchés, les restaurants, les cafés, les zincs, enfin, toute l'humanité, à quelque classe de la société qu'elle appartienne et quelque fonction qu'elle remplisse, chez elle, dans les hospices, dans les bastringues, au théâtre, dans les squares, dans les rues pauvres ou dans ces vastes boulevards dont les américaines allures sont le cadre nécessaire aux besoins de notre époque. (VI, 140–41)

In his own early Naturalist fiction such as *Marthe* and *Les Soeurs Vatard,* and in his *Croquis parisiens* of 1880 Huysmans had already treated some of these subjects.

From the point of view of technique, Huysmans is convinced that the Impressionists have made a significant breakthrough, recognizing, as they did, that the effect of natural light on colors is different from the effect of artificial light. In "L'Exposition des Indépendants en 1880" we find the fullest analysis of Impressionism, in which one is impressed by the perception Huysmans shows of its theories but is surprised at his disappointment in the final results:

> Did this attempt at rendering the teeming masses in the powdery light, or at separating them with their crude tints, without gradations, without half-tones, in certain straight shafts of sunlight, shortening and almost eliminating shadows, as in Japanese pictures, succeed during the period in which it was ventured?—I have to say it: almost never.

> Cette tentative de rendre le foisonnement des êtres et des choses dans la pulvérulence de la lumière ou de les détacher avec leurs tons crus, sans dégradations, sans demi-teintes, dans certains coups de soleil tombant droit, raccourcissant et supprimant presque les ombres, comme dans les images des Japonais, a-t-elle abouti, à l'époque où elle fut osée?—Presque jamais, je dois le dire. (VI, 104)

Using epithets of softness, subtlety, and nuance, Huysmans suggests the type of landscape he feels the Impressionists were attempting to paint. In a totally contrasting vocabulary of hardness, aggression, and brutality, he describes what the Impressionists, in his opinion, were actually painting.

They began from a correct point of view: they fervently observed—contrary to the habits of Corot, who is pointed out, I don't know why, as a precursor—how nature appeared, modified according to the time of the year, the climate, the hour of the day, the more or less violent heat of the sun or the more or less pronounced threats of rain; they have wandered, hesitated, seeking, like Claude Monet, to render the movement of water struck by the changing reflections of the shoreline. The result was a crushing, opaque heaviness, where nature had a delightful delicacy of fleeting shades. None of them has conveyed either the fluid glassiness of water mottled by the sky's changing flecks, whipped by the reflected tops of leaves, twisted by the spiral of the tree trunk that seems to turn upon itself as it sinks; or, on solid ground, the floating of the tree whose outlines blur when the sun flashes behind it. These irizations, these reflections, these hazes, these powderings, were transformed, on their canvases, into chalky sludges, hatched in harsh blue, gaudy lilac, surly orange, cruel red.

Partant d'un point de vue juste, observant avec ferveur,—contrairement aux us de Corot qu'on signale, je ne sais pourquoi, comme un précurseur,—l'aspect de la nature modifiée, suivant l'époque, suivant le climat, suivant l'heure de la journée, suivant l'ardeur plus ou moins violente du soleil ou les menaces plus ou moins accentuées des pluies, ils ont erré, hésité, voulant, comme Claude Monet, rendre les troubles de l'eau battue par les reflets mouvants des rives. Ç'a été, là où la nature avait une délicieuse finesse de fugitives nuances, une lourdeur écrasante, opaque. Ni le vitreux fluide de l'eau, jaspée par les taches changeantes du ciel, fouettée par les cimes réfléchies des feuillages, vrillée par la spirale du tronc d'arbre, paraissant tourner sur lui-même, en s'enfonçant; ni, sur la terre ferme, le flottant de l'arbre dont les contours se brouillent, quand le soleil éclate derrière, n'ont été exprimés par l'un d'entre eux. Ces irisations, ces reflets, ces vapeurs, ces poudroiements, se changeaient, sur leurs toiles, en une boue de craie, hachée de bleu rude, de lilas criard, d'orange hargneux, de cruel rouge. (VI, 104–5)[6]

There is an irony in the fact that this is a very poetic passage in which Huysmans seems to express a real feeling for the subtle, fleeting moment. In his own fiction, however, he only rarely[7] describes such scenes. The predominant colors in his early, Naturalist fiction, corresponding in time to these articles on Impressionism, are grey, black, red, and purple. Contrary to the Impressionists, who studied the objective color values of things in nature, Huysmans was always much closer to the Symbolists in the way he exploited the emotional and symbolic impact of colors.[8] Whatever Huysmans' sympathy with the Impressionist movement, there is certainly a discrepancy between his alleged admiration for their aims and his own instinctive interpretation of nature.

Huysmans rationalized his disappointment in many of the Impressionist works by ascribing the predominance of certain colors, especially blue, to the fact that the artists were suffering from what he calls "these ophthalmias and these nervous conditions" ("ces ophtalmies et ces névroses") (VI, 107). This theory, suggested by poorly executed scientific experiments, was widely believed at that time. It naturally distressed those artists whom Huysmans accused of having this ailment, especially since he was otherwise regarded as a highly intelligent and perceptive critic. In the letter, for instance, which Pissarro wrote to his son about *L'Art moderne,* he complains that "Even Huysmans, in his book, deplores this disease of the visual organ; to qualify, however, he declares us cured" ("Même Huysmans, dans son livre, déplore cette affection de l'organe visuel; comme correctif cependant il nous déclare guéris").[9] In a letter which Pissarro wrote to Huysmans personally about *L'Art moderne* he asked why the critic had not included a discussion about Cézanne, whom the artists considered one of the greatest influences on modern art. Huysmans replied:

> Yes, this is a temperament, an artist, but overall—except for a few still lifes that hold up—the rest, in my opinion, was not born viable. It is interesting, curious, thought-provoking, but there is definitely an eye problem there, which he himself is aware of, they assure me.
>
> In my humble opinion, the Cézannes are the models of unsuccessful Impressionism.— You may thus imagine that after so many years of struggle, it is no longer a question of intentions made more or less manifest, more or less visible, but of total works, serious births, works that are not monsters.
>
> Oui, c'est un tempérament, un artiste, mais en somme, si j'excepte quelques natures mortes qui tiennent, le reste, à mon avis, n'est point né viable. C'est intéressant, curieux, suggestif en réflexions, mais il y a là un cas oculaire certain, dont lui-même se rend compte, m'assure-t-on.
>
> A mon humble avis, les Cézanne sont les types de l'impressionnisme non abouti.— Songez donc qu'après tant d'années de lutte, il ne s'agit plus d'intentions plus ou moins manifestes, plus ou moins visibles, mais d'oeuvres pleines, d'accouchements sérieux, d'oeuvres qui ne soient point des monstres.[10]

In *Certains* Huysmans does include a brief article on Cézanne in which he praises "some brutal, rough pears and apples, plastered with a trowel, gone over with a roll of the thumb" ("des poires et des pommes brutales, frustes, maçonnées avec une truelle, rebroussées par des roulis de pouce") (X, 38–39). These solid, sculpted, forceful still lifes are far removed from the evanescent scenes Huysmans claimed to look for in Impressionism. Indeed, he continues to criticize Cézanne's landscapes for being sketchy and unrealistic, the product of "an artist with diseased retinas" ("un artiste aux rétines malades") (X, 40). This sketchy, so-called unfinished quality of the Impressionist works was, besides the "crude" colors, the one most frequently criticized by Huysmans, which shows that Huysmans was still very bound to the classical demands of drawing and, in spite of his support of the general direction of these new paintings, could not accept the new technique. There is a passage in *En Ménage* in which Jeanne looks around André's room and comments on his art collection. Since Jeanne is unlikely to have knowledge of these art works, one must presume that it is the writer talking and one wonders whether the comment about the Impressionists is indeed a moment of self-mockery on the part of Huysmans:

> She looked around the morning-room where they were, recognized old knick-knacks, an engraving by Daullé after Teniers, an old print by Breughel the Droll, earthenware plates . . . contemplated the Impressionist watercolors, which she had never seen; look, this is something new, it's pretty; but why ever is it unfinished?

Elle regardait le petit salon où ils étaient, reconnaissait d'anciens bibelots, une gravure de Daullé d'après Teniers, une vieille estampe de Breughel-le-Drôle, des assiettes de faïence . . . contemplait les aquarelles impressionnistes qu'elle n'avait jamais vues; tiens, voici du nouveau, c'est joli, mais pourquoi donc ce n'est pas terminé? (IV, 250)

So Huysmans, in spite of defending modern art in general terms, rejected most of the Impressionists in the final analysis, and admired only those, who, like Caillebotte, "rejected the system of Impressionist blobs that force the eye to squint in order for it to restore the focus of people and things" ("a rejeté le système des taches impressionnistes qui forcent l'oeil à cligner pour rétablir l'aplomb des êtres et des choses") (VI, 115), or Raffaëlli, who "also rejected works which, under the pretext of impressionism, lacked drawing and corrupted color" ("n'a pas accepté non plus, sous prétexte d'impression, les pénuries de dessin et les vices de la couleur") (VI, 116).

We have noted that Huysmans, at the beginning of *L'Art moderne,* put "la manière" above "le sujet" (VI, 8), but he understood the treatment to be an emotional concept as well as a pictorial one. It was on these grounds that he rejected totally any art form which he understood to be dealing with form alone and was not interested in the Neo-Impressionists, who developed the Impressionist color theories on a more scientific basis and painted pictures which certainly looked more "finished" but which, according to Huysmans, had "too many systems, and not enough crackling flame, not enough life!" ("trop de systèmes, et pas assez de flamme qui pétille, pas assez de vie!")[11] The qualities Huysmans was looking for in modern art, even in landscapes, and wrongly ascribed to the Impressionist program, were temperament and human interest:

Such as it is, and above all, such as it will be, Impressionist art shows a very astute sense of observation, a very particular and very profound analysis of depicted temperaments.

Tel qu'il est, et tel qu'il sera surtout, l'art impressionniste montre une observation très curieuse, une analyse très particulière et très profonde des tempéraments mis en scène. (VI, 44)

Huysmans' indifference to landscape painting which does not have any human interest was expressed as early as 1867 in his very first piece of art criticism. It was an article on contemporary landscape painting, written for the *Revue Mensuelle* of November 25 and never published in his collected works. It shows a very muted enthusiasm for French contemporary art and one can hardly imagine that the article was written by the same man who produced such colorful and forceful articles about the independent painters some ten years later. It does, however, lay down those criteria about landscape paintings on which he based his later criticism. He talks briefly about Courbet, Corot, Rousseau, and mainly about Diaz. He criticizes the latter, however, "for not deigning to paint his characters" ("de ne pas daigner peindre ses personnages") and says that "above all, it would be better if he took the trouble (he could, I am convinced) to come down to Man" ("mieux vaudrait surtout qu'il se donnât la peine (il le pourrait, j'en suis convaincu) de descendre jusqu'à l'homme").[12]

Raffaëlli

As far as contemporary landscape painting was concerned, Huysmans looked to Raffaëlli as the one who understood the modern Parisian temperament. As we have discussed, Huysmans was not very interested in the typical Impressionist landscapes, although he genuinely welcomed any attempt to break away from the old schools. He did love Raffaëlli, though, because his work depicted one of the sordid aspects of Parisian life and thus complemented the works of his other favorite painters and corresponded to the kind of landscape he was describing in his own writing. Raffaëlli painted the decaying suburbs of Paris with their poor and miserable peasants living in the shadow of the new factories which blackened the little vegetation still remaining. There is a reoccurring imagery of dilapidated shacks, puny rivers, dirty children, undernourished horses, lanky poplar trees, old carts, and smoke erupting from factory chimneys. These scenes confirmed Huysmans' belief that modern society was dying, was sterile, and that his only possible escape from mediocrity and decay was to live a life of intellectual and, eventually, religious escape.

Just as his study of Degas, Forain, Moreau, and Rops helped Huysmans focus his thoughts about women and develop a vocabulary with which to describe them, in Raffaëlli he found the imagery which corresponded to his views on nature. When we compare the art critical texts to his fiction we see the striking interplay between the two. Raffaëlli himself, as we shall see in a letter he wrote to Huysmans, was amazed at the insight the writer seemed to have into the artist's own feelings.

There are certain elements which Huysmans focuses on both in his analysis of Raffaëlli's work and in the treatment of nature in his own prose poems and novels. These are the beauty of melancholy landscape; the calming solitude; the sickliness, which is connected in Huysmans' mind to women; black water, which acts as a mirror; and black soot, which complements the water and is symbolic of death.

Huysmans' predilection for melancholy landscapes goes back to his Dutch and Flemish period when he had chosen Ruysdael as one of his favorites because of the melancholy winter scenes with setting suns and bare trees. In "En Hollande" of 1877 Huysmans writes of one of Ruysdael's windmill paintings that

Never has the great master's melancholy—further quickened by nature's desolation at the oncoming somber days of winter—been rendered thus! Never has the suffering of a place that shivers and complains, when the snow comes, cried or bled in such a way in a canvas.

Jamais la mélancolie du grand maître, ravivée encore par le navrement de la nature aux approches des sombres journées d'hiver, n'a été ainsi rendue! jamais la douleur d'un site qui frissonne et se plaint, aux arrivées des neiges, n'a ainsi crié, n'a ainsi saigné dans une toile.[13]

Then in "Notes sur le salon de 1877: tableaux militaires et paysages," published in *L'Actualité* on July 8, 1877, Huysmans sets down for the first time, in more general, theoretical terms, his beliefs about landscape painting:

I do not, of course, require that one paint only sickly and shabby wastes, or else the prettified and joyous small gardens of the Paris outskirts; I have no difficulty accepting that many artists understand nothing of the doleful charm or the artificial joys of walled-in landscapes; moreover, I have no difficulty imagining that many people admire Ruysdael and Rousseau, do not see that the beauty of a landscape lies chiefly in its melancholy; and, further, I understand that many people do not think, as I do, that the sadness of wallflowers drying in a pot is more interesting than the sun-filled laughter of roses grown outside in the earth. . . .

Je ne demande pas, bien entendu, qu'on ne peigne que les landes souffreteuses et rapées ou les jardinets maquillés et joyeux des environs de Paris; j'admets parfaitement que beaucoup d'artistes ne comprennent rien du tout au charme dolent ou aux joies factices des paysages enserrés dans des murs; je me figure parfaitement que bien des gens admirent cependant Ruysdael et Rousseau, ne voient pas que la beauté d'un paysage est faite surtout de mélancolie; et plus encore je conçois que nombre de personnes ne pensent comme moi que la tristesse des giroflées séchant dans un pot est plus intéressante que le rire ensoleillé des roses poussées en pleine terre. . . .[14]

This aesthetic of melancholy is central to Huysmans' taste in landscape painting and two years later, in "Le Salon de 1879" in *L'Art moderne,* he repeats that

I know of few great landscape artists who convey a carefree and joyful impression in their canvases. Rousseau, Millet, Constable, and, drawing from the ancients, Ruysdael, painted landscapes from which emanates a sorrowful grandeur. One could say that the beauty of a landscape lies chiefly in its melancholy.

Je ne connais guère de grands paysagistes qui vous fassent éprouver devant leurs toiles une impression rieuse et légère. Rousseau, Millet, Constable et, en prenant dans les anciens, Ruysdael, ont peint des paysages d'où se dégage une grandeur triste. On pourrait dire que la beauté d'un paysage est surtout faite de mélancolie. (VI, 34)

These words are repeated verbatim in *La Bièvre* (VIII, 87). The attitude is perhaps best summed up when he describes Raffaëlli's *Vue de Gennevilliers* in "L'Exposition des Indépendants en 1880" as an expression of

the melancholy grandeur of bloodless places lying beneath infinite skies; here, then, is expressed at last that poignant note of the spleen of landscapes, of the plaintive delights of our outskirts!

la mélancolique grandeur des sites anémiques couchés sous l'infini des ciels; voici donc enfin exprimée cette note poignante du spleen des paysages, des plaintives délices de nos banlieues! (VI, 117)

It is one of the fundamental ambivalences in Huysmans' approach that he hated the industrialization, the Americanization of modern society, yet found in the ugliness it produced, the wretched people who suffered under it, part of the modernity which he found appealing. He also felt strongly that it was an important subject matter for art. This attempt on his part to come to terms with society ended with *A Rebours,* but meanwhile he threw himself enthusiastically into the new aesthetic.

One of the central images of this new society was the factory and the new colossal metal buildings such as the railway stations.[15] In the early seventies many of the Impressionists, including Pissarro, Guillaumin, and Monet, painted scenes of factory smokestacks, still a rather daring theme for artistic representation. Huysmans is certainly progressive in his attitude when, in "Le Salon de 1879," he refutes a statement that engineers were ruining nature:

> But no! They only modify them and give them, most of the time, a more penetrating and livelier accent. The factory smokestacks that rise in the distance mark the North, Pantin, for example, with a stamp of melancholy grandeur that it would never have had without them.
>
> Mais non! ils les modifient simplement et leur donnent, la plupart du temps, un accent plus pénétrant et plus vif. Les tuyaux d'usines qui se dressent au loin marquent le Nord, Pantin par exemple, d'un cachet de grandeur mélancolique qu'il n'aurait jamais eu sans eux. (VI, 88)

This idea is repeated in the prose poem "Vue des remparts du Nord-Paris" of 1880, in which he writes:

> Created incomplete in anticipation of the role that Man will assign her, Nature awaits from her master her completion, the finishing touch. . . . And we have delegated the engineers to apply it, to make manifest the instinct for harmony that obsesses us, so that we may suit Nature to our needs, bring her in unison with those pleasant or pitiful lives it is her mission to frame and reflect.
>
> Créée incomplète dans la prévision du rôle que l'homme lui assignera, la nature attend de ce maître son parachèvement et son coup de fion. . . . Et c'est pour l'appliquer, c'est pour réaliser l'instinct d'harmonie qui nous obsède, que nous avons délégué les ingénieurs afin d'assortir la nature à nos besoins, afin de la mettre à l'unisson avec les douces ou pitoyables vies qu'elle a charge d'encadrer et de réfléchir. (VIII, 107–8)

In his "Salon des Indépendants" of the same year he also puts in an impassioned plea to painters to include factories and stations in their works:

> which artist will now render the imposing grandeur of the factory towns . . . the colossal scale of locomotives and train stations; which landscapist will render the terrifying and awe-inspiring solemnity of the tall furnaces blazing in the night, the gigantic blast furnaces crowned at their summits with pale fires?
>
> quel artiste rendra maintenant l'imposante grandeur des villes usinières . . . la colossale ampleur des locomotives et des gares; quel paysagiste rendra la terrifiante et grandiose solennité des hauts fourneaux flambant dans la nuit, des gigantesques cheminées, couronnées à leur sommet de feux pâles? (VI, 141)[16]

Huysmans incorporated his antipathy towards sunny, lush scenes and his fascination with factories in the novel *En Rade,* 1887, long after he ceased to hold any interest in either Raffaëlli or the more popular Impressionists, having discovered Redon and other more imaginative, fantastic painters. Could this be, like Jeanne's comment about the Impressionists in *En Ménage,* another example of self-mockery on the part of Huysmans? The reference to the crude, dirty color of the haystacks certainly leads one to believe so:

What an oven! thought the young man, who sat down cross-legged and huddled, trying to shelter his body within the circle of shade cast by the brim of his large straw hat. And what a joke, that golden wheat! he said to himself, looking at the dirty-orange bundles gathered into piles in the distance. No matter how much he spurred himself, he could not manage to find truly grand this harvest picture so incessantly celebrated by painters and poets. Beneath a sky of imitable blue, there were shirt-sleeved and hairy people, stinking of grease, monotonously cutting down blighted underbrush. How paltry this picture seemed, compared with a scene of a factory or the belly of an ocean liner lit by the fires of a forge!

Quelle fournaise! pensa le jeune homme, qui s'assit en tailleur et se tassa, cherchant à s'abriter le corps dans le cercle d'ombre projeté par les ailes de son large chapeau de paille. Et quelle blague que l'or des blés! se dit-il, regardant au loin ces bottes couleur d'orange sale, réunies en tas. Il avait beau s'éperonner, il ne pouvait parvenir à trouver que ce tableau de la moisson si constamment célébré par les peintres et par les poètes, fût vraiment grand. C'était, sous un ciel d'un imitable bleu, des gens dépoitraillés et velus, puant le suint, et qui sciaient en mesure des taillis de rouille. Combien ce tableau semblait mesquin en face d'une scène d'usine ou d'un ventre de paquebot, éclairé par des feux de forges! (IX, 174–75)

Huysmans never found an artist who represented "the terrifying and awe-inspiring solemnity of the tall furnaces blazing in the night" ("la terrifiante et grandiose solennité des hauts fourneaux flambant dans la nuit") (VI, 141). He himself came closest to describing such scenes in his nightmarish perception of the setting sun in the opening scene of *En Rade.*

In Raffaëlli's work, however, he discovered the drama of the factories. As in Huysmans' own early works, the emphasis is not so much on the threatening fire but on the soot which they spew out across the countryside in a very human fashion, contrasted strongly to the scanty vegetation, the pale sunlight, and the weak, pathetic movements of the people. This soot, one of the notable characteristics of the landscapes Huysmans loved, is associated with death and destruction and is, ironically, their most forceful and striking element. Certain phrases which describe these clouds of soot being poured out into the landscape are found in nearly every description of Raffaëlli's paintings and in Huysmans' own prose poems.

Huysmans first mentions Raffaëlli in the *Salon* of 1879. He singles him out as one of the few artists "vraiment moderne" (VI, 52). He is especially impressed by one of Raffaëlli's melancholy landscapes in which "factory chimneys spew boiling soot onto a livid sky" ("des cheminées d'usine crachent sur un ciel livide des bouillons de suie") (VI, 52). Huysmans already uses this phrase in the prose poem "Autour des fortifications" (I, 127), and repeats it, in part, in "Vue des remparts du Nord-Paris" in *Croquis parisiens,* in which "tall brick chimneys, round and square, vomit boiling soot into the clouds . . ." ("de longues cheminées rondes et carrées de briques vomissent dans les nuages des bouillons de suie . . .") (VIII, 105), and again in the description of Raffaëlli's *Vue de Gennevilliers,* 1880, where "On the right, factory stacks vomit boiling black smoke that rips apart and separates, all in the same direction" ("A droite, des tuyaux d'usines vomissent des bouillons de fumée noire qui se déchirent et s'écartent, toutes, du même côté") (VI, 117).

This discussion of Raffaëlli's work in 1879 typifies Huysmans' criticism of those painters he most liked. For he talks above all of his emotional reaction to them—"I saw few paintings at the Salon that so painfully and so delightfully gripped me" ("J'ai vu au Salon peu de tableaux qui m'aient aussi douloureusement et aussi délicieusement poigné") (VI, 52)—and he uses them as a springboard for personal memories and fantasies. The degree to which he likes the art is in direct relationship to the degree to which it corresponds to his own experience. In this case, Raffaëlli's painting

> evoked in me the sorrowful charm of the ramshackle shanties, the slender poplars that stand out along those endless roads that disappear, beyond the town walls, into the sky . . . all the distress of the old outskirts rose before me.
>
> a évoqué en moi le charme attristé des cabanes branlantes, des grêles peupliers en vedette sur ces interminables routes qui se perdent, au sortir des remparts, dans le ciel . . . toute la détresse des anciennes banlieues s'est levée devant moi. (VI, 52)[17]

Similarly, of a watercolor in the same exhibition Huysmans writes that

> As I have in front of this excellent painter's paintings, I have seen again, standing in front of his watercolors, lives of toil and wretchedness; I have seen again, on plains where an old white horse grazes by a cart that stands sadly and raises its arms, those scenes that unfailingly offer themselves to those who go beyond the town walls.
>
> Comme devant les tableaux de cet excellent peintre, j'ai revu, devant son aquarelle, des existences de labeurs et de misères; j'ai revu, dans des plaines où broute un vieux cheval blanc près d'une charrette tristement assise et levant les bras, ces scènes qui s'offrent immanquablement aux gens qui sortent des remparts. (VI, 89)

In "L'Exposition des Indépendants en 1881" which concludes *L'Art moderne,* Huysmans returns to the discussion of the portrayal of people in the landscape of Raffaëlli. He feels strongly that a landscape painting is not complete without people or the buildings which symbolize them. He expects a strictly naturalistic rendering of these figures—"a very profound and very particular analysis of temperaments" ("une analyse très particulière et très profonde des tempéraments mis en scène") (VI, 44)—and this implies a detailed portrayal of the people and their milieu. In 1881 he places Raffaëlli alongside the Le Nain brothers as sensitive and accurate painters of the poor, for "no one had dared to place them in the sites where they live and which are inevitably appropriate to their destitution and their needs" ("personne n'avait osé les installer dans les sites où ils vivent et qui sont forcément appropriés à leurs dénûments et à leurs besoins") (VI, 269). One of his figures in particular "no longer exceeds painting's rights in blending philosophic or literary elements into it" ("n'outrepasse plus les droits de la peinture, en y mêlant des éléments philosophiques ou littéraires") (VI, 268). Although Huysmans had been very enthusiastic in his praise of Raffaëlli in his accounts of the 1879 and 1880 exhibitions, he now admits that he had been disturbed by "a tendency toward that maudlin humanitarianism that spoils Millet's peasants for me . . . that useless pomposity" ("une tendance à cette humanitairerie qui me gâte les paysans de Millet . . . cette inutile emphase") (VI, 268).

Huysmans' own interest in the lower classes was certainly aesthetic to a large degree, consistent with his belief that modern art, as well as criticism, should be impartial and objective. He interprets working class scenes as descriptions of shapes, colors and movements; and his fascination for the attire of the peasants, their bent, weary bodies, their tools, and their houses is on the same level as his interest in the makeup and dress of the prostitute, the actress, and the dancer. In spite of this, however, one can detect on his part, in all the descriptions of Raffaëlli's work, a certain compassion and pity for the peasants, which goes beyond a strictly Naturalist rendering. Thus, throughout his articles we find expressions of sympathy such as "Two people drag themselves painfully along," "painfully gripped," "these wretches who make their way," "the distress of the old outskirts" ("Deux se trainent péniblement," "douloureusement poigné," "ces malheureux qui cheminent," "la détresse des anciennes banlieues") (VI, 52), "existences of toil and wretchedness," "difficulties that the world of the poor encounters in living" ("des existences de labeurs et de misères," "difficultés qu'éprouve le pauvre monde à vivre") (VI, 89) and

All the horrors of winter are there. This impression of the great cold that penetrates you to the marrow, this restlessness and this sort of malaise that grip the human machine . . . have never been expressed before.

Toutes les horreurs de l'hiver sont là. Jamais l'impression du grand froid qui vous pénètre jusqu'aux moelles, jamais cette inquiétude et cette sorte de malaise qui saisissent la machine humaine . . . n'ont été exprimées. (VI, 120)

Helen Trudgian exaggerates greatly when she claims that Huysmans "becomes almost the confidant of those who have come down in the world" ("devient presque le confident des déclassés"),[18] but there is certainly a dichotomy in Huysmans between his attempt to observe nature dispassionately and a true sympathy with the suffering working classes. His sympathy, in turn, is always mitigated by his decadent fascination with everything ugly and sickly, leading him to find beauty in the most sordid of scenes. Classical beauty and symmetry are anathema to him. These conflicting attitudes are manifest, not only in Huysmans' art criticism but, as we shall see, in his prose poems and novels.

Le Drageoir aux épices, 1874

This collection of prose poems consists of *transpositions d'art* based on seventeenth-century Dutch paintings and character studies. "La Rive gauche," however, is a poem about a river. It is Huysmans' earliest description of a local landscape, written the same year as the first independent exhibition, before Huysmans developed his great interest in Impressionist artists. It is largely anecdotal in its account of the narrator's walk along the Bièvre river as it meanders through the poor areas outside of Paris. He mainly describes the people he meets and the popular entertainment he observes. His landscape descriptions, however, are poetical, and subtly incorporated into this very naturalistic account of a Sunday stroll are attitudes and observations which form the basis of all Huysmans' later landscape descriptions and lend insight into his approach to the work of Raffaëlli.

The walk, according to Huysmans, is prompted by a need to escape the noise of Paris and the vulgarity of the masses. When the Impressionist painters sought fresh scenes outside Paris they went much further afield, but given Huysmans' hatred of the open countryside, it is not surprising that his walks did not take him far from Paris and that refuge, rather than the beauty of nature, was what called him:

> This is not the real countryside, so green, so merry in the clear sunlight; this is a world apart, sad, arid, yet, because of those very qualities, solitary and charming.

> Ce n'est pas la vraie campagne, si verte, si rieuse au clair soleil; c'est un monde à part, triste, aride, mais par cela même solitaire et charmant. (I, 68)

The opening line of the prose poem—"Weary of the crowds' murmur" ("Las du bruissement des foules") (I, 65)—can be considered the first step in his retreat from the everyday life of Paris which leads him eventually to the Church. One is reminded of des Esseintes' desire to find a place "far from the incessant flood of human folly" ("loin de l'incessant déluge de la sottise humaine"); of Jacques Marles in *En Rade,* who escapes to

> the only refuge on which he and his wife could now rely, . . . a shelter, a berth, where they could cast anchor and put their heads together, during a momentary truce, before reentering Paris to take up the struggle. . . .

> le seul refuge sur lequel lui et sa femme pussent maintenant compter . . . un abri, une rade, où ils pourraient jeter l'ancre et se concerter, pendant un passager armistice, avant que de rentrer à Paris, pour commencer la lutte. . . . (IX, 6)

of the Carhaix' belltower home in *Là-Bas,* where Durtal finds "a warm haven" ("un havre tiède"), where he can dream of existing "outside of time" ("à l'écart du temps") (XII, 58–59); of Durtal's refuge in the Church of Saint-Sulpice in *En Route,* where "he kept himself, at the time, so far from everything, so far from that city in full cry only a stone's throw away" ("il se tenait alors si loin de tout, si loin de cette ville qui battait, à deux pas de lui, son plein") (XIII, 1, 148); and finally, of Huysmans' own attempt to escape completely by joining an oblature.

In spite of its fairly objective account of nature and a relatively optimistic mood, "La Rive gauche" contains images which mark the incipient fear and pessimism that typify his later work. For example, Huysmans describes an old lantern which is attached to two houses by many pieces of string. This view is transformed into "a gigantic spider spinning its web" ("une gigantesque araignée tissant sa toile") (I, 67), a frightening image which reappears in *En Rade,* 1887. Jacques is making his way to the château of Lourps and comes first to an old church. He is at first encouraged that he recognizes his way, but then

> that black and red church . . . those crossings, with their rose windows starred with lead wire, like gigantic spiderwebs suspended over a furnace, seemed sinister to him.

> cette église noire et rouge . . . ces croisées semblables avec leurs rosaces étoilées de filets de plomb, à de gigantesques toiles d'araignées pendues au-dessus d'une fournaise, lui parurent sinistres. (IX, 9)

A further example in "La Rive gauche" of a vocabulary of fear and sickness, which sets Huysmans apart from the majority of the Impressionists with their objective and optimistic view of nature, is found in this description of the setting sun. Unlike "these irizations, these reflections, these vapors, these powderings" ("ces irisations, ces reflets, ces vapeurs, ces poudroiements") (VI, 105), which Huysmans demands of the Impressionist painters in *L'Art moderne,* he here writes that "The sun was setting, and the clouds that surrounded it seemed spattered with droplets of blood" ("Le soleil se couchait et les nuages qui l'entouraient semblaient éclaboussés de gouttelettes de sang") (I, 70).

In "La Rive gauche" some temporary refuge is found in the poor areas surrounding the Bièvre river, a puny flow of water which is, as Huysmans writes, "soot-black in Paris" ("d'un noir de suie à Paris") (I, 65). By relating the blackness of the water to the blackness of the soot, Huysmans connects the sky (the tall chimneys which pour out soot in the characteristic Huysmansian landscape) and the land. This universal blackness, associated with decay and death, is present throughout Huysmans' work, and this is the earliest example. The black water is also related to the imagery of mirrors, which play an important symbolic role in Huysmans, as in so many poets of the turn of the century. For dark mirrors can be, according to Michael Riffaterre, "melancholy reflections, mirrors of distressful memory or bad conscience. These are characterized by a shadowy or dim reflection, or the reflection that lets you see beyond, as in dark stagnant waters."[19] Certainly, in "La Rive gauche" the dark, dank river, bordered by rows of tall poplar trees, acts as a catalyst and prompts flights of memory and revery which typify even the most Naturalist of Huysmans' works:

> it [that little river] is . . . framed by bizarrely sad sights that evoke in me something like distant memories or the desolate rhythms of Schubert's music.
>
> elle [cette petite rivière] est . . . encadrée d'aspects bizarrement tristes qui évoquent en moi comme de lointains souvenirs ou comme les rythmes désolés de la musique de Schubert. (I, 65–66)

"Autour des fortifications," written at the same time as "La Rive gauche" but only added later to the edition of Huysmans' collected works, is further evidence of his fascination with the poor, desolate districts surrounding Paris. Incorporated into the lengthy, detailed descriptions of the landscape, the distant views of trains and factory chimneys, the anecdotes about cafés and cabarets, are rich poetic images which hint at Huysmans' later articles.

It is in this poem that Huysmans introduces his fundamental metaphor of disease with which he describes such landscapes. From using the adjective "morbide" (I, 109) to describe the district's charm, he develops the comparison between the subtle appeal of a sickly woman to the beauty of this ruined neighborhood:

> Who has not remarked, indeed, that many women, common and red-faced, become more refined when an illness strikes them and lingers? Who has not followed pain's terrible quarterings, the delicate pallors and the subtle graces of convalescent women?
>
> Qui n'a, en effet, remarqué que bien des femmes, communes et rougeaudes, s'affinent lorsqu'une maladie s'abat sur elles et se prolonge? Qui n'a suivi les terribles équarrissements corporels de la douleur, les pâleurs délicates et les grâces subtiles des convalescences? (I, 110)

The suffering, of which Huysmans is certainly aware, does not interfere with the calming influence of these landscapes: "These walks are rich in peace and reveries" ("Ces promenades sont fécondes en apaisements et en rêveries") (I, 111). Huysmans even seems to end the poem on a note of defiance. Following the description of the factories spewing out "their inky flakes" ("leurs flocons d'encre") (I, 131) is a lyrical passage describing the sunny, joyful landscape, more typical of the scenes portrayed by the Impressionists than by Huysmans in his fiction:

> And, as though indifferent to the sorrows that the neighborhood conceals, above the Point-du-Jour the sky, its clouds now swept away, sifts gold dust across its blue sieve and floods with luminous joys the river's water, which seems to sparkle with pleasure.

Et comme indifférent aux douleurs que ce quartier recèle, au-dessus du Point-du-Jour, le ciel, maintenant balayé de nuages, blute au travers de son bleu tamis de la poussière d'or et inonde de joies lumineuses l'eau du fleuve, qui semble pétiller d'aise. (I, 131)

In Huysmans' subsequent work there is little evidence of any such positive view of nature. The darkness and the barrenness which characterize "La Rive gauche" remain the dominant images in his later poems and in the relatively few landscape descriptions which are interspersed in his novels.

Marthe, 1876

There is a description of the Seine in chapter 5 of *Marthe* in which black and darkness also predominate. It comes at the point where Marthe is about to commit suicide, and her state of mind is both explained by and reflected in the oppressive, destructive nature of her surroundings:

The Seine, that evening, carried water the color of lead, with occasional stripes formed by the reflection from the street lamps. To the right, on a coal-boat, moored to an iron ring the size of a hoop, shadows of men and women moved about confusedly. To the left arose the platform of the bridge, with its statue of the King. Some distance down, near a concert, a tree pinked its frail outline against the slate gray of the sky. Still further on, the Pont des Arts shaded off into the night, with its crown of gaslights, while the shadow of its pillars died in the river, forming a long black mark. A fenboat shot through the arch of the bridge, casting a puff of warm steam in Marthe's face and leaving behind it a long wake of white spray that gradually extinguished in the soot of the water.

La Seine charriait ce soir-là des eaux couleur de plomb, rayées çà et là par le reflètement des réverbères. A droit, dans un bateau de charbon, amarré à un rond de fer grand comme un cerceau, des ombres d'hommes et de femmes se mouvaient confusément; à gauche, se dressait le terre-plein du pont avec la statue du Roi. Planté au bas, près d'un concert, un arbre déchiquetait ses linéaments frêles sur le gris ardoisé du ciel. Plus loin enfin, le pont des Arts s'estompait dans la brume avec sa couronne de becs de gaz et l'ombre de ses piliers se mourait dans le fleuve en une longue tache noire. Une mouche fila sous l'arcade du pont, jetant une bouffée de vapeur tiède au visage de Marthe, laissant derrière elle un long sillage de mousse blanche qui s'éteignit peu à peu dans la suie des eaux. (II, 72–73)

Here we have a series of words to describe blackness—"couleur de plomb," "un bateau de charbon," "des ombres," "le gris ardoisé," "une longue tache noire," and, finally, "la suie des eaux," the reference to soot which we find in all of Huysmans' descriptions of water. Claire Wade, in an interesting analysis of color and light in the work of Huysmans, points out that

"Couleur de plomb" and "gris ardoisé" tie the blacks of air and water to certain heavy minerals. Such a union gives a density and an impenetrability to both and, in consequence, transforms them from the customary source of life to sources of death. The link with destruction is further amplified through the use of "la suie des eaux" and is reinforced by the verbs *se mourait* and *s'éteignait* which indicate that all signs of life completely disappear when they come in contact with the dark water.[20]

The stylistic treatment of this scene fits the pattern we have already seen in the chapter on women, whereby Huysmans creates the impression that the protagonist is looking at a painting. It is as if he has inserted a *transposition d'art* into the narrative. Here again he introduces the description with a verb of seeing: "Elle regarda" (II, 72), leads the reader around the space with adverbs such as "A droite," "à gauche," and "Plus loin" (II, 72), and ends the description with the protagonist awakening suddenly, as if from a dream: "Elle se réveilla comme d'un songe" (II, 73). The description is not based obviously on any particular painting, but it is no coincidence that in 1881 Huysmans singles out for praise Raffaëlli's *Vue de Seine,* for it depicts the same dark, depressing, slow-moving water of the Seine under a dense, oppressive sky:

> a canvas where water flows, sea-green, between two snowbanks, beneath an impervious and ghastly sky, blurred by dingy gusts of smoke. We are far from that apple-green taffeta water and those white trails of cotton wool that the official snow-painters so pleasantly arrange. The Seine is terrifying in Mr. Raffaëlli's panel; it rolls, slow and muffled, and it seems that it will never again become clear or blue between its banks, so keen is the impression of anguish left by this landscape of desolation.

> une toile où l'eau coule, glauque, entre deux rives de neige, sous un ciel imperméable et blême que brouillent des fumées fuligineuses. Nous sommes loin de cette eau en taffetas vert-pomme et de ces traînées de blanche ouate que les neigistes officiels disposent si gentiment. La Seine est terrible dans le panneau de M. Raffaëlli; elle roule, lente et sourde, et il semble que jamais plus elle ne s'éclaircira et bleuira entre ses rives, tant demeure aiguë l'impression d'angoisse que laisse ce paysage de désolation. (VI, 266)

Les Soeurs Vatard, 1879

In *Les Soeurs Vatard,* the novel which follows *Marthe,* Huysmans inserts a description of the poor suburbs to which he was so attracted in spite of his feeling that they represented the collapse of civilization. It comes at the end of chapter 2, after Céline and Désirée leave the book bindery after a hard night's work and wend their way slowly through the streets of Paris till they reach the outskirts. Huysmans' attitude towards the men and women in the bindery is one of disdain, but suddenly a note of pity creeps in when he describes the type of scene with which he was familiar through his Sunday walks and was discovering at this point in the work of Raffaëlli:

> The area became sadder as it climbed toward the town walls. This swarming street, those deserted boulevards that collided with it then fled as far as the eye could see, this population that teemed on the pavement, the women coming from wiping the sweating plaster walls, the men smoking Turkish-style pipes and lounging about, hands in pockets, the children reluctantly scrubbing themselves in the water of the gutters, all cried out the shocking poverty of the old outskirts, the endless desolation of wages eroded by drunkenness and finished off by illness!

> Le quartier s'attristait à mesure qu'il montait vers les remparts. Cette rue grouillante, ces boulevards désertés qui la prenaient en écharpe et fuyaient à perte de vue, cette population

qui fermentait sur la chaussée, les femmes sortant d'essuyer les plâtres en sueur des corridors, les hommes fumant des têtes de sultanes et se prélassant, les mains dans les poches, les enfants se frottant à l'écorche-cul dans l'eau des ruisseux, criaient la détresse lamentable des anciennes banlieues, la désolation sans fin des paies écornées par les pochardises et achevées par les maladies! (III, 27–28)

As we saw in his criticism of Raffaëlli, there is a dichotomy between his sympathy for the suffering working classes and his attempt to observe nature dispassionately, and in so doing, to find beauty in the most sordid of scenes.

Croquis parisiens, 1880

This second book of prose poems, as the title suggests, faithfully reflects Huysmans' interest in the contemporary Parisian themes which he believed were the right subject matter for fiction and painting. This includes the cabarets, prostitutes, the tramway conductor, the washerwoman, cafés, and, under the subheading "Paysages," four descriptions of the Parisian landscape. There are clear similarities between these poems, composed at the time Huysmans was writing about Raffaëlli, and the descriptions of the paintings he so loved.

In "La Bièvre" Huysmans regrets the modernization of the poor areas surrounding the Bièvre river, already described in "La Rive gauche." His decadent, aesthetic attraction to things which are sickly and ugly is here expressed even more intensely and explicitly. Starting with the opening line. "Nature is interesting only when she is sickly and woebegone" ("La nature n'est intéressante que débile et navrée") (VIII, 87), he continues to describe the river in images of disease and concludes the poem with the complaint that

the uniform whiteness of the limewash will mask the mottled ulcers of the ailing neighborhood. . . . Soon, they will end forever, the Intimists' eternal and charming stroll across the plain furrowed by the toil of the active and wretched Bièvre.

le lait de chaux va masquer de son uniforme blancheur les ulcères diaprés du quartier souffrant. . . . Bientôt sera à jamais terminée l'éternelle et charmante promenade des intimistes, au travers de la plaine que sillonne, en travaillant, l'active et misérable Bièvre. (VIII, 91)

In this poem Huysmans develops more strongly, by using the anthropomorphic vocabulary with which he always describes the river, the relationship between sickly, desperate nature and the poor people who live there.

He describes the Bièvre with "its despairing attitude and the reflective air of those who suffer" ("son attitude désespérée et son air réfléchi de ceux qui souffrent") (VIII, 87), and the dirt and blackness described already in "La Rive gauche" and in *Marthe* here reflect even more vividly the weight of the narrator's negativism

that strange river, that outlet for all filth, that sink the color of slate and molten lead, boiling here and there in greenish eddies, dotted with turbid mucosities. . . . In places, the water seems paralyzed and gnawed by leprosy; it stagnates, then stirs its flowing soot and once more takes up its slow, mired progress.

cette étrange rivière, cet exutoire de toutes les crasses, cette sentine couleur d'ardoise et de plomb fondu, bouillonnée ça et là de remous verdâtres, étoilée de crachats troubles. . . . Par endroits, l'eau semble percluse et rongée de lèpre; elle stagne, puis elle remue sa suie coulante et reprend sa marche ralentie par les bourbes. (VIII, 89)

Nature, which in the early seventies Huysmans perceived as dark, dirty, and melancholy, is now thoroughly rotten and reflects the general collapse of civilization. The increasing intensity of Huysmans' depression can be traced in the very use of the word "suie," which we have been analyzing. In "La Rive gauche" the word is part of an adjectival phrase describing "noir." In *Marthe* he talks of "la suie des eaux," so that the soot becomes more dominant than the water, and now, in the "suie coulante" of "La Bièvre," there is no direct mention of the water, as it becomes soot itself.

The image of the soot-black water, acting as a mirror of man's conscience, reappears in *En Route*, 1895, the story of Huysmans' conversion as told through Durtal. The Abbé Gévresin persuades Durtal to go to a monastery, partly by appealing to his longing for escape, humidity and warmth:

The abbey is situated in the hollow of a valley . . . Saint Bernard sought out the low and humid plains, to found there his monasteries

L'abbaye est située dans le fond d'une vallée . . . saint Bernard recherchait les plaines basses et humides pour y fonder ses cénobies (XIII, 1, 251)

and again,

There, you will walk along delightful ponds, and I recommend to you, at the edge of the cloister wall, a path between age-old walnut trees where you may take soothing strolls at daybreak.

Vous y longerez de délicieux étangs et je vous recommande, à la lisière de la clôture, une allée de noyers séculaires où vous pourrez faire d'émollientes promenades, au point du jour. (XIII, 1, 251–52)

Durtal takes the advice of L'Abbé Gévresin and it is on the edge of the "pond of the Cross" that he experiences his first crisis over confession. The pond received its name from a large crucifix in the center which is reflected in the water and it is this reflective quality which Durtal observes when he calls it "this black ice . . . this inky expanse" ("cette glace noire . . . cette étendu d'encre") (XIII, 2, 86). Durtal perceives the Christ figure as alive and sees two "white arms that extended beyond the instrument of torture and twisted in the waters' soot" ("bras blancs qui dépassaient l'instrument de supplice et se tordaient dans la suie des eaux") (XIII, 2, 87). As Joyce A. Lowrie writes,

The reflection of the white arms of Christ in the blackened waters of the pool causes Durtal to internalize the image: "Assis sur l'herbe, Durtal regardait l'obscur miroir de cette croix couchée et, songeant à son âme qui était, ainsi que cet étang, tannée, salie, par un lit de feuilles mortes, par un fumier de fautes. . . ." ["Seated on the grass, Durtal contemplated the dim mirror of this jacent cross and, considering his soul, which was, like this pond, brown, soiled, by a bed of dead leaves, by a dunghill of transgressions. . . ."] [XIII, 2, 87][21]

This image of dead leaves (memory) lying in the mirror of one's soul is reminiscent of the passage from *Hérodiade* which des Esseintes recites in front of the Moreau painting, thus connecting again similar experiences in Huysmans' spiritual journey:

> O miroir!
> Eau froide par l'ennui dans ton cadre gelée
> Que de fois, et pendant les heures, désolée
> Des songes et cherchant mes souvenirs qui sont
> Comme des feuilles sous ta glace au trou profond. . . .
>
> (VII, 297)

The symbolism of the Bièvre river and its surrounding areas was vital to Huysmans' thought at this time and he continued to work on the poem. The definitive version appeared in a Dutch review called *De Nieuwe Gids* in 1886 and was published in book form by Genonceaux in 1890.[22] Huysmans describes in more detail the changing river as it flows from its source, through the new industrial neighborhoods, till it joins the Seine in Paris. The most significant change in the six years which separate the two versions, however, is the degree of symbolism and spiritual significance attached to the river. In the first version, as in the other prose poems in *Croquis parisiens,* Huysmans' stylistic treatment of the river certainly indicated that he related the destruction of the Bièvre to the destruction of civilization and, in particular, of working women. In the final version he begins the work quite explicitly with the symbolic value of what he is about to describe: "The Bièvre represents today the most perfect symbol of female misery exploited by a large city" ("La Bièvre représente aujourd'hui le plus parfait symbole de la misère féminine exploitée par une grande ville" (XI, 9). The account of the river is in strictly female terms and it ends with another clear statement about its symbolism:

Symbol of the miserable condition of women drawn into the snare of the cities, isn't the Bièvre also the emblematic image of those abbatial races, those old families, those castes of dignitaries that fell little by little and ended, in descending steps, by confining themselves within the shameful mire of a profitable business?

Symbole de la misérable condition des femmes attirées dans le guet-apens des villes, la Bièvre n'est-elle pas aussi l'emblématique image de ces races abbatiales, de ces vieilles familles, de ces castes de dignitaires qui sont peu à peu tombées et qui ont fini, de chutes en chutes, par s'interner dans l'inavouable boue d'un fructueux commerce? (XI, 23)

Added to the collapse of the modern woman is the collapse of the aristocracy, a subject which Huysmans had used as the basis of his novel *A Rebours*, 1883, written in the time which separates the two versions of "La Bièvre."

In "Le Cabaret des peupliers," which describes a country inn in one of the poor neighborhoods surrounding Paris, we find a further episode in the demise of the Bièvre river. As in "La Bièvre," Huysmans establishes a clear symbiotic relationship between nature and its poor inhabitants, stressing their proximity to the earth:

> weak-sapped trees sit at unequal distances, showing their paralyzed arms like beggars, shaking heads that stammer in the wind, curving trunks poorly nourished by the miserliness of an incurable soil.

> des arbres aux sèves affaiblies siègent à d'inégales distances, montrant comme des mendiants leurs bras paralysés, hochant des têtes qui bégaient dans le vent, courbant des troncs chétivement nourris par la lésine d'un incurable sol. (VIII, 93–94)

This vocabulary of abuse and sterility is developed further as Huysmans, describing the Bièvre in female terms reminiscent of those describing the prostitutes in *Marthe,* follows the changing face of this pathetic river. He is quite explicit in the connection between the destruction of the river and the destruction of Paris and modern life:

> that disheartening image of life that is evoked in us by the Bièvre, so joyous and blue at Buc, sicklier, blacker as it advances, exhausted by the constant labors inflicted upon it, crippled and putrid when, after finishing its heavy work, it falls, worn out, into the sewer that sucks it in at once and will spit it out farther on, in a forgotten stretch on the Seine.

> cette désolante image de la vie, qu'évoque déjà en nous la Bièvre, si joyeuse et si bleue à Buc, plus malingre, plus noire à mesure qu'elle s'avance, épuisée par les constants labeurs qu'on lui inflige, impotente et putride alors qu'ayant terminé sa lourde tâche, elle tombe, exténuée, dans l'égout qui l'aspire d'un trait et va la recracher au loin, dans un coin perdu de Seine. (VIII, 97)

In "La Rue de Chine," in which Huysmans describes the peaceful area of Ménilmontant, he is less bitter and does not see nature as a painful reflection of man's condition. He is able to detach himself from the "éternelles privations" (VIII, 101) of the inhabitants and states with confidence that

> It is no longer, as in the plains of the Gobelins, a poverty of nature proportionate to the ruthless distress of those who live there . . . it is the spot desired by artists seeking solitude; it is the haven longed for by the aching souls who ask only for a salutary rest far from the crowd.

> Ce n'est plus comme dans la plaine des Gobelins une chétivité de nature en rapport avec l'impitoyable détresse de ceux qui la peuplent . . . c'est le coin souhaité par les artistes en quête de solitude; c'est le havre imploré par les âmes endolories qui ne demandent plus qu'un bienfaisant repos loin de la foule. (VIII, 101–2)

In "Vue des remparts du Nord-Paris" the impact of Raffaëlli's work of 1879 is particularly apparent. Looking down on the "marvellous and terrible view of the plains that lie exhausted at the city's feet" ("merveilleuse et terrible vue des plaines qui se couchent, harassées, aux pieds de la ville") (VIII, 105), the narrator takes the reader's view systematically from "A l'horizon" (VIII, 105), where the chimneys vomit black soot, to "plus bas" (VIII, 105), where white steam escapes from "slender metal smokestacks" ("minces tuyaux de fonte") (VIII, 105), to "plus loin" (VIII, 106), where "a goat grazes, tied to a stake" ("une chèvre broute attachée à un piquet"),[23] to "au loin enfin, tout au loin" (VIII, 106), where "the beggar . . . returns to his resting place, sweating, tired to death, broken down, painfully climbing the hill . . . followed by dogs" ("le mendiant . . . retourne au gîte, suant, éreinté, fourbu, gravissant péniblement la côte . . . suivi de chiens") (VIII, 107).[24]

In this poem Huysmans displays no hint of the maudlin humanitarianism ("l'humanitairerie") of which he accuses Raffaëlli. Turning the suffering of the peasants into a thing of beauty, he declares:

And it is then especially that the plaintive charm of the outskirts has its effect: it is then especially that the all-powerful beauty of nature is resplendent, for the place is in perfect harmony with the profound distress of the families that live there.

Et c'est alors surtout que le charme dolent des banlieues opère: c'est alors surtout que la beauté toute puissante de la nature resplendit, car le site est en parfait accord avec la profonde détresse des familles qui le peuplent. (VIII, 107)

Although *A Rebours,* 1884, marks the official end to Huysmans' Naturalism, its treatment of nature, as we shall see, is the logical development of the approach seen in his previous work. Huysmans makes a point of establishing explicit connections between *A Rebours* and his preceding novels and prose poems. *A Rebours* is set in the countryside to which des Esseintes has gone to escape the mediocrity, ugliness, and difficulties of life in Paris. Des Esseintes does not, however, find it beautiful and rarely ventures outside his "thébaïde raffinée," the fantastic, artificial world he creates for himself at Fontenay. The novel, as the title suggests, is an experiment in the non- or antinatural, an attempt by one man to take control over his environment and to adapt it to his changing moods. Huysmans' references to nature are a fascinating combination of the melancholy countryside admired in Raffaëlli and featured in his prose poems and a view of nature as woman, which has more to do with Huysmans' preoccupation with sex and artifice than with nature itself.

The only time des Esseintes enjoys the view from his home is one night, when the light plays on the surface and color of the earth in such a way that it is metamorphosed into a woman's face, described in the female vocabulary that was discussed in the previous chapter of this study. Introducing this description with "Par sa fenêtre," which frames the view, and using art vocabulary such as "silver-painted" ("gouachés avec de l'argent") (VII, 38), Huysmans again creates the impression that the protagonist is looking at a painting, which is, of course, appropriate for this novel above all others:

> The plain, lying partly in the shadow of the hills, appeared to have shrunk in size; and in the middle it seemed as if it were sprinkled with face-powder and smeared with cold-cream. . . . On account of its artificial, made-up appearance, Des Esseintes found this landscape not unattractive.

> Rétrécie par l'ombre tombée des collines, la plaine paraissait, à son milieu, poudrée de farine d'amidon et enduite de blanc de cold-cream. . . . En raison de son maquillage et son air factice, ce paysage ne déplaisait pas à des Esseintes. (VII, 38)

This preference for the artificial over the natural typifies the kind of decadence which des Esseintes strives for. At the same time, however, he compares the open, lush countryside around Fontenay unfavorably to the Parisian banlieue for which he has obviously maintained a weakness:

> The greenery of this part of the country had no appeal whatever for him, lacking as it did even that languid, melancholy charm possessed by the pitiful, sickly vegetation clinging pathetically to life on the suburban rubbish-heaps near the ramparts.

> La verdure de ce pays ne lui inspirait, du reste, aucun intérêt, car elle n'offrait même pas ce charme délicat et dolent que dégagent les attendrissantes et maladives végétations poussées à grand' peine, dans les gravats des banlieues, près des remparts. (VII, 38)

Many critics are disturbed by this seeming ambivalence in Huysmans which leads him, on the one hand, to strive for the beautiful and artificial, to hate the "Americanization" of Paris, the general ugliness and mediocrity of his surroundings and the people he has to deal with in everyday life and, on the other hand, to love the ugly countryside around Paris, ruined by the industrialization which he deplores and tries to escape. Michael Lemaire, for example, writes that

> it seems to me that one thereby arrives at a contradiction: how can the dandy's desire to escape the ugliness of the world lead him to praise these miserable landscapes, destroyed by man, even if one accepts that it is possible to find in them a special charm?

> il me semble qu'on arrive là à une contradiction: comment le désir du dandy de fuir la laideur du monde peut-il l'amener à faire l'éloge de ces paysages misérables, détruits par l'homme, même si l'on admet qu'il est possible d'y trouver un charme spécial?[25]

For the decadent, however, it is not the question of beauty or ugliness which is the main issue. It is a matter of health versus illness, natural versus unnatural, boring versus stimulating, fresh versus rotten. So Huysmans' taste for a countryside which has been spoiled and is sickly, changed and ruined by *man* is not so far removed from all the unnatural, artificial, perverse elements of *A Rebours*, such as the flowers created by gardeners to look artificial, the turtle which is altered and ultimately killed by des Esseintes, and the young man introduced to a life of crime and decadence as an amusement for des Esseintes.

A further incident in *A Rebours* which connects it to Huysmans' preceding works is the wonderful description of the rainy weather which inspires des Esseintes to plan a journey to England. It is a development of the soot, dirt, and river imagery used in the prose poems, in the early novels, and in the descriptions of Raffaëlli's paintings. The sky is described in vocabulary usually associated with the land, so that the whole of nature is combined in an overwhelming and depressing presence. Once again the description is introduced by a verb of observing. Des Esseintes

scrutinized the clouds from his study window. . . . Sooty river flowing across the grey plains of the sky carried along an endless succession of clouds, like so many boulders torn out of the earth. . . . The floods of ink had dried up . . . the countryside was enveloped in a water mist. . . . Daylight in the village dimmed to a ghastly twilight, while the village itself looked like a lake of mud, speckled by the quicksilver needles of rain pricking the surface of the slimy puddles. From this desolate scene all color had faded away, leaving only the roofs to glisten brightly above the supporting walls.

parcourait son cabinet de travail où il continuait à scruter les nuages. . . . Des fleuves de suie roulaient, sans discontinuer, au travers des plaines grises du ciel, des blocs de nuées pareils à des rocs déracinés d'un sol. . . . Les flots d'encre s'étaient volatilisés et taris . . . une brume d'eau enveloppa la campagne. . . . un jour livide éclaira le village maintenant transformé en un lac de boue pointillé par les aiguilles de l'eau qui piquaient de gouttes de vif-argent le liquide fangeux des flaques; dans la désolation de la nature, toutes les couleurs se fanèrent, laissant seuls les toits luire sur les tons éteints des murs. (VII, 189–90)

I have noted that in "La Rive gauche," 1874, Huysmans writes that the Bièvre evokes in him the "desolate rhythms of Schubert's music." He develops this image of Schubert in the chapter on music in *A Rebours,* but in this case it is not nature which reminds him of music but the sound of Schubert songs which recalls memories of desolate landscapes. He talks of the devastating effect that the music has on his physical and psychological health:

it was chiefly Schubert's lieder that had excited him, carried him away, then prostrated him as if he had been squandering his nervous energy, indulging in a mystical debauch. . . . This desolate music, surging up from the uttermost depths of the soul, terrified and fascinated him at the same time.

c'étaient surtout des lieders de Schubert qui l'avaient soulevé, jeté hors de lui, puis prostré de même qu'après une déperdition de fluide nerveux, après une ribote mystique d'âme. . . . Cette musique de désolation, criant du plus profond de l'être, le terrifiait en le charmant. (VII, 312–13)

The very horror and suffering appeal to des Esseintes, just as Huysmans is drawn to the melancholy and desolation of Raffaëlli's landscapes. Indeed, the discussion of Schubert songs serves as a starting point for a lengthy description of a lonely, melancholy landscape very similar to those in Huysmans' Naturalist writing. It is characteristic of *A Rebours* that the only Naturalist description of nature is a memory provoked by the arts:

> these exquisite, funereal laments called to mind a suburban scene, a shabby, silent piece of waste land, and in the distance, lines of men and women, harassed by the cares of life, shuffling away, bent double, into the twilight, while he himself, steeped in bitterness and filled with disgust, felt alone in the midst of tearful Nature, all alone, overcome by an unspeakable melancholy, by an obstinate distress, the mysterious intensity of which precluded any prospect of consolation, of pity, of repose.

> ces exquises et funèbres plaintes évoquaient pour lui un site de banlieue, un site avare, muet, où sans bruit, au loin, des files de gens, harassés par la vie, se perdaient, courbés en deux, dans le crépuscule, alors qu'abreuvé d'amertumes, gorgé de dégoût, il se sentait, dans la nature éplorée, seul, tout seul, terrassé par une indicible mélancolie, par une opiniâtre détresse, dont la mystérieuse intensité excluait toute consolation, toute pitié, tout repos. (VII, 313)

En Rade, 1887

The search for consolation, pity, and rest drives Jacques and Louise Marles in *En Rade* to visit an old aunt and uncle in the castle of Lourps near the village of Jutigny:

> a shelter, a berth, where they could cast anchor and put their heads together, during a momentary truce, before reentering Paris to take up the struggle.

> un abri, une rade, où ils pourraient jeter l'ancre et se concerter, pendant un passager armistice, avant que de rentrer à Paris pour commencer la lutter. (IX, 6)

As in *A Rebours,* the protagonist in *En Rade* fails to find peace of mind and the novel consists of his painful attempts to fight "cette lutte intime" (IX, 55). Jacques' psychological torment is expressed most obviously by the dream sequences and the descriptions of the castle itself. His wanderings through the corridors, empty spaces, and deep cellars of the castle clearly represent his psychological and metaphysical search. Nature, as it is treated in *En Rade,* is also a clear extension of Jacques' innermost feelings revealing, as Claire Wade writes, "Jacques's animosity towards and distrust of the tangible world in which he lives."[26]

There is a good example of this in the opening chapter of the book, where Huysmans describes Jacques' arrival at the castle after a particularly harrowing journey. Typically, the scene takes place at sunset, for this allows the confusion of line and color which encourages the interchange between sky and land, mind and reality, and, later, dream and reality. The scene introduces the conflict between nature—the external world—and Jacques' tormented mind, which is momentarily soothed by the outside "real" world but which, on the whole, dominates any objective view of reality and deforms it into frightening visions. It will be seen that the vocabulary used in the descriptions of the countryside suggests a painting, as do some of the descriptions in *Marthe, Les Soeurs Vatard,* and the *Croquis.* They are introduced by a verb of seeing and Jacques scans the countryside as if looking at a picture, noting the spatial structure and the colors. This stylistic device helps to emphasize the distance which Jacques basically feels from "reality."

After noting that Jacques is terrified at the thought of finding his wife even sicker at the end of the journey than she had been in Paris, Huysmans writes that

> the external *sight* of the landscape checked the internal visions for a few minutes. *His eyes rested* on the road, sought to *see,* and their attention distracted the heart's fears, which fell still.

> l'extérieur *spectacle* du paysage refoula pour quelques minutes les visions internes. *Ses yeux s'arrêtèrent* sur la route, cherchèrent à *voir* et leur attention détourna les transes du coeur qui se turent. (IX, 8) [my italics]

A description of the view continues as Jacques' eyes try to make out where his path leads:

> *On his left,* he noticed at last the path that had been pointed out to him. . . . Around him stretched successions of fields whose boundaries were blurred by the dusk that melted them into darkness. *On the hillside, in the distance,* a great building filled the sky, like an enormous barn with black, hard outlines, above which flowed silent rivers of red clouds.

> *A sa gauche,* il aperçut enfin le sentier qu'on lui avait signalé. . . . Autour de lui s'étendaient des enfilades de champs dont le crépuscule confondait les limites, en les fonçant. *Sur la côte, au loin,* une grande bâtisse emplissait le ciel, pareille à une énorme grange aux traits noirs et durs, au-dessus de laquelle coulaient des fleuves silencieux de nuées rouges. (IX, 8–9) [my italics]

This is followed by the description of the church, which he compares to "gigantic spiderwebs suspended above a furnace" ("de gigantesques toiles d'araignées pendues au-dessus d'une fournaise") (IX, 9), which immediately shifts the physical setting from the real and tangible to the unreal, so that the natural order of things is overturned and imagination and fear take over.

When Jacques turns his eyes down from the red, fiery sky, he sees once again the melancholy landscape of the poor peasant which could be one of Raffaëlli's subjects:

> He *looked* higher still; crimson waves continued to break into foam in the sky; lower down, the landscape was completely deserted, the peasants gone home, the cattle brought in; in the expanse of the plain, if one listened, one heard only, in the distance, on certain hillsides, the imperceptible barking of a dog.

> Il *regarda* plus haut; des ondes cramoisies continuaient à déferler dans le ciel; plus bas le paysage était complètement désert, les paysans tapis, les bestiaux rentrés; dans l'étendue de

la plaine, en écoutant, l'on n'entendait, au loin, sur des coteaux, que l'imperceptible aboie-
ment d'un chien. (IX, 9) [my italics]

Jacques is overcome by "that inexpressible melancholy breathed by landscapes dozing beneath the heavy rest of the evenings" ("cette indicible mélancolie qu'exhalent les paysages assoupis sous le pesant repos des soirs") (IX,
10), but Huysmans no longer talks of the charm of such a countryside but of
its mystery, which corresponds to the psychological and spiritual dimension
that his work takes on with *En Rade* and *Certains,* 1889. The pacifying effect
of the landscape anticipates the cleansing, mystical effect of prayer in his post-
conversion novels:

this vague and swimming distress that precludes reflection, cleansing the soul of its precise
fears, lulling the painful parts, relieving the certainty of suffering with its mystery, soothed
him.

cette détresse vague et noyée, excluant la réflexion, détergeant l'âme de ses transes précises,
endormant les points douloureux, lénifiant la certitude des exactes souffrances par son mystère, le soulagea. (IX, 10)

Corresponding to the castle as part of Jacques' symbolic metaphysical
search, the melancholy countryside also, at nighttime, takes on a metaphysical
perspective as it becomes infinite and frightening. It is described by a series of
words associated with depth, holes, emptiness, and darkness:

The immense landscape, without depth during the day, now plummeted like an abyss; the
bottom of the valley, vanished in the blackness, seemed to hollow into infinity, while its
edges, brought closer together by the shadow, seemed less broad; a funnel of darkness took
shape where, in the afternoon, a cirque descended from its terraces in a gentle slope.

L'immense paysage, sans profondeur pendant le jour, s'excavait maintenant comme un
abîme; le fond de la vallée disparu dans le noir semblait se creuser à l'infini, tandis que ses
bords rapprochés par l'ombre paraissaient moins larges; un entonnoir de ténèbres se dessinait
là où, l'après-midi, un cirque descendait de ses étages en pente douce. (IX, 10)

In Huysmans' post-conversion novel, *La Cathédrale,* this ambiguous landscape, in which land and sky lose their clear definition and both seem to disappear into the darkness, appears again as Durtal makes his way back from
Notre Dame de la Salette. It is an expression of Durtal's spiritual anguish and
uncertainty which he tries to sooth by studying Chartres Cathedral:

the landscape was sinister; one felt an extraordinary malaise in contemplating it, perhaps because it confused the idea of infinity that is within us. The firmament was now of only sec-
ondary importance, like a castoff of the mountains' forsaken summits, and the abyss became
everything.

Le paysage était sinistre; l'on éprouvait un extraordinaire malaise à le contempler, peut-être
parce qu'il déroutait cette idée de l'infini qui est en nous. Le firmament n'était plus qu'un

accessoire relégué, tel qu'un rebut, sur le sommet délaissé des monts et l'abîme devenait tout. (XIV, 1, 19)

Consistent with the pattern we have noted in the preceding chapter, this trance or "picture looking" is suddenly broken as the protagonist returns to reality and has to deal with his immediate problem:

> He lingered in that fog; then his thoughts, diluted in the mass of melancholy that enveloped him, touched each other and, revived by that joining, struck him straight in the heart with a sudden blow. He thought of his wife, shivered, started walking again.
>
> Il s'attardait dans cette brume; puis ses pensées, diluées dans la masse de mélancolie qui l'enveloppait, s'atteignirent et, redevenues par cohésion actives, le frappèrent en plein coeur d'un coup brusque. Il songea à sa femme, frissonna, reprit sa marche. (IX, 10)

The novel continues to develop Jacques' pitiful attempt to escape his depression, his melancholy view of nature, his nightmares, and his fears. Jacques is intelligent and self-aware and fights to relate rationally and calmly to the world around him but is constantly defeated by his subconscious. In *A Rebours* des Esseintes quite consciously alters his surroundings to fit his moods. In *En Rade* the subconscious takes over and we see the world totally transformed by Jacques' perception of it. Although he continually tries to escape his own troubled mind by analyzing his experiences, most of the descriptions in the novel reveal a depressed and tormented person.

The melancholy nature of his earlier years, when "a landscape's beauty lies chiefly in melancholy" ("la beauté d'un paysage est surtout faite de mélancolie") (VI, 14), has lost all its charm and is becoming increasingly threatening. This is especially true of the garden attached to the castle which Jacques visits the morning after his first nightmare in an attempt to clear his head. The garden, real as it may be, turns into a further extension of his troubled mind. His first perception of it is "a crazy garden, an ascent of trees, rising dementedly into the sky" ("un jardin fou, une ascension d'arbres, montant en démence, dans le ciel") (IX, 48), an expression of insanity which reflects on the observer more than the observed. The garden contains some fresh, strong, colorful plants (symbolic of hope) attempting to break through the layer of dead, neglected ones, but it is too late and the dominant images are ones of threat, aggression, entrapment, sterility, and death, reminding Jacques of his own and his wife's sicknesses, old age, and death.[27] The imagery used to describe this garden is very similar to Jacques' and des Esseintes' dream sequences.

Frightened, yet intrigued, Jacques stumbles on through this overgrown garden, painfully aware of his own neuroses and that his moods are so easily dominated by the outside world that he is "subjected totally against his will to external impressions" ("soumis contre toute volonté à des impressions externes") (IX, 55). He is ashamed of the fact that, in spite of the bright sunshine, "An inexpressible sadness once more gripped his heart" ("Une indicible tristesse lui serrait à nouveau le coeur") (IX, 54) and that he allowed this corner of nature to remind him of the "sickly and dull melancholy" ("mélancolie maladive et sourde") (IX, 55) of the castle.

In spite of the fear that the garden instills in Jacques, it attracts him more than the open countryside. One morning he observes a landscape from a high embankment, which allows the kind of wide view favored by the Impressionists. Indeed, inserted into this nightmarish novel is a long description of the way colors change according to the time of day and the prevailing winds. For instance:

> the sky drizzled imperceptible filings of very pale blue, almost lilac, like those powders that sift the heated firmaments in the morning, and whose color deepens in the afternoon.

> le ciel bruinait en une imperceptible limaille d'un bleu très pâle, presque lilas, comme ces poudres que blutent les firmaments chauffés, le matin, et dont le ton, dans l'après-midi, se fonce. (IX, 145)

The tone of the description changes suddenly as Huysmans, reflecting his own criticism of Impressionist painting, comments on the cruelty and harshness of the colors and the fact that Jacques prefers the more meaningful melancholy of the garden.

The return to the garden introduces, not nightmarish descriptions this time, but erudite accounts of the flora, which are closer to the type of intellectual descriptions found in *A Rebours*. Nature here becomes transformed in Jacques' mind into a world of metals which remind him of fifteenth-century engravings "whose heraldic aspects made him dream" ("dont les allures héraldiques le faisaient rêver") (IX, 149). Once again, nature, like a painting, puts the protagonist into a state of revery which ends with an abrupt noise that forces him back to reality:

> The creaking of the winch set into motion over the well drew him from his reflections. He noticed, through the screen of leaves, Aunt Norine in clogs furiously turning the crank.

> Le grincement du treuil mis en branle au-dessus du puits le tira de ses réflexions. Il remarqua, au travers du tamis des feuilles, la tante Norine en sabots, qui tournait furieusement la manivelle. (IX, 149)

Là-Bas, 1891

In *En Rade* the treatment of nature indicates that Jacques finds it increasingly hard to look at the external world dispassionately and find any solace in it. In *Là-Bas* nature is also a reflection of the protagonist's state of mind and the descriptions of nature parallel closely the description of the castle of Tiffauges, where Gilles de Rais carried out his gruesome, nightmarish deeds: "The countryside of Tiffauges remained in perfect harmony with the immense chateau, erect among its ruins" ("La campagne de Tiffauges . . . restait en parfait accord avec le château, debout, dans ses décombres") (XII, 1, 179). The images with which Huysmans portrays this countryside and the peasants are those whose development we have been tracing, namely melancholy, sterility, darkness, confusion, sickly vegetation, and death:

> the same melancholy, heavy sky, the same sun, which seemed older than in other parts of the world and which but feebly gilded the sorrowful, age-old forests and the mossy sandstone. There were the same endless stretches of broken, rocky soil, pitted with ponds of rusty water. . . .

> un ciel mélancolique et grave, un soleil qui paraissait plus vieux qu'autre part et qui ne dorait plus que faiblement le deuil des forêts séculaires et la mousse âgée des grès; une terre qui vagabondait, à perte de vue, en de stériles landes, trouée de mares d'eau rouillée. . . . (XII, 1, 178)

This landscape is far removed from the typical Impressionist painting with its bright colors and its sense of immediacy and change. It is, quite to the contrary, characterized by its permanency and solidity:

> One felt that this iron-grey sky, this starving soil . . . these crippled beggars, eaten by vermin, plastered with filth, even the cattle, undersized and wasted . . . had perpetuated their primordial state, preserving an identical landscape through all the centuries.

> On sentait que ce firmament couleur de fer, que ce sol famélique, . . . que ces mendiants estropiés, mangés de vermine et vernis de crasse, que ce bétail même, fruste et petit . . . se perpétuaient, absolument semblables dans un paysage identique, depuis des siècles! (XII, 106)

In chapter 11 of *Là-Bas* Durtal describes the sadistic crimes which Gilles de Rais perpetrated against children, including rape, sodomy, murder, vampirism, and necrophilia. These horrors are carried out between moments of exalted religious penitence. Indeed, chapter 11 ends with Gilles sacrilegiously biting the foot of the cross in a vain attempt to expiate his crimes. His hysterical confusion is expressed by a vivid, surreal description of the forests surrounding Tiffauges, through which Gilles gropes, distraught, after an episode of particular cruelty. The animistic description is a phallic representation of nature and is the most extreme example in Huysmans of nature as a projection of the protagonist's mind. We have seen that in *En Rade* the garden contained many elements of aggression and entrapment. Whereas most of the plants and trees are sterile or dead, however, the "deep, thick, black forests" ("forêts noires et épaisses, profondes") (XII, 2, 19) around Tiffauges are aggressively alive and fecund, perhaps more closely related to Huysmans' sexual fantasies than his usual view of nature; the imagery, therefore, has more in common with the discussions of Rops than of Raffaëlli. This type of sexual view of nature is found already in chapter 8 of *A Rebours,* in which des Esseintes orders horticulturalists to create flowers which have the voracious and sexual characteristics of humans and animals. In *A Rebours* "The horticulturists are the only true artists left" ("les horticuiteurs sont les seuls et les vrais artistes") (VII, 143); in *Là-Bas* it is the protagonist himself who alters nature: "his very presence . . . depraves it" ("sa présence même . . . la déprave") (XII, 2, 19).

At the beginning of the chapter Huysmans explains that Gilles had developed "a dislike for the feminine form" ("le mépris des formes féminines") (XII, 2, 8), so the phallic description of the forest is an expression of Gilles' fear of women combined with his nevertheless profound sexual urge:

> Here a tree appears to him as a living being, standing on its root-tressed head, its legs waving in the air and spread wide apart, subdivided into new thighs, which again open and subdivide. Here between two limbs another branch is jammed, in a stationary fornication which is reproduced in diminished scale from bough to twig to the top of the tree. There it seems the trunk is a phallus which mounts and disappears into a skirt of leaves or which, on the contrary, issues from a green clout and plunges into the glossy belly of the earth.

> Ici, l'arbre lui apparaît comme un être vivant, debout, la tête en bas, enfouie dans la chevelure de ses racines, dressant des jambes en l'air, les écartant, puis se subdivisant en de nouvelles cuisses qui s'ouvrent, à leur tour, deviennent de plus en plus petites, à mesure qu'elles s'éloignent du tronc; là, entre ces jambes, une autre branche est enfoncée, en une immobile fornication qui se répète et diminue, de rameaux en rameaux, jusqu'à la cime; là encore, le fût lui semble être un phallus qui monte et disparaît sous une jupe de feuilles, ou bien il sort au contraire d'une toison verte et plonge dans le ventre velouté du sol. (XII, 2, 19)

Just as the flower chapter in *A Rebours* ends with the syphilis nightmare, the fornicating forest in *Là-Bas* becomes diseased, an aspect of sex and women which was one of Huysmans' constant preoccupations:

> He observes exostoses and ulcers, membranous sores, tubercular chancres, atrocious caries. It is a natural lazaret, a venereal clinic of trees from which, at a turning of a pathway, rises a red beech.

> Il constate des exostoses et des ulcères, des plaies taillées à pic, des tubercules chancrelleux, des caries atroces; c'est une maladrerie de la terre, une clinique vénérienne d'arbres dans laquelle surgit au détour d'une allée, un hêtre rouge. (XII, 2, 20–21)

This last view of nature is certainly very different from the naturalistic landscape descriptions found in *Le Drageoir aux épices* of 1874. There are elements of the fantastic in *En Rade* and *Là-Bas* which show that Huysmans was becoming increasingly unable to describe the outside world objectively, as something separate from himself. All external phenomena, including nature, had, by 1891, become in his mind an extension or even a creation of his own temperament.

I have shown that this development in his fiction is not inconsistent with the views on nature seen in Huysmans' discussions of Raffaëlli, the only landscape artist who really satisfied his very personal perception of nature. For in Raffaëlli he found an expression of ugliness, solitude, and decay which coincided with his own view of man's destructive instincts and of the collapse of society.

In spite of these attitudes, Huysmans was also a staunch defender of the Impressionists, a position with which he himself never truly came to terms. He criticized them on certain technical details but genuinely believed that Impressionism was an artistic experiment which was appropriate to the times. Certainly, there was a true coincidence of subject matter between Impressionism and Huysmans' fiction of that period. There was, however, a philosophical and intellectual gap between his and their ideas, and his interest in Impressionism turned out to be merely a brief, albeit important, phase. The Impressionists wanted to paint nature dispassionately, to record the particular and the momentary; Huysmans approached everything subjectively and always looked for general, more lasting, truths. For the Impressionists nature alone was an adequate subject for study; for Huysmans the human element was essential. Color to the Impressionists was an object of scientific analysis; Huysmans always had the inclination to use color symbolically. The Impressionists were interested in crowd scenes, whereas the characters in Huysmans' fiction are all isolated, either physically or psychologically. Where nature became a retreat for the Impressionists, it increasingly added to Huysmans' depression and pushed him further along the road to the fantastic, the subconscious, and the mystical.

Between 1879 and 1881, when Huysmans was writing his articles on the Impressionist exhibitions, he was very excited about the developments in modern art. He did not have the perspective to understand that his basic outlook precluded a true appreciation of the Impressionist works, with the exception, of course, of Degas, Forain, and Raffaëlli, who are not, strictly speaking, Impressionists, but who did have enormous impact on his fiction. By 1895, however, Huysmans understood that his criticism was more than an argument with technique: it was a fundamental dissatisfaction with the emphasis on form over meaning. This led him, twelve years after the publication of *L'Art moderne,* to write to his friend Gabriel Mourey, writer and critic:

> Permit me to thank you also, my dear Mourey, for your kind citing from books that seem to me to be already over and done with, lost in the hazy distance—especially *L'Art moderne.* I do not know if it affects you as it does me, but after some years, when one sees them again, one can no longer understand why one ever wrote books that it would no longer occur to one to write.

> Que je vous remercie aussi, mon cher Mourey, des aimables citations que vous faites de volumes qui me semblent déjà abolis, dans de vagues lointains—*L'Art moderne* surtout. Je ne sais si ça vous fait le même effet qu'à moi, mais après des ans, quand on revoit cela, on finit par ne plus comprendre pourquoi on a écrit des livres qu'il ne vous viendrait plus à l'idée de faire.[28]

4

Redon and the Terrifying World
of the Subconscious

The work of Odilon Redon, which Huysmans discovered in 1881, acted as a catalyst in a process of self-discovery. He had found some temporary excitement in the bustling new mechanical world of Paris but, on the whole, he had found that the material of everyday life was ugly and uninspiring. His interest in the artificial world of the theater and the brothel provided some escape, but Huysmans' misogyny interfered with any real pleasure he could have derived from it. He had found some solace in the surrounding countryside of Paris, but his ambivalence towards the Impressionists, his love for Raffaëlli, and his treatment of nature in his imaginative works show that he always saw in nature signs of decay and collapse and a confirmation of life's ugliness and loneliness. The discovery of Redon thus came at a time when Huysmans was showing more interest in the subconscious and in this pre-conversion period Huysmans increasingly resorted to fantasy and dream as material for his work. And for the Huysmansian protagonist dream and fantasy provided a new form of attempted escape.

Redon, one of the main artists represented in des Esseintes' collection, exerted such an important influence on Huysmans' writing that most of this chapter will focus on him. Following the pattern set out in the preceding two chapters, we look at Huysmans' views expressed in his art criticism and correspondence and see how these are integrated into his fiction. First, though, we give a brief survey of the role of dream in Huysmans' work prior to the discovery of Redon, and its development afterwards.

Structurally, dreams and the descriptions of dream-provoking art play the dual role of introducing a whole new descriptive world into the otherwise naturalistic novels of Huysmans[1] and of acting as a tool whereby the reader, if not the protagonist himself, is given additional insight into the mind of the protagonist, especially in those areas which most frighten him, namely sex and physical suffering. For the protagonist himself these psychological, spiritual escapes do not always have the expected positive results, because the hallucinations and dreams which they have are always frightening or, at the least, disturbing. Even des Esseintes, who tries to control his experiences by choosing to surround himself by specific paintings of dreamlike nature, fails because the real nightmare which they partially stimulate is the central (literally coming in the middle chapter of the novel) and most frightening experience of his stay in Fontenay. So dreams and art of the fantastic do not, in the end, afford the escape from everyday life which Huysmans' characters look for.

Huysmans showed an interest in dreams and visions as artistic material as early as 1874 in *Le Drageoir aux épices*. In one of these prose poems called "Camaïeu rouge" he presents a first-person narrative by a character remembering a vision of a room dominated by reds and inhabited by "the all-powerful goddess" ("la toute-puissante déesse") (I, 14), dressed also in reds. The narrator, dazzled, closes his eyes and when he opens them again, the vision has gone. The reader is left to wonder whether this room or woman existed in reality or whether it was a vision, a product of the narrator's imagination. This early prose poem thus contains several elements of dream sequences that occur in Huysmans' later and more mature works. It is set at nightfall, in a bedroom, with a mirror, all of which are conducive to dreaming; it has a character who closes his eyes and on opening them finds himself forced to confront a part of himself which he had previously ignored or suppressed; moments in which the reader, as well as the fictional character, is in suspense about the "reality" of the experience; and finally, relief on the part of the dreamer on discovering that what has just happened to him was, in fact, merely a dream.

"Ballade chlorotique," another prose poem in this collection, is the first instance of a hallucinatory female character of a fantastic, unreal nature. Again, it is set at nightfall, and as this frightening figure approaches with her "hollow eye" and her "sickly laugh" ("oeil creux," "rire maladif") the young people "writhed beneath the wind of her kiss like grasses beneath the gust of a storm" ("se tordaient sous le vent de son baiser comme des herbes sous le souffle d'un orage") (I, 51). This female character, symbolic of death and disease, occurs frequently in Huysmans' subsequent works, most notably in the nightmare in *A Rebours*. Both "Camaïeu rouge" and "Ballade chlorotique" show Huysmans' fascination with the bizarre as a subject for literary creation. This is in the tradition of Baudelaire, the Goncourts, and Bertrand and as yet does not represent, on Huysman's part, any conscious reaction against Naturalism.

These early experiments in the artistic possibilities of amazing and fantastic visions were not developed by Huysmans in his early novels. His interest in the role of the subconscious, as seen in these prose poems, is temporarily suppressed in his fiction until the publication of *A Rebours* in 1884. So in *Les Soeurs Vatard, En Ménage,* and *A Vau-l'eau* there are no dreams or visions. The publication of these strictly Naturalistic works coincides with the beginnings of Huysmans' friendship with Zola, to whom he was introduced in 1876 by his friend Henry Céard. Some letters, however, show that he still retained a fascination for nonnaturalistic subjects and did not work on them for fear they would not be accepted for publication.[2]

Beginning with the year 1880 we find increasing evidence, especially in his art criticism, that his interest in fantasy and dreams was still strong. In the Salon review of 1880 for *La Réforme,* a periodical patronized by Zola's Médan group, Huysmans writes of his discovery of Gustave Moreau. Aware of the inconsistency of a defender of the Impressionist school expressing admiration for paintings far removed from scenes of contemporary everyday life, he is almost apologetic:

> Whether or not one enjoys these enchantments blossomed in an opium mind, one must admit that Mr. Moreau is a great artist. . . .

> Que l'on aime ou que l'on n'aime pas ces féeries écloses dans le cerveau d'opium, il faut bien avouer que M. Moreau est un grand artiste. . . . (VI, 155)

When, in the following year, 1881, Huysmans discovered Odilon Redon, another painter of the fantastic and the macabre, he found the dreamlike quality lacking in the Impressionist school. He at last found a painter who seemed to him to believe in Poe's "consoling aphorism: 'All certainty is in dreams'" ("consolant aphorisme: 'Toute certitude est dans les rêves'") (VI, 301). When one considers that in 1882 Huysmans published *A Vau-l'eau,* in which the protagonist systematically fails in all attempts to escape the dreary, everyday world, the appeal of Redon's work, which opened new vistas, becomes evident. As Huysmans writes in the appendix to *L'Art moderne,* 1882, "with him, we enjoy losing our footing and drifting in a dream world . . ." ("avec lui nous aimons à perdre pied et à voguer dans le rêve . . .") (VI, 301).

This is exactly what des Esseintes does as he contemplates the work of Redon, which he has chosen, among other paintings, to decorate his house. The use of Redon's work was just one of the elements of *A Rebours* which proved to Zola that Huysmans had dealt a final blow to Naturalism, and relations between the two authors became increasingly strained. In response to a criticism of Zola's, in which the master questioned the logic of the novel, Huysmans replied:

> It's true! that book should have been set completely in dreams and not moored to the ground even by a thread. Hence its confusions, its inevitable waverings.

> C'est vrai! il aurait fallu mettre ce bouquin-là complètement dans le rêve et ne pas attacher par un fil au sol. De là des confusions, des ballottages inévitables.[3]

Whereas Zola had tried to draw Huysmans back into a more strictly naturalistic, logical world, Huysmans was now openly espousing the more surrealistic world of dreams.

After *A Rebours* Huysmans developed further his interest in the role of dreams in literature at the same time as he was becoming more involved in the art of Redon. In November 1885 he wrote to Jules Destrée of his increasing admiration for Redon: "one has to have seen it to imagine how far the art of dreams can go" ("il faut avoir vu ça pour se figurer jusqu'où peut aller l'art du rêve"). In the same letter he describes how he and Mallarmé were stunned by Redon's most recent works: "we were left gaping in front of strange primitive beings, to which he brought new but totally nightmarish life" ("nous demeurâmes béants devant d'étranges primitifs qu'il renouvelait, en plein cauchemar").[4] Huysmans' new viewpoint, in which dreams and nightmares predominate, is seen likewise in a letter he wrote to Zola in 1885, thanking him for a copy of *Germinal* which Zola had just sent him. Huysmans singles out the least naturalistic aspect of the novel, namely the hallucinatory description of the mine itself: "the mine is gigantic and grips you like a nightmare" ("la mine est gigantesque et vous étreint comme un cauchemar").[5]

In 1886, the highpoint of Huysmans' interest in dreams, he wrote a letter to the Dutch novelist Arij Prins in which he openly admitted that there was a growing rift between himself and Zola, that there was

> an immense difference between Zola's ideas . . . and mine. He loves his age, and celebrates it—I detest it. . . . Basically, I am for the art of dreams as much as for the art of reality.
>
> une différence immense entre les idées de Zola . . . et les miennes. Lui aime son temps qu'il célèbre—moi je l'exècre. . . . Au fond, je suis pour l'art du rêve autant que pour l'art de la réalité.[6]

Huysmans' explicit admission that the realm of the mind is as valid a subject for literature and art as that of the physical world led him to add some new pieces to the 1886 edition of *Croquis parisiens:* three prose poems which are based on visions, hallucinations, and nightmares. They are "Damiens," "Cauchemar," and "Obsession."

At this time Huysmans also began work on a short story which he eventually developed into the novel *En Rade,* in which he tries to integrate the world of dream and the world of reality, the subconscious and the conscious. At the same time Huysmans began to record his own dreams in a personal notebook, known as the "carnet vert," including observations which he thought might be useful material for future books. Indeed, Huysmans used some of his nightmares about underground labyrinths to portray the castle of Lourps in which *En Rade* takes place. Two of the three actual dream sequences of *En Rade,* however, are based, not on Huysmans' own dreams, but on the work of Moreau and Redon.

After the appearance of *En Rade* in serial form in 1886, Zola wrote Huysmans a letter in which he criticized the division between reality and dream in the novel, claiming it was too abrupt and the author's purpose unclear. Huysmans replied,

I trapped myself in a preconceived idea, a division fixed before the fact—daytime, reality, nighttime, dreams . . . I would have done infinitely better had I applied this in all its rigor—alternating a chapter of reality with one of dream.

Je me suis mis dedans, en vertu d'une idée préconçue, d'une division arrêtée d'avance—le jour, la réalité, la nuit, le rêve . . . j'eusse infiniment mieux fait de l'appliquer dans toute sa rigueur—de faire alternativement, un chapitre de réalité, et un de songe.[7]

Yet in his next novel, *Là-Bas,* which he began in 1887, he disregards his own criticism. The whole "reality" of the novel is distinctly dreamlike and nightmarish with only one, albeit important, dream or hallucination. Just as des Esseinte's nightmare appears in the structural center of *A Rebours,* so the hallucination of Gilles de Rais is set in the eleventh of the twenty-two chapters of *Là-Bas.* In this dream, already discussed in the chapter on nature, Gilles has a vision of fornicating nature which reveals his own, and, vicariously, the protagonist Durtal's, fears and obsessions.

Huysmans' formulation of the doctrine of "naturalisme spiritualiste" seems to have been the direct result of his growing sense that mystery, that dreams and visions, and psychic phenomena, are all an essential dimension of the human condition and therefore of art. He had exhausted the resources of Naturalism to explain the human mind and was increasingly sure that there was an inexplicable force which governed the world. In no uncertain terms in *Là-Bas* he thus accuses the Naturalists of

wanting to limit themselves to the filth of the flesh; they deny wonder and reject the extrasensual. I don't believe they would know what you meant if you told them that artistic curiosity begins at the very point where the senses leave off!

Vouloir se confiner dans les buanderies de la chair, rejeter le suprasensible, dénier le rêve, ne pas même comprendre que la curiosité de l'art commence là où les sens cessent de servir! (XII, 6)

The inclusion of man's subconscious as subject matter for literature and painting thus led Huysmans slowly from simple visions and hallucinations, as seen in *Le Drageoir aux épices,* through *A Rebours,* where nightmares and nightmarish art are important elements in the description of the protagonist himself, through *En Rade,* where the realm of dream becomes indistinct from the realm of reality, through *Là-Bas,* where Durtal investigates the mysterious through Satanism, and finally through Catholic mysticism, where, at last, Huysmans finds release from himself.

Odilon Redon

The discovery of the artist Odilon Redon in 1881 came, as we have said, at a time when Huysmans was showing increasing interest in dreams and the fantastic. The impact of Redon's work, with its disturbing distortions of natural forms, was far-reaching. Huysmans wrote about Redon in *L'Art moderne* and in *Certains;* Redon features alongside Moreau as one of the important artists in des Esseintes' collection; and Huysmans based a major prose poem on his work. Huysmans was primarily interested in Redon's charcoal drawings and lithographs. According to his criticism and his correspondence, he was familiar with the early series executed between 1879 and 1889, namely *Dans le Rêve, A Edgar Poe, Les Origines, Hommage à Goya, La Nuit, La Tentation de Saint Antoine,* and *A Gustave Flaubert,* and with some individual works such as *Profil de lumière, Araignée, Des Esseintes,* and *Les Yeux clos.* As usual, Huysmans' selection is very subjective, for he concentrates on those of Redon's works which could be interpreted as expressions of fantastic, nocturnal, and frightening experiences. Huysmans was less interested in Redon's work after 1890 when he used color to create lyrical, iridescent paintings of people, flowers, and mythological subjects. In a letter to Jules Destrée of October 1885 Huysmans even writes that Redon was "not worth a dime as a painter" ("pas peintre pour un sou").[8]

For Huysmans, the appeal of Redon's work lies in its complex, detailed execution of imaginative, fantastic figures and landscapes. He found them disturbing and threatening in their weird juxtaposition of human, animal, and plant forms and in the distortion of their size. He liked the fact that their intent is ambiguous, open-ended, and that they do not lend themselves to easy interpretation. As Redon writes in his autobiography *A Soi-même,*

> My drawings inspire and cannot be defined. They determine nothing. They place us, as music does, in the ambiguous world of the indeterminate.
>
> Mes dessins inspirent et ne se définissent pas. Ils ne déterminent rien. Ils nous placent, ainsi que la musique, dans le monde ambigu de l'indéterminé.[9]

Huysmans is sensitive to this musical quality of Redon's work, and it is its non-naturalist, dreamlike character which appeals to him. He classifies Redon, along with Moreau, as one of the artists who go beyond the normally accepted confines of the visual arts. Comparing him to poets and musicians, he writes in *L'Art moderne* that

> we will find his progenitors only among musicians, perhaps, and certainly among poets. His is, indeed, a true transposition of one art into another.
>
> nous ne lui trouverons d'ancêtres que parmi des musiciens peut-être et certainement parmi des poètes. C'est, en effet, une véritable transposition d'un art dans un autre. (VI, 300–301)

In *A Rebours* Huysmans reiterates that

> These drawings defied classification, most of them exceeding the bounds of pictorial art and creating a new type of fantasy, born of sickness and delirium.

Ces dessins étaient en dehors de tout; ils sautaient, pour la plupart, par-dessus les bornes de la peinture, innovaient un fantastique très spécial, un fantastique de maladie et de délire. (VII, 97)

At the time that Huysmans came across Redon's first exhibition of charcoal drawings in the offices of *La Vie Moderne* in 1881, the artist was very little known. Redon maintained that Emile Hennequin was the first to write about him, for in a letter to Edmond Picard of June 15, 1894, he says,

Of the earliest journalists to call attention to my art, Emile Hennequin was the very first, at the time of the exhibition of *Le Gaulois* in 1882. He did it with amazing insight, in an article that appeared in the *Revue Artistique et Littéraire* (March 4, 1882). Many of the writers that came later did no more with respect to me than expatiate on what he had briefly suggested.

Des publicistes qui les premiers signalèrent mon art, tout d'abord fut Emile Hennequin, lors de l'exposition du *Gaulois* en 1882. Il le fit avec une merveilleuse clairvoyance, dans un article paru à la *Revue Artistique et Littéraire* (4 mars 1882). Beaucoup des écrivains qui le suivirent n'ont fait, à mon égard, que développer ce qu'il avait sommairement indiqué.[10]

It was, in fact, Huysmans who first drew the public's attention to Redon the year before when, in "Le Salon officiel de 1881," in a footnote to a discussion of the two illustrators of children's fairy tales, Crane and Doré, he wrote:

Another artist has recently come to the fore in France, as a painter of the fantastic; I speak of Mr. Odilon Redon.
    Here, nightmare is transported into art. If you blend, in macabre surroundings, somnambulistic figures vaguely related to those of Gustave Moreau, with an element of fear, you will perhaps form an idea of the bizarre talent of this singular artist.

Un autre artiste s'est récemment affirmé en France, dans la peinture du fantastique; je veux parler de M. Odilon Redon.
    Ici, c'est le cauchemar transporté dans l'art. Mêlez dans un milieu macabre, de somnambulesques figures ayant une vague parenté avec celles de Gustave Moreau, tournées à l'effroi, et peut-être vous ferez-vous une idée du bizarre talent de ce singulier artiste. (VI, 214)

In this brief footnote Huysmans comes much closer to a definition of the fantastic than in his discussion of Crane and Doré where he simply compares the degree of realism in their whimsical and magical worlds.[11] When he introduces the concept of the dreamlike, the macabre, and the frightening in the case of Redon, he is dealing with those moments of unnerving hesitation[12] when one is not sure whether one is dreaming or whether one is confronted by a supernatural event. It is this tension in Redon's work which makes it so suitable a springboard for des Esseintes' imagination and fearful revery and a perfect basis for a prose poem describing a nightmare. Huysmans' sensitivity towards these works is important in understanding his own aesthetic and creative development and is also remarkable from the art-historical point of view, as the first exhibition was, according to Redon's own son Arï, ignored by everyone else:

The drawings were hung in the offices, but there was no publicity. There was a cold and a reserve that will remain a puzzle in my memory.

Les dessins furent accrochés dans les bureaux, mais on ne fit aucune réclame. Il y eut un froid et une réserve qui resteront dans mon souvenir comme une énigme.[13]

Redon's second exhibition ran from February to March 1882 in the offices of *Le Gaulois*. Huysmans was very enthusiastic about the work and decided to contact the artist. Fully aware that his interest in non-Impressionist art could be considered strange, as he was a well-known Naturalist writer and supporter of the Impressionist school, he wrote the following tentative letter to Redon in February 1882:

You will, no doubt, be quite astonished to know that a naturalist writer is so enthusiastic about your delightfully and cruelly whimsical works.

Vous allez être sans doute fort étonné de voir qu'un écrivain naturaliste se soit passionné pour vos oeuvres si délicieusement et si cruellement fantaisistes. (ibid., p. 98)

This letter, however, led to a very close relationship between the two men, Redon becoming one of Huysmans' few close, personal friends. Huysmans did a great deal to promote the artist's work, both in Paris and among his Belgian literary acquaintances such as Jules Destrée, Edmond Picard, Octave Maus, and Emile Verhaeren. Through them Redon was invited to exhibit twice in Belgium, once in 1886 and again in 1890, in the Salon des XX, and in 1894 he exhibited in the first Salon of *La Libre Esthétique*.

Being a shy person himself and very loathe to promote his own work, Redon was, in fact, extremely grateful for the exposure which Huysmans' articles gave him:

It is a broad study on what has been produced over the last four years. He devoted two pages at the end to me, wherein I am judged in an entirely new fashion. I am very pleased, since one's reputation, public opinion, in short, what passes through the minds of others, is totally outside of us, and are things that are difficult to assess. These writings render them perceptible, especially to recluses like myself.

C'est une large étude sur ce qui a été produit durant les quatre dernières années. Il m'a consacré deux pages à la fin où je suis jugé d'une façon toute neuve. Je suis bien content: la réputation, l'opinion, en un mot, ce qui se passe dans l'esprit des autres étant totalement hors de nous, sont choses difficilement appréciables. Ces écrits les rendent sensibles, surtout aux solitaires comme moi. (ibid., p. 12)

After Redon read the description of his work in *A Rebours* he wrote: "I am especially pleased and proud of the chapter that Huysmans devotes to me" ("je suis singulièrement content et fier du chapitre que me consacre Huysmans) (ibid., p. 98).

The discussion of Redon's 1882 exhibition in *L'Art moderne* begins with a composite description of his disturbing, dreamlike drawings in which Huysmans is particularly aware of eyes which dominate the otherwise inhuman and uncommunicative apparitions. The oversized eyes work on the observer's conscience and the image remains in his mind as an unresolved force:

> There were feverish prints, unimaginable, hallucinated visions, battles of human bones, strange figures, faces like dried pears and like cones, heads with brainless skulls, receding chins, low foreheads connecting directly with the noses, then immense eyes, insane eyes, spring from human faces, deformed as if through bottle-glass, by nightmares.

> Il y avait là des planches agitées, des visions hallucinées inconcevables, des batailles d'ossements, des figures étranges, des faces en poires tapées et en cônes, des têtes avec des crânes sans cervelets, des mentons fuyants, des fronts bas, se joignant directement au nez, puis des yeux immenses, des yeux fous, jaillissant de visages humains, déformés, comme dans des verres de bouteille, par le cauchemar. (VI, 299)[14]

Next, Huysmans discusses in particular the series called *Le Rêve,* among which was "a gigantic female figure that stares, almost mesmerizes, with her great, deep-black eyes" ("une gigantesque figure de femme qui le fixe, le magnétise presque, de ses grands yeux d'un noir profond") (VI, 299). In a letter to André Mellerio of July 21, 1898, Redon himself said of this series that

> This album may be one of my favorites, because it is wrought without any literary alloy. The title, *Dans le Rêve,* being, as it were, only the key the opens it.

> Cet album est peut-être l'un de mes préférés, parce qu'il est façonné sans aucun alliage de littérature. Le titre de *Dans le Rêve* n'étant en quelque sorte qu'une clé d'ouverture.[15]

Huysmans continues the 1882 article with a description of some drawings which "went even further into the horror provoked by dreams tormented by congestion" ("partaient plus avant encore dans l'effroi des rêves tourmentés par la congestion"), among which he is struck by another eye, "a cube wherein palpitated a dejected eyelid" ("un cube où palpitait une paupière morne") (VI, 299). Another series shown at this exhibition was *A Edgar Poe,* in which the artist translates visually the "the poet's most subtle and abstruse thoughts" ("pensées les plus subtiles et les plus abstruses du poète") (VI, 300). Again Huysmans is most impressed by the one in which

> a white eye rolls in a patch of shadows, while, emerging from subterranean and glacial water, a bizarre being . . . looks at us, raising its finger, and crinkles its mouth into a mysterious and childlike smile.

> un oeil blanc roule dans un pan de ténèbres, tandis qu'émerge d'une eau souterraine et glaciale, un être bizarre . . . lequel nous regarde, en levant le doigt, et plisse sa bouche en un mystérieux et enfantin sourire. (VI, 300)

The contrast between the white (purity) and the shadows (sexuality) is repeated in a drawing of a mythical woman, whose rigidity reminds Huysmans of both medieval virgins and of Moreau's goddesses: "a white fairylike figure sprang up, like a lily, into a black sky" ("une blanche figure de fée jaillissait, comme un lys, dans un ciel noir") (VI, 300).

Huysmans added a note to this article concerning some color drawings of Redon he had seen since the *Gaulois* exhibition of 1882, mentioning especially the figure of a woman. Unlike all the previously discussed themes, which were disturbing or terrifying, this woman inspires compassion:

> an indescribable Melancholy, in colored grease paints, a woman seated, reflective, alone in space, who sobbed for me the mournful lamentations of the spleen.

> une indicible Mélancolie, aux crayons gras de couleur, une femme assise, réfléchie, seule dans l'espace, qui a sangloté pour moi les douloureux lamentos du spleen. (VI, 300)

This last phrase is the most personal one in this article on Redon and, indeed, this drawing was to play an important part in des Esseintes' artistic experience.

A Rebours, 1884

Since Huysmans interprets Redon's drawings and lithographs as expressions of hallucinatory or nightmarish experience, fantastic and imaginative in execution, they are a perfect addition to des Esseintes' art collection, consisting as it does of

> evocative works which would transport him to some unfamiliar world, point the way to new possibilities, and shake up his nervous system by means of erudite fancies, complicated nightmares, suave and sinister visions.

> quelques oeuvres suggestives le jetant dans un monde inconnu, lui dévoilant les traces de nouvelles conjectures, lui ébranlant le système nerveux par d'érudites hystéries, par des cauchemars compliqués, par des visions nonchalantes et atroces. (VII, 79–80)

Moreau fulfilled a large part of des Esseintes' need to escape temporarily into a fantastic and stimulating world far removed in time and space from his own. His taste for the macabre and his somewhat prurient interest in physical pain and suffering (probably a sublimation of his own intense fear of physical illness and suffering) is satisfied by the engravings of Jan Luyken—"this artist in lugubrious fantasy and ferocious cruelty" ("cet artiste fantasque et lugubre, véhément et farouche") (VII, 92)—and his fascination with totally perverted nature, recreated by man's tormented mind, was partly satisfied by the works of Bresdin.

Huysmans was developing his ideas on *A Rebours* while writing the articles in *L'Art moderne,* so his discovery of Redon in 1881 was a significant revelation to him. In Redon's drawings he found the "cauchemars compliqués" which were to play increasingly important roles in the fiction of his middle period. In *A Rebours* he fictionalizes and personalizes his fairly objective art criticism, as he does in the case of Moreau also, by stressing the relationship between the works of art and des Esseintes, the looker. He does this firstly by describing the placement of the works in des Esseintes' house, beginning the section on Redon with:

> he paused more often in front of the other pictures that decorated the room. These were all signed Odilon Redon. In their narrow gold-rimmed frames of unpainted pearwood, they contained the most fantastic of visions.

> des Esseintes s'arrêtait plus particulièrement devant les autres cadres qui ornaient la pièce. Ceux-là étaient signés: Odilon Redon. Ils renfermaient dans leurs baguettes de poirier brut, liséré d'or, des apparitions inconcevables (VII, 95–96)

and concluding it with:

> Besides this collection of Redon's works, covering nearly every panel in the vestibule, he had hung in his bedroom an extravagant sketch by Theotocopuli.

> En outre de cette série des ouvrages de Redon, garnissant presque tous les panneaux du vestibule, il avait pendu dans sa chambre à coucher, une ébauche désordonnée de Théocopuli [*sic*]. (VII, 98)

Secondly, Huysmans records the reaction of des Esseintes to the works so that the reader shifts back and forth from the art works to the protagonist of the novel. Further, Huysmans underlines the intimate connection between des Esseintes and the art by speculating on the morbid origins of Redon's work. As if projecting des Esseintes' own sick body and mind, he writes, "These drawings . . . created a new type of fantasy, born of sickness and delirium" ("Ces dessins . . . innovaient un fantastique très spécial, un fantastique de maladie et de délire") (VII, 97).

Unlike the descriptions of Moreau's paintings in the same novel, Huysmans does not mention any drawing or series of drawings by name,[16] but by the structure of the description, which he retained from *L'Art moderne,* the reader is given the impression that there are very many drawings in des Esseintes' room. We read, for instance, that there are:

> the most fantastic visions . . . there were other drawings which plunged even deeper into the horrific realms of bad dreams and fevered visions . . . there, studies of bleak and arid landscapes, of burnt-up plains . . . sometimes Redon's subjects actually seemed to be borrowed from the nightmares of science.

> *des* apparitions inconcevables . . . puis des fusains partaient plus encore dans l'effroi du rêve tourmenté par la congestion . . . là, *des* paysages, secs, arides . . . parfois même *les sujets* semblaient empruntés au cauchemar de la science. (VII, 96) [my italics]

The image of the eye set in outsize bodies remains an important one in *A Rebours* and provokes the first personal reaction of des Esseintes to Redon's work, reaffirming that immediate relationship between the protagonist and his art collection:

In fact, there were some of these faces, dominated by great wild eyes, and some of these bodies, magnified beyond measure or distorted as if seen through a carafe of water, that evoked in Des Esseintes' mind recollections of typhoid fever, memories which had somehow stayed with him of the feverish nights and frightful nightmares of his childhood.

Et, en effet, tels de ces visages, mangés par des yeux immenses, par des yeux fous; tels de ces corps grandis outre mesure ou déformés comme au travers d'une carafe, évoquaient dans la mémoire de des Esseintes des souvenirs de fièvre typhoïde, des souvenirs restés quand même des nuits brûlantes, des affreuses visions de son enfance. (VII, 97)

He continues this connection in the following paragraph when he writes that

Overcome by an indefinable malaise at the sight of these drawings . . . he would rub his eyes and turn to gaze at a radiant figure which, in the midst of all these frenzied pictures, stood out calm and serene: the figure of Melancholy, seated on some rocks before a disk-like sun, in a mournful and despondent attitude.

Pris d'un indéfinissable malaise, devant ces dessins . . . il se frottait les yeux et contemplait une rayonnante figure qui, du milieu de ces planches agitées, se levait sereine et calme, une figure de la Mélancolie, assise, devant le disque d'un soleil, sur des rochers, dans une pose accablée et morne. (VII, 97)

The figure of Melancholy, a mere footnote in *L'Art moderne,* but described here as if she were actually in the room rather than in a painting, at this moment becomes an important, consoling character for des Esseintes, who has no meaningful relationships with people. As if afraid to submerge himself too deeply in emotions, however, and also needing an appropriate transition to other painters, Huysmans quickly reverts from what has become a rather subjective description of art to a more objective art-critical approach, in which he concentrates on colors and materials:

He would meditate for hours in front of this work, which, with its splashes of gouache amid the heavy pencil-lines, introduced a refreshing note of liquid green and pale gold into the unbroken black of all these charcoal drawings and etchings.

Il méditait longuement devant cette oeuvre qui mettait, avec ses points de gouache, semés dans le crayon gras, une clarté de vert d'eau et d'or pâle, parmi la noirceur ininterrompue de ces fusains et de ces estampes. (VII, 97–98)

In the examples just discussed Huysmans uses his studies of Redon in *L'Art moderne* for the novel *A Rebours* with relatively minor changes. He incorporates them meaningfully into the body of the novel by describing the reaction of des Esseintes to the works and by pointing to the similarities between the tone of the works and des Esseintes' own mind and experiences.

The impact of the images in Redon's work was so great on Huysmans, however, that he incorporated them, not only in the obvious case of des Esseintes' art collection, but also in contexts quite unrelated to it. In one notable instance the same lithograph appears in two places in *A Rebours,* both as part of the collection and in another context where the connection is not obvious. I shall first discuss these two texts and later those parts of the prose poem "Cauchemar" and the novel *En Rade*, where the lithograph appears yet again in different guises. Beginning with the appendix to *L'Art moderne* one finds the description of a Redon landscape which reads:

> a deserted, arid, desolate site, like landscapes on lunar maps, in the middle of which a stalk rose, bearing something like a host, like a round flower, a cadaverous face with pensive features.

> un site désert, aride, désolé, pareil aux paysages des cartes sélénographiques, au milieu duquel une tige se dressait supportant comme une hostie, comme une fleur ronde, une face exsangue, aux traits pensifs. (VI, 299)

In the description of Redon's work in *A Rebours* one again finds

> studies of bleak and arid landscapes, of burnt-up plains, of earth heaving and erupting into fiery clouds, into livid and stagnant skies . . . a monstrous flora spread over the rocks.

> des paysages, secs, arides, des plaines calcinées, des mouvements de sol, des soulèvements volcaniques accrochant des nuées en révolte, des ciels stagnants et livides . . . une flore monstrueuse s'épanouissait sur les roches. (VII, 96)

These images appear again in chapter 8 of *A Rebours*, during which des Esseintes suffers his worst nightmare, that of "the Pox" ("La grande vérole"). It is in this chapter that Huysmans develops most explicitly the very close connections between flowers and sickness and flowers and women.[17] The first part of the chapter is the account of the exotic flowers des Esseintes orders for his house as part of his attempt to exclude all that is banal and experience everything rarified and aristocratic. They represent the ultimate in Decadence because they are real flowers bred to look like artificial ones. Some look like minerals, some can attack and devour like animals, and many, "as if ravaged by syphilis or leprosy, displayed livid patches of flesh, mottled with roseola, damasked with dartre" ("comme rongées par des syphilis et des lèpres, tendaient des chairs livides, marbrées de roséoles, damassés de dartres") (VII, 135). None of the flowers are natural or healthy looking—all remind des Esseintes of disease and death. The stultifying atmosphere of these flowers exhausts des Esseintes and he lies down to rest. He is unable to relax, however, because his mind is too active and

> engrossed in a single subject, as if wound up by a spring, his mind went on playing out its chain even in sleep, and he soon fell victim to the sombre fantasies of a nightmare.

> absorbé par un sujet unique, comme monté par un ressort, l'esprit, bien qu'endormi, continua de dévider sa chaîne, et bientôt il roula dans les sombres folies d'un cauchemar. (VII, 143)

Even asleep des Esseintes is analytic and rational, trying to understand

who the frightening characters in his dream are. He fails to place "la femme
bouledogue" whom he finds walking next to him in the woods, but he does rec-
ognize the green, sexless creature with the piercing eyes as the personification
of syphilis. After several attempts to escape this apparition, des Esseintes gives
up and closes his eyes—all within the dream. When he reopens them he sees
in front of him a landscape which clearly derives from the Redon paintings described above:

> a hideous mineral landscape now lay before him, a wan gullied landscape stretching away
> into the distance without a sign of life or movement. This desolate scene was bathed in light;
> a calm, white light, reminiscent of the glow of phosphorus dissolved in oil.

> un paysage minéral atroce fuyait au loin, *un paysage blafard, désert,* raviné, mort; une
> lumière éclairait *ce site désolé,* une lumière tranquille, blanche, rappelant *les lueurs du phos-*
> *phore* dissous dans l'huile. (VII, 147) [my italics]

In this lunar landscape he sees "an ashen-faced woman, naked but for a pair
of green silk stockings. . . . Her eyes gleaming ecstatically, she called to him
in a low voice" ("une femme très pâle, nue, les jambes moulées dans des bas
de soie verts. . . . Les yeux pâmées, elle l'appela tout bas") (VII, 147). This
must surely be a reincarnation of the passage in *L'Art moderne* in which "une
tige se dressait supportant comme une hostie, comme une fleur ronde, une face
exsangue" (VI, 299). This Redonesque image is then combined with descriptions of the phallic flowers which began the chapter; the symbolism of the ambivalent, destructive "Femme-Fleur" is complete. Des Esseintes wakes up from
this ghastly nightmare, relieved to discover that "Ah, thank God it was only a
dream" ("Ah, ce n'est, Dieu merci, qu'un rêve") (VII, 149).

Again, an attempt to escape reality—in this case by falling asleep and
dreaming—provides no relief for des Esseintes but, on the contrary, makes
him confront his latent fears with even greater intensity, so that waking up to
reality is a relief, albeit temporary. In spite of the statement of Poe, quoted by
Huysmans, that "Toute certitude est dans les rêves" (VI, 301), and Huysmans'
knowledge of contemporary dream analysis, discussed in *En Rade,* Huysmans'
fictional characters do not appear to consider dream experiences an integral part
of the self. For they can dismiss dreams and nightmares, as des Esseintes does
here, as a passing event and do not seem to reach any greater understanding of
themselves as a result of them. They regard them with fascinated detachment.

Des Esseintes himself believes he can cure the ailment which results in
these nightmares with physical remedies. He is only partially successful:

> He had tried to install a set of hydropathic appliances . . . but without success . . . he was
> reduced to brief aspersions in his bath . . . to mere cold affusions followed by an energetic
> rub-down.

> Il avait sans succès tenté d'installer des appareils hydrothéraphiques . . . il fut réduit aux
> courtes aspersions dans sa baignoire . . . aux simples affusions froides, suivies d'énergiques
> frictions. (VII, 151)

When all this fails and he is again faced with boredom and his sick health, he reverts, once more, to art—this time to some Goya prints and watercolors which allow him to escape for several hours into a fantastic and macabre universe.

It is ironic that des Esseintes submits voluntarily to the nightmarish experiences of other artists and can interpret their meaning with perception, yet when he is confronted with the first nightmare which is not a vicarious experience but a real one, he is incapable of understanding, as we readers do, that it reflects his own passions and fears regarding women, castration, disease, and death.

"Cauchemar," 1886

The section on Redon in *A Rebours* was instrumental in spreading Redon's reputation, and Huysmans' admiration for his work grew more intense at this period. The mysterious, poetic, frighteningly bleak quality of the artist's imagery corresponded to Huysmans' spiritual gropings in the years between 1884 and 1891. In February 1885 he wrote an article for *La Revue Indépendante* called "Le Nouvel Album d'Odilon Redon." It is a significant discussion of the series of lithographs called *Hommage à Goya*. Huysmans included the article, virtually unchanged, but for the title, in the second edition of *Croquis parisiens* of 1886. He named it "Cauchemar," under the subheading "Paraphrases," and if it were not for that clue and the brief explanation at the end of the prose poem that it is based on the work of Redon, it would be read as an autobiographical account of a nightmare or a fantastic experience. The fact that Huysmans included it in his collection of prose poems indicates that he considered it to be more fiction than art criticism.

The prose poem is written in a combination of third-person narrative in the *passé simple* and first-person meditation with occasional appeals to the "vous" of the spectator/reader. The images described in this album are familiar—the strange figures appearing out of the darkness, huge eyes in bodiless heads, heads disconnected from their bodies, ambiguous plant people, Biblical kings, lunar landscapes. Here, however, Huysmans steps beyond the purely visual to describe Redon's work, just as he did in some of his descriptions of Degas and Moreau, for the more Huysmans likes a work of art, the more dramatic his descriptions. In one passage, for instance, Huysmans talks of the deathly silence, the icy cold, in which "an irrepressible, intense fear nailed you, gasping, to the stone bench that extended like a dock along the stagnant water" ("une peur irrépressible, intense, vous clouait, haletant, sur la banquette de pierre qui s'étendait, ainsi qu'un quai, le long de cette eau morte") (VIII, 160). What further objective account of Redon in *L'Art moderne* is the extent of the narrator's interpretation and personal emotions which he allows to enter into the descriptions. Corresponding to the rest of the *Croquis parisiens,* the orientation is much more psychological than in earlier poems, in which the presence of the narrator is not felt.

In "Cauchemar" the immediacy of the experience is established by the "ce fut" of the opening phrase "It was first an enigmatic figure, sorrowful and noble, that loomed out of the darkness" ("ce fut d'abord une énigmatique figure, douloureuse et hautaine qui surgit des ténèbres") (VIII, 157), since the pronoun "ce," with no stated antecedent, implies the reader's prior information about the situation. This first image is immediately complemented by a personal comment on the part of the narrator which typifies Huysmans' pessimistic view of life at this time:

> desolate and pensive, watching the river of the ages flow by that river even swollen by the turgid torrents of human stupidity.

> regardant, désolé et pensif, couler le fleuve des âges, le fleuve toujours grossi par les emphatiques flots de la sottise humaine. (VIII, 157)

The ambiguous, disturbing eye is the dominant image at the beginning of this nightmare, just as it was in the previous discussion of Redon. It acts as a starting point for the narrator/poet's meditation on "the eternal sorrows that pass through and reverberate in the souls of couples ever since Genesis" ("les éternelles douleurs qui se transmettent et se répercutent dans l'âme des couples, depuis la Genèse") (VIII, 157), on man's aggressive nature, on Melancholy, and "the absolute uselessness of everything" ("l'inutilité absolue de toute chose") (VIII, 158), on truth and hypocrisy—in other words, all the metaphysical concerns which were occupying Huysmans' mind at this time and were slowly drawing him closer to Catholicism, where these questions could be answered with certainty.

The narrator's presence is established through all these meditations. It is explicitly expressed when Huysmans writes, "In any case, that mysterious visage haunted me" ("Quoi qu'il en soit, ce mystérieux visage me hantait") (VIII, 158). Each lithograph in the series is the basis for a new phase in this nightmare and Huysmans creates very natural transitions with expressions like

> a ghastly landscape *followed upon* that modern vision of olden days.

> à cette moderne vision des anciens âges, *succéda* un paysage atroce. (VIII, 158)

> The frightening flower of ignominy and suffering, that fantastic and living lotus *had wilted* and its phosphoric halo had faded. The pale attorney, the cadaverous clown, the ghastly lord *were replaced* by a no less horrible vision.

> L'effroyable fleur d'ignominie et de souffrance, le fantastique et vivant nelumbo *s'était fané* et son nimbe phosphorique s'était éteint. Au pâle avoué, à l'exsangue clown, au blême lord, *s'était substituée* une vision non moins horrible. (VIII, 160)

> And now this formation of living matter *disappeared in its turn*, the unspeakable type of this head *grew dim*, the obsession of this motionless water finally ceased.

> Et voilà que cette formation de la matière vivante *disparut à son tour*, que le type ignoble de cette tête *s'effaça*, que l'obsession de cette eau immobile cessa enfin. (VIII, 161)

Finally *there was a lull* . . . but the spectacle that had passed *continued its procession*, recalling an ancient and similar sight nearly forgotten for years. . . . Then the water, that water of terror, *dried up, and in its place rose a desolate steppe.*

Enfin une accalmie eut lieu . . . mais le spectacle parcouru *défila encore,* rappelant un ancien et analogue spectacle presque oublié depuis des ans. . . . Alors, l'eau, cette eau d'épouvante, *se tarit, et à sa place surgit un steppe désolé.* (VIII, 162)

And in the desolate planet, there *emerged from the white ground* the same stalk that had just sprung from the black water.

Et dans la planète désolée, *sortait du sol blanc* la même tige qui jaillissait tout à l'heure de l'eau noire. (VIII, 163) [my italics][18]

Earlier versions of this moonscape appeared in *L'Art moderne* and twice in *A Rebours,* and have been discussed above. In "Cauchemar" Huysmans elaborates the descriptions and, using the Béer and Maedler map as a source of information, he gives proper names to the seas, mountains, and craters of the moon. The relatively brief description, the last scene in the nightmare, serves as the basis of the whole second dream sequence in *En Rade.* The fundamental elements of the *En Rade* text are present in "Cauchemar"—the silence, the cold, the rarefied atmosphere, and even the names of the moon's craters. In *En Rade* Huysmans further develops these elements and intersperses the description with Jacques' comments and movements as he makes his way through this volcanic landscape. Relating the metallic flower which emerges out of the white earth in this last lithograph to the earlier one in which "the monstrous stalk of an impossible flower" ("la monstrueuse tige d'une impossible fleur") (VIII, 159) was growing out of black water gives additional unity to the description. When meditating on the first flower Huysmans uses vocabulary similar to that used in his discussions of good and evil and punishment in "L'Ouverture de Tannhaeuser" and in *Là-Bas:*

I asked myself from what excessive evils this pallid face could have suffered and what solemn expiation caused it to shine above the water.

Je me demandais de quels maux excessifs cette face blafarde avait pu souffrir et quelle solenelle expiation la faisait rayonner au-dessus de l'eau. (VIII, 159)

He is less clear in his interpretation of the second flower but is very moved by the more unspecific sense of misery and doom which it projects: "its more ambiguous sorrow melted into the irony of a dreadful smile" ("sa douleur plus ambiguë se fondait dans l'ironie d'un affreux sourire") (VIII, 163). This is the final image of the nightmare, for this ominous ambiguity is suddenly replaced by "l'inflexible figure de la Certitude" (VIII, 163) which brings the narrator abruptly back to reality. The prose poem ends with this explanatory statement:

Such were the visions evoked by an album dedicated to Goya's glory by Odilon Redon, the prince of mysterious dreams . . . lost, for the pleasure of a few of art's aristocrats, in the democratic environment of modern-day Paris.

Telles les visions évoquées dans un album dédié à la gloire de Goya, par Odilon Redon, le prince des mystérieux rêves . . . égaré pour le plaisir de quelques aristocrates d l'art, dans le milieu démocratique du Paris moderne. (VIII, 163)

"Damiens," 1886

"Damiens," another addition to the 1886 edition of *Croquis parisiens,* is also a nightmare account based on a work of art. The integration of the work of art is more sophisticated than in "Cauchemar." In "Damiens" the narrator records a nightmare or hallucination in which he confuses his own reflection and a painting of Damiens, the man who was tied and quartered for the attempted assassination of Louis XV in 1757. In this structurally complex prose poem there is constant interplay between the different levels of reality, beginning with a realistic description of a room, moving to the account of Damiens, and returning at the end to the narrator's meditations on suffering and sin. Huysmans also makes a more explicit statement here than anywhere previously about the relationship between the work of art and the narrator and between physical suffering and spiritual suffering. The latter concept is basic to his Catholic novels.

"Damiens" is a poem in which the narrator expresses his disgust and self-recrimination for having gone to a prostitute. It is a development of the thoughts on prostitution expressed earlier in *Marthe,* where Huysmans lends these feelings to the young prostitute herself, and in his discussions of Forain's paintings in *L'Art moderne,* where Huysmans describes the viewpoint of both the prostitutes and the men who frequent them. Although ten years separate *Marthe* from "Damiens," the details of the room bear a great deal of resemblance to those of the earlier text. These descriptions are the setting for the main part of the poem, which is based on the painting of Damiens, a totally unrelated subject but one which Huysmans uses as a metaphor for his own suffering at the hands of the prostitute.

The opening line of "Damiens," like "Cauchemar," refers to an unspecified preceding event, thereby giving the poem a sense of immediacy and also of mystery. The narrator talks of "The keenness of these painful delights" ("L'acuité de ces douloureuses délices") (VIII, 115) which put him into a state of nervous tension during which he nearly loses his sense perceptions and his grip on reality: "my ears filled with buzzings and my eyes closed . . . I nearly lost consciousness" ("mes oreilles s'emplirent de bourdonnements et mes yeux se fermèrent . . . je perdis à peu près connaissance") (VIII, 115). This leaves him very vulnerable to dreams and fantasy and his awareness of the room round him is felt "ainsi que dans un rêve" (VIII, 115). After this suggestion of a dream, it remains unclear whether we are dealing with reality or dream. The sense of mystery continues.

In the second paragraph the narrator's senses return one by one and his sight, especially, becomes very alert. He describes the room in which he finds himself alone—its red wallpaper, its net curtains, its mirror, its washbasin, its clock, and its worn couch, images which are all familiar to a reader of Huysmans' earlier work.

We find them first in the early prose poem "Camaïeu rouge." It treats the same subject as "Damiens"—the narrator waking up in a room where he has visited a prostitute. Whereas "Damiens" is concerned with the psychological impact of this experience, symbolized by the dream sequence, "Camaïeu rouge" is merely a playful symphony in red. It is fascinating to see, however, that Huysmans retains many of the details from this very early work.

Red, with its sexual connotations, is a dominant color in his early Naturalist fiction and he always draws attention to reds in his early art criticism. We thus find the first version of the "red-papered room" ("chambre tendue de papier rouge") of "Damiens" (VIII, 116) in "Camaïeu rouge," which begins: "The room was hung in rose-colored satin figured with a crimson floral pattern" ("La chambre était tendue de satin rose broché de ramages cramoisis") (I, 13). We find it again in the scene in *Marthe* where the young prostitute lies abjectly in her bed, disgusted by "her self-abdication" ("cette abdication d'elle-même") (II, 33). She looks around and sees "those walls covered in dull-red satin" ("ces murs tendus de satin, d'un rouge mat") (II, 34). In the study of Forain in "L'Exposition des Indépendants en 1880" Huysmans mentions with particular interest a watercolor of a private room in a restaurant where men would take their mistresses or a prostitute. The color of the room, once again, is red. In a watercolor of a brothel Huysmans points out that the room is "hung with rich red" ("tendue de rouge pourpre") (VI, 125). In chapter one of *A Rebours,* in which des Esseintes chooses the furniture and color scheme to suit his sensitive and artistic nature, Huysmans explains why the protagonist prefers orange to red, the favorite color of his earlier characters:

> The hearty, blustering type on the other hand, the handsome, full-blooded sort, the strapping he-men who scorn the formalities of life and rush straight for their goal, losing their heads completely, these generally delight in the vivid glare of the reds and yellows, in the percussion effect of the vermilions and chromes, which blind their eyes and intoxicate their senses.

> Les gens, au contraire, qui hussardent, les pléthoriques, les beaux sanguins, les solides mâles qui dédaignent les entrées et les épisodes et se ruent, en perdant aussitôt la tête, ceux-là se complaisent, pour la plupart, aux lueurs éclatantes des jaunes et des rouges, aux coups de cymbales des vermillons et des chromes qui les aveuglent et qui les soûlent. (VII, 23)

The other features of the room in "Damiens" are similarly found in the early texts, among others "a sofa covered with crocheted point lace, a round mirror . . . a mantelpiece without candles" ("un canapé recouvert d'une guipure au crochet, une glace ronde . . . une cheminée surmontée sans bougies") (VIII, 115–16). Whereas in "Damiens" these details are all negative, in

"Camaïeu rouge," with the exception of the mirror, the description is more positive:

> The divan, the armchairs, the chairs were covered in a fabric to match the hangings, with pink fringes, and on the mantel, surmounted by an unsilvered mirror that revealed an autumn sky all empurpled by a setting sun . . . blossomed, in a vast window box, an enormous cluster of crimson azaleas, salvias, foxglove and amaranths.

> Le divan, les fauteuils, les chaises, étaient couverts d'étoffe pareille aux tentures, avec crépines incarnates, et sur la cheminée que surmontait une glace sans tain, découvrant un ciel d'automne tout empourpré par un soleil couchant . . . s'épanouissait, dans une vaste jardinière, un énorme bouquet d'azaléas carminées, de sauges, de digitales et d'amarantes. (I, 13–14)

In the Forain watercolors Huysmans again points out the negative aspects of the room, symbolizing as they do the depressed feelings of its occupants. The one is "furnished with a tired divan, a mantel embellished by a clock that didn't work" ("meublée d'un divan fatigué, d'une cheminée embellie par une pendule ne marchant pas") (VI, 123).

The third paragraph in "Damiens" describes the mirror, an important image in this poem because it marks the onset of the narrator's psychic suffering and his introspection. As in *Alice through the Looking Glass,* it is the entry to a world of fantasy, confusion, and self-observation. Huysmans describes the mirror "Like a blinding patch of tulips surrounding a clear pool" ("Comme un plant d'aveuglantes tulipes rangées tout autour d'un bassin clair") (VIII, 116). He cannot take his eyes from the mirror, but they suffer from the sight of his own reflection: "I wanted to rip them from that border of flaming flowers and plunge them, to freshen them, into the very water of the looking glass" ("je voulus les arracher de cette margelle d'ardentes fleurs et les plonger, pour les rafraîchir, dans l'eau même de la glace") (VIII, 116). This suffering is far removed from the beautiful autumn sunset seen in the mirror in "Camaïeu rouge." In *Marthe,* however, the mirror plays the role of conscience as the young prostitute lies back and sees her reflection:

> She could not believe it was her image. . . . Her eyes frightened her; set in dark shadows, they seemed to be strangely hollowed out and she discovered, in their unexpected depth, a sort of childish and vulgar expression which made her blush beneath her makeup.

> Elle ne pouvait croire que cette image fût la sienne. . . .Ses yeux l'effrayèrent, ils lui parurent, dans leur cerne de pensil, s'être creusés bizarrement et elle découvrit, dans leur subite profondeur, je ne sais quelle expression enfantine et canaille qui la fit rougir sous son fard. (II, 34–35)

The imagery Huysmans uses in "Damiens" to describe the mirror, with its clear, cool water surrounded by flaming flowers, seems to be influenced by two totally disparate texts of his own. He developed the tulip image as early as 1875, in a prose poem called "La Tulipe," published on April 1 in the *Musée des Deux-Mondes* and never published in his collected works. The narrator addresses the tulip with words of praise:

> your splendid banners . . . your brocades of purple and gold . . . your variegated rose and maize-colored robes . . . glow red in your dalmatics, more flashing than scarlet and copper copes.

> tes splendides oriflammes . . . tes brocarts de pourpre et d'or . . . tes robes diaprées de rose et de maïs . . . rutile dans tes dalmatiques plus étincelantes que les chapes écarlates et cuivrées.[19]

The other text which appears to have been in Huysmans' mind while writing this description is the segment of Mallarmé's *Hérodiade* which des Esseintes recites in *A Rebours* while looking at the Moreau painting. The self-revelation, expressed by the nudity, is also reminiscent of the naïve expression which Marthe discovered in herself when staring at her mirror.

When the narrator in "Damiens" tries to escape this mirror image by looking upwards, he is confronted by "un affreux spectacle" (VIII, 116). In a structure similar to Mallarmé's "Le Démon de l'analogie," Huysmans first describes the vision and then begins to solve its mystery. He soon remembers having seen an old engraving of Damiens in a dealer's shop in the rue Bonaparte.[20] He describes the engraving, adding to it the details of the soldiers and judges who were not present in his vision. In a gradual process of self-awareness, the narrator first expresses sympathy with the criminal and then realizes that

> his image, which I noticed above my head, was my own, reflected by the mirror built into the tester of the bed on which I lay, face discomposed, eyes sunken, arms rigid against the sides of my body, shirt drawn up to the knees.

> son image que j'apercevais, au-dessus de ma tête, était la mienne réfléchie par le miroir encastré dans le ciel du lit sur lequel j'étais couché, la face défaite, les yeux hâves, les bras roides, collés au corps, la chemise ramenée sur les genoux. (VIII, 118)

This subjective view of a work of art, expressed explicitly here for the first time in a work of Huysmans, is, in fact, typical of his whole approach. He is attracted to a work to the extent that it reveals his own state of mind.

Huysmans breaks the mystery and tension of the frightening vision by referring to the banging of the door and the footsteps of the prostitute and the money he has left for her on the mantlepiece. He then continues with further meditations on the significance of the vision he has just suffered:

> That physical similarity that I notice between the posture of a clumsy assassin and my own is perhaps, from the spiritual point of view, even more correct. . . . Had not I, too, been pulled, shaken on a [place de la] Grève of the mind, by four different reflections; quartered, as it were: first by a thought low and lewd; then by an immediate disillusion of my desire, upon entering that room; then by my penitential regret for the money spent; finally by that expiating distress that the fraudulent crimes of the senses, once committed, leave behind them.

Cette analogie physique que je relève entre l'attitude d'un maladroit assassin et la mienne est peut-être, au point de vue spirituel, plus juste encore. . . . N'avais-je pas été, moi aussi, tiré, cahoté, sur une idéale Grève, par quatre réflexions diverses; écartelé en quelque sorte:— d'abord par une pensée de basse concupiscence;—puis par une désillusion immédiate du désir dès l'entrée dans cette chambre;—ensuite par le pénitentiel regret de l'argent versé;— enfin par cette expiatrice détresse que laissent, une fois commis, les frauduleux forfaits des sens. (VIII, 118–19)

So the poem concludes with a typically depressing Huysmansian attitude to life—disgust with material and physical pleasures, magnified by the sense of guilt which ensues and leading to total spiritual malaise.

En Rade, 1887

In the chapter on women it has been shown how the set of images developed by Huysmans when describing paintings by Moreau and Degas was used as the basis of the first dream sequence in *En Rade.* This type of connection abounds in Huysmans' work and provides insight into the mind and writing methods of this author.

The reader, probably unaware of its immediate source, is nevertheless well prepared for the onset of the dream/hallucination in *En Rade* because it occurs after Huysmans describes Jacques' depressed state of mind. We read that, like the King, he is "overwhelmed by an infinite spiritual fatigue, by a limitless dispondency" ("assommé par une fatigue spirituelle infinie, par un découragement sans bornes") (IX, 27), that "an indefinable sensation of malaise obsessed him" ("une indéfinissable sensation de malaise l'obséda") (IX, 28), so that when "a bizarre phenomenon took place" ("un phénomène bizarre se produisit") (IX, 29) we are not surprised by this hallucinatory experience. The word "dream" is not actually used till page fifty-seven, when Jacques begins to ponder its meaning. Previously it appeared as a hallucination and contained that ambiguity which Todorov considers one of the crucial elements of the fantastic.

So when Jacques launches on lengthy hypotheses about the possible source of this first dream, he realizes that it based on the biblical story of Esther but fails to see why this should suddenly enter his sleeping mind after many years. He is quite explicit in ruling out the influence of paintings in this scene, although we know that Huysmans himself has drawn from the works of the two artists Degas and Moreau: "he had seen no engraving, no painting whose subject could have led him to think of it" ("il n'avait vu aucune gravure, aucun tableau dont le sujet pût l'induire à y penser") (IX, 59). After three pages of different dream theories, which are evidence that Huysmans was truly fascinated by and well informed on current thought on the subject, he dismisses them all as inadequate in explaining Jacques' particular experience. He ends the discussion on a typical note of scepticism about contemporary thought: "whatever opinions they profess, scholars talk nonsense" ("quelle que soit l'opinion qu'ils professent, les savants ânonnent") (IX, 62). Having rejected all naturalistic or scientific explanations of dreams, especially when the relationship between the dream and its significance seems to be so obscure, Jacques finally ascribes to them a supernatural cause:

> Would he finally have to admit supernatural cause, believe in the designs of a Providence that incites the incoherent swirlings of dreams, and thereby accept the inevitable visits of incubi and succubi, all the remote hypotheses of the demonists?
>
> Fallait-il enfin admettre des causes surnaturelles, croire aux desseins d'une Providence incitant les incohérents tourbillons des songes, et accepter du même coup les inévitables visites des incubes et des succubes, toutes les lointaines hypothèses des démonistes? (IX, 76)

This question is not answered in any definitive fashion in *En Rade,* but in writing *Là-Bas* Huysmans seems to have opted for the demonic and magical explanation of dreams. Having thus accepted the existence of another world, of spirits who try to contact man in strange ways, Huysmans is no longer interested in the phenomenon of dreams as a way of exploring the nonrational world. His attempt to add a non-Naturalistic dimension to man by describing and analyzing dreams ends with *En Rade.* His interests are channeled into demons and finally, with *La Cathédrale,* into symbolism as an explanation of man's existence.

Jacques' preoccupation with the possible explanation of dreams has the beneficial effect of distracting his mind from the dream itself, but Jacques fails to gain any deeper insight into his own neuroses. The fact that the dream is not about himself makes it harder for Jacques to understand any possible connection between himself and the suppressed eroticism of the frustrated King,

> lost in a dream, absorbed by an argument within his soul, weary, perhaps, of the uselessness of omnipotence and the inaccessible aspirations that it breeds. . . .
>
> perdu dans un rêve, absorbé par un litige d'âme, las peut-être de l'inutilité de la toute-puissance et des inaccessibles aspirations qu'elle fait naître. . . . (IX, 32)

For the second dream also there are indications in the preceding chapter that Jacques is in a hallucinatory state of mind, for his perception of his surroundings is confused. He has gone for a walk with his wife and is overcome by worry and fear, about both her health and his inability to cope with the responsibilities of married life. His neurosis is expressed by a terror of "the countryside's enormous silence" ("le silence énorme de la campagne") (IX, 95) and a deformation of nature in which stone and water, earth and sky are confused. The church, for instance, seems to be filled with "a shadowy and turbid water" ("une eau ténébreuse et trouble") (IX, 94) and "felt that weakening of the entire body" ("dans le ciel dur, sourdaient les froides eaux des arbres") (IX, 95). The sense of distance and void and silence overwhelms Jacques; he "felt that weakening of the entire body" ("se sentait cette défaillance de tout le corps")

(IX, 96). Yet the introduction of the dream is less explicit than the first and, contrary to the opinion of most critics, Huysmans attempts rather unsuccessfully to integrate reality and fantasy, Jacques' daytime world and his dreams. The first dream about Esther occurs well into the chapter, is introduced by the statement "un phénomène bizarre se produisit" (IX, 29), and is not about Jacques. In the second dream Jacques himself, accompanied by his wife Louise, journeys to the moon. There is no clear beginning to the dream, for the opening sentence of chapter 5 marks its beginning: "It went beyond all bounds, in an indefinite flight of the eye, an immense desert of dry plaster . . ." ("C'était au-delà de toutes limites, dans une fuite indéfinie de l'oeil, un immense desert de plâtre sec . . .") (IX, 99).

This "c'était" which opens the dream gives it the same immediacy as the "ce fut" of "Cauchemar," and there is no stylistic indication that it is anything but a continuation of the surrealistic description of the sky at the end of the preceding chapter. The reader only learns in the middle of the second page that Jacques and his wife are on the moon. Huysmans makes a natural transition between the conclusion of chapter 4, which describes the moon, and the opening of chapter 5, which, as we learn, also describes the moon. The characterization of these two moonscapes, however, is radically different. The "real" moon in the sky at the end of chapter 4 is more closely related to the castle dungeons, for it is

> like a gaping well that descends to the depths of the abysses and raises to the level of its silver coping buckets of pale fires.
>
> pareille à un puits béant descendant jusqu'au fond des abîmes, et ramenant au niveau de ses margelles d'argent des seaux de feux pâles. (IX, 97)[21]

In marked contrast to this deep, dark, and narrow well surrounded by light, the moon described in the dream is open, vast, white, and hard. Whereas Jacques and Louise are haunted by noises in the castle, on the moon there is an all-pervasive silence, like the "silence énorme" which terrified Jacques immediately before the dream, and the sterile landscape is described in a series of negatives:

> No exhalation . . . no charnel-house, the void, nothing, the nonexistence of fragrance and the nonexistence of noise, the suppression of smell and of hearing.
>
> Nulle exhalaison . . . aucun charnier, le vide, rien, le néant de l'arôme et le néant du bruit, la suppression des sens de l'odorat et de l'ouïe. (IX, 104-5)

This second dream, clearly drawn from the Redon lithographs discussed earlier, is an antidote to the first one, which abounds in sexual imagery like the Moreau paintings which influenced its account. The second dream is dominated by an imagery of whiteness, petrification, and sterility (the dream landscape is covered in cristal, salt, plaster, ice, frost, diamonds, sand, whitewash, snow, calcium, etc.), modified by a vocabulary of illness and destruction. This contradictory landscape seems to reflect Jacques' ambivalent desire for purity, both sexual and spiritual, and his awareness that purity will always be tarnished. So we find that the landscape which is dotted with mountains of plaster and salt is also "inflated with tubercles, swollen with cysts, scorified like slag" ("gonflé de tubercules, boursouflé par des kystes, scorifié tel que du mâchefer") (IX, 102), and of the "marsh crystallized like a lake of salt" ("marais cristallisé tel qu'un lac de sel") we read that "incurable sores raised pink vesicles on this flesh of pale ore" ("d'inguérissables plaies soulevaient de roses vésicules sur cette chair de minerai pâle") (IX, 105). This dry, arid, largely pure landscape appears again in Huysmans' novel of conversion, *En Route,* as Durtal contemplates his own soul:

> On a day of an eclipse, in a rarified air, he perceived in his innermost depths the panorama of his soul, a deserted twilight, its horizons brought nearer by a kind of night; and it was, beneath an ambiguous light, something like a levelled moor, like a swamp filled in with rubble and ashes.

> Dans un jour d'éclipse, dans un air raréfié, il apercevait au fond de soi le panorama de son âme, un crépuscule désert, aux horizons rapprochés de nuit; et c'était, sous une lumière louche, quelque chose comme une lande rasée, comme un marécage comblé de gravats et de cendres. (XIII, 361)

These images thus make an interesting transition in the work of Huysmans from an art critical essay on Redon to a prose poem, to a description of a dream, and finally to a description of his own mind, represented by Durtal in the autobiographical novel.

Jacques' hallucinatory vision of the moon provides some temporary escape from the physical and mental abuse of his daily life. He attains the sensation "that he was finally rid of the outer shell of the body" ("qu'il était enfin débarrassé de l'écorce d'un corps") (IX, 110), but is brought rudely back to reality by a banal comment of Louise. Whereas in the dream he turns to his wife for comfort, this comment makes him realize again that he cannot tolerate her presence. He is "himself surprised by the stupidity of his wife, who until then had seemed to him less abundant and less firm" ("surpris lui-même de la sottise de sa femme qui lui était jusqu'alors apparue moins abondante et moins ferme") (IX, 111). Jacques' distaste for women and his fear of the ills of his own body and mind, here forgotten temporarily, foreshadow Durtal's mystical experience of release from the self through the liturgy in *La Cathédrale* and *L'Oblat.*

A few days after this dream, again contemplating the possibilities "of forgetting his existence, of growing a new soul and a new skin" ("d'oublier son existence, de faire âme nouvelle et peau neuve") (IX, 139), he thinks about his imaginary journey to the moon. He is pleased with himself because he believes he understands the source of his dream and, unlike the first time, gives no further thought to any theoretical interpretation of his experience:

this time, he told himself, the source of my dream is clear, its filiation easier to follow than the one about Esther, for the evening before I left for the old luminary, I looked at the stars and the Moon and I remember that at that moment I distinctly recalled the details of the maps of the moon that I own.

cette fois, se dit-il, la source de mon rêve est claire, la filiation plus facile à suivre que celle d'Esther, car la soirée qui précéda mon départ pour le vieil astre, j'ai regardé les étoiles et la Lune et je me souviens qu'à ce moment je me rappelais nettement les détails des cartes sélénographiques que je possède. (IX, 139)

This supremely naturalist explanation lends no credence to any psychological interpretation of dreams. It is left to the readers of each generation to understand the further significance of the dream and to enjoy the relationship between Huysmans' dream fantasies and art.

The third dream describes Jacques' mad climb to the top of a bell tower, his fear of falling into the void beneath it, his descent from the tower, and his discovery of a witches' Sabbath. The dream contains an abundance of sexual imagery expressing an obvious fear of impotence and is an early version of the novel *Là-Bas,* in which Huysmans contrasts the forces of good and evil. It does not seem to be inspired by any painting.

"Le Monstre," 1889

Huysmans' last text on Redon, part of a historical survey of the monster in art, appeared in 1889, in *Certains.* It contains some wonderful and sensitive descriptions of a new album of Redon lithographs based on Flaubert's *Tentation de Saint Antoine,* a second album dedicated to Flaubert and an earlier album called *Les Origines* The focus of Huysmans' interest has changed. He is less interested in the dreamlike quality of the finished work but is fascinated by the process which produced it. Redon questioned the very basis of the article and it became the cause of tension between the two friends. He objected to Huysmans' claim that he produced monsters aimed at scaring the viewer, and that they were based on plant and animal life seen through a microscope.

Huysmans talks of the traditional form of the monster as an incoherent juxtaposition of animal and human forms with a view to "symbolizing evil divinities and crime" and "arousing horror" ("symboliser les divinités mauvaises et le crime", "susciter l'horreur") (X, 123). He traces such monsters from antiquity to the Middle Ages, where, he believes, "the beauty of terror" ("la beauté de l'épouvante") (X, 132) came to an end. He briefly discusses Callot, who "suggests neither anxiety nor laughter" ("ne suggère ni l'émoi, ni le rire") (X, 132), then Goya, who "attained, in the end, simply the macabre" ("aboutit simplement au macabre") (X, 132–33),[22] and finally certain Japanese such as Hokousai, who "are decorative" ("sont d'allure décorative") (X, 133). He completes the survey with Redon, whom he considers the only contemporary artist to treat the subject, managing to "wed the horror of man's face to the convoluted hideousness of caterpillars, to create a new monster" ("marier l'horreur du visage de l'homme aux hideurs enroulées des chenilles, pour créer à nouveau le monstre") (X, 136). He regrets, however, that the monster, as conceived by Redon, has lost its religious symbolism, which was one of the main elements in medieval art and one of increasing importance to Huysmans.

He confirms here that the idea of monsters "is perhaps born in man from visions generated by nights of evil dreams" ("est peut-être née chez l'homme des visions enfantées par des nuits de cauchemar") (X, 134), which is how Huysmans has interpreted Redon in the previous articles and, implicitly, in his fiction where he bases nightmare sequences on works of Redon. Redon also objected to this view of his work. In May 1904 Emile Bernard wrote an article in *L'Occident* on Redon and in the margin of his own copy, next to "Here is a work of nightmare and splendor" ("Voici une oeuvre de cauchemar et de splendeur"), Redon wrote, "I don't think this a work of nightmare" ("Je ne crois pas que ce soit oeuvre de cauchemar").[23]

Huysmans elaborates here for the first time the idea that Redon used microscopically small animals as models for his monsters. He had made this point briefly in *L'Art moderne,* where we read that "they were vibrios and volvoces, the animalcules of vinegar that crawled in soot-tinged glucose" ("c'étaient des vibrions et des volvoces, les animalcules du vinaigre qui grouillaient dans de la glucose teintée de suie") (X, 299), and again in passing in *A Rebours,* where he explains that "sometimes Redon's subjects actually seemed to be borrowed from the nightmares of science" ("parfois même les sujets semblaient empruntés au cauchemar de la science") (VII, 96). In "Le Monstre" he claims that Redon's genius lies in having discovered "the world of animalcules, infusoria, and larvae, whose supreme horror the microscope reveals" ("le monde des animalcules, des infusoires et des larves, dont le microscope nous révèle la souveraine horreur") (X, 134). Unlike the descriptions in "Cauchemar" which are subjective and poetic, reflecting the psychological mood of Huysmans as much as the art of Redon, the descriptions in this last article attempt to be very objective and are dominated by the scientific vocabulary of microscopic life, on which Huysmans believed Redon based his work. He uses words of movements and fluidity to describe the "monde onduleux et fluent" (X, 135), which contrasts strongly to the image of rigidity which Huysmans describes in *L'Art moderne* and which caused him to compare Redon to Moreau.

In spite of these secular, scientific images, and the lack of religious symbolism, Huysmans attempts to link Redon to the mystical artists of the Middle Ages, to whom he himself was beginning to turn:

> Despite its entirely modern structure, this figure harks back across the centuries, by virtue of the profound, unique expression of its features, to the doleful works of the Middle Ages.
>
> En dépit de sa structure toute moderne, cette figure ramène à travers les siècles, par l'expression profonde, unique des traits, aux oeuvres dolentes du Moyen Age. (X, 138)

Huysmans felt confident in his suggestion that Redon's work was influenced by the plant and animal life revealed by the microscope because he knew that Redon was a close friend of the botanist Armand Clavaud, but Redon denied strongly any such straightforward explanations of his art. He felt that Huysmans' article misunderstood the essentially imaginative quality of his work. Gauguin also felt Huysmans was taking a simplistic, pedestrian view of Redon's work and in one of his notebooks wrote, "I don't see in what way Redon makes monsters. They are imaginary beings. He is a dreamer, a man of the imagination" ("Je ne vois pas en quoi Redon fait des monstres. Ce sont des êtres imaginaires. C'est un rêveur, un imaginatif").[24]

Redon discusses this issue at some length in his journal *A Soi-même*. He refutes Huysmans' theory, saying that

> I think that I obeyed the suggestions of instinct in creating certain monsters. They do not depend, as Huysmans insinuated, on the aid of a microscope that explores the frightening world of the infinitely small.
>
> Je crois avoir obéi à ces indications de l'instinct dans la création de certains monstres. Ils ne relèvent pas comme l'a insinué Huysmans des secours du microscope devant le monde effrayant de l'infiniment petit. (p. 28)

Yet his description of his own artistic aims and methods is not so different from Huysmans' demands for imaginative, fantastical, and, later, "mystical" subject matter combined with extremely rational, realistic execution:

> My most productive method . . . has been to . . . copy reality directly, carefully reproducing objects of external nature, in its tiniest, its most particular, its most accidental detail. After making the effort to copy scrupulously . . . I feel a mental surge come on.
>
> Mon régime le plus fécond . . . a été . . . de copier directement le réel en reproduisant attentivement des objets de la nature extérieure, en ce qu'elle a de plus menu, de plus particulier, de plus accidental. Après un effort pour copier minutieusement . . . je sens une ébullition mentale venir. (ibid.)

Redon claims that his aim was to

> make unlikely beings seem human, according to the laws of verisimilitude, applying . . . the logic of the visible to the invisible.
>
> faire vivre humainement des êtres invraisemblables, selon les lois du vraisemblable, en mettant . . . la logique du visible au service de l'invisible. (ibid.)

Redon's definition of Mysticism even seems to coincide with that of Huysmans at this time, for he writes:

> In the broad sense in which we wish to place ourselves, it appears that Mysticism is nothing other than the feeling of the Beyond, of the incomprehensibility of the infinite.

Au sens large où nous voulons nous placer, il semble que le Mysticisme ne soit pas autre chose que le sentiment de l'Au-delà, de l'incompréhensible de l'infini.[25]

Yet when it became clear to Redon that Huysmans' flirtations with mysticism and spiritualism were drawing him closer to Catholicism and blinding him to earthly and artistic concerns, he could no longer respect Huysmans' views and the friendship came to an end. In May 1904 Emile Bernard wrote an article on Redon in *L'Occident,* and in the margin of that article Redon wrote that

Huysmans only partially understood me. I believe I helped his evolution, but I kept my feet on the ground. And my works are *real,* whatever they say. . . . And three cheers for a good game of tennis.

Huysmans ne me comprit qu'incomplètement. Je crois avoir aidé à son évolution, mais je suis resté sur le sol. Et mes ouvrages sont *vrais* quoiqu'on en dise. . . . Et vive une bonne partie de tennis.

Next to the part of the same article which reads "le surnaturel est sa nature," Redon wrote "the supernatural is not my nature; I like external nature too much" ("le surnaturel n'est pas ma nature; j'aime trop la nature externe").[26]

After his conversion Huysmans, in his turn, denied having entertained any serious interest in Redon:

I did not fall into that snare; but it was so amusing to talk about a man who distorts as though he had in his eye a glass ball filled with water! Oh, Goya's monsters are far more lively and impressive than those manufactured by that lithographer! To be sure, I do not deny his virtuosity in his trade as an engraver; his pastels, too, have some brilliance; but all that is, after all, unbalanced and cracked! Yes, it really is nature seen, as I said to you earlier, through an aquarium!

Je ne suis pas tombé dans ce panneau-là; mais c'était si amusant de parler d'un homme qui déforme comme s'il avait une boule de verre pleine d'eau dans l'oeil! Ah! les monstres de Goya sont autrement vivants et impressionnants que ceux qu'a fabriqués ce lithographe! Je ne nie pas, certes, sa virtuosité dans son métier de graveur; ses pastels aussi ont quelque éclat; mais tout cela, en résumé, est déséquilibré et absurdement loufoque! Oui, c'est bien la nature vue, comme je vous le disais tout à l'heure, à travers un aquarium![27]

Given the quality of the articles Huysmans dedicated to Redon, the place he gave him in *A Rebours,* the way in which he incorporated the painter's images into his own fiction, and the manner in which he helped Redon personally, it is impossible to take this statement as a serious comment on Redon. Huysmans did easily forget his enthusiasm for certain styles and artists after he moved on to new ones. This we have already noted in his own avowed amazement, expressed in the letter to Gabriel Mourey in 1895, that he could ever have loved the Impressionists.

On the other hand, it is true that dreams, like women and nature, had failed to provide a true escape for Huysmans or add further insight into his existence.

The inclusion of dreams in his fiction was the result of Huysmans' conviction that there was more to life and art than the physical world. He wanted to blend the inner and outer worlds by substituting the "vision of a reality for the reality itself" ("rêve de la réalité à la réalité même") (VII, 35) and to counteract Naturalism, which had grounded itself in filth and flesh, denied the extrasensual and had not understood that interesting art begins where the senses leave off.

Through his studies of Redon's work and the transposition of its images into his own fiction, Huysmans had been successful in adding a rich new dimension to his work, whereby the reader has greater insight into the mind of the protagonist. The protagonist himself, however, except in "Damiens," fails to learn from the experience. The dreams are an expression of his suffering and are, therefore, intolerable to him. Only the art of dreams is palatable and, indeed, provides temporary relief from life's banality which all of Huysmans' characters are trying to escape. It is ultimately in religious faith that Huysmans finds his peace and equilibrium.

Conclusion

Since ancient times critics have tried to establish relationships of subject matter, style, and function among the arts. James Merriman, in an article on the interrelationship between painting and literature, points to some of the difficulties of such studies:

> The investigation of paintings or other non-literary art works as direct or diffused sources of literature does not differ theoretically or in intellectual result from the more usual kinds of *Quellenforschung*. Of course such study poses its own delicate problems in verification, dissemination mechanisms, and the history of taste, since influence tends to take place in very subtle ways and only rarely by means of a writer's having been verifiably led to an innovation in his own work by looking at some specific painting, for example.[1]

In this study on J.-K. Huysmans, I hope to have thrown another light on the problem concerning the relationship between painting and literature, in a "verifiable" way. For his lifelong preoccupation with the visual arts, both as an educated art lover and as an art critic, was an influential element throughout his development as a writer. In the case of Huysmans we have an author who not only saw paintings but wrote about them at great length—about their subject matter, their style, and their impact on him. I have not, as some other critics such as Cressot and Trudgian, tried to find literary texts whose style "parallels" paintings which he wrote about in his criticism. Nor have Huysmans' gifts or failings as an art critic been of major concern to me, so I have not evaluated his analyses of the actual paintings he saw or compared them to contemporary criticism. My specific purpose has been more modest but at the same time I believe that the study has led to a greater understanding of Huysmans. I have shown that Huysmans turned to art as a source of inspiration on many levels and that his creative works benefit greatly from frequent passages which evoke paintings. I strongly refute a derogative statement by one of the most highly reputed Huysmans scholars that "It [Huysmans' style] is afflicted, however, with the literary disease . . . *la peinturite*—the tendency to evoke the memory of paintings in descriptive passages."[2] Far from seeing such pictorial descriptions in this negative light, I have illustrated their beauty, originality, and creative importance in the writing of Huysmans.

I have shown, by textual comparisons between his discussions of art in his criticism and passages in his fiction and prose poems, that Huysmans frequently used art as a filter through which to experience reality. This is certainly not an isolated phenomenon in French or other literature, but in Huysmans it happens to an unusual degree. This is due to the fact that his particularly passive, neurotic existence cut him off from the "reality" that was the material of art for at least most of the writers of that Naturalist period and led him constantly closer to the visual arts as a source of experience and truth and as a confirmation of his own feelings.

Sometimes a description of a painting is explicit and Huysmans shows imaginative pleasure in experimenting with the various methods of inserting such descriptions into the narrative. Often a description of a painting is implicit and has required more "detective work" on my part to point out its sources in Huysmans' art criticism. Again, Huysmans demonstrates great skill in manipulating stylistic devices to indicate to the reader that he is being invited to view "reality" through the frame of a picture.

The close interrelationship between Huysmans' art criticism and his creative writing stems from the undisputed fact that both are subjective to a more than ordinary degree. Although he had a sensitive and often penetrating understanding of the painter's craft, he did not try to base his critical assessments mainly on objective standards derived from a general theory of art. He truly cared for relatively few works and only those which, at a given time, were in harmony with his state of mind and seemed to hold an answer to his personal, psychological, and aesthetic questions. It is generally agreed that his novels, and some prose poems, are autobiographical insofar as the leading protagonists share many of his thoughts, feelings, and aesthetic tastes.

In my analyses of Huysmans' works one aspect of his writing which I hope to have elucidated is the metaphorical role of descriptions of paintings. I have shown that, just as des Esseintes lived a brief, vicarious episode with Salome in *A Rebours,* there is an unusually strong personal involvement in all of Huysmans' descriptions of paintings. Through art Huysmans sublimates his feelings and thoughts and by describing paintings and architecture, he expresses ideas on life in general.

This phenomenon is first noted in some of Huysmans' early prose poems in the collection *Le Drageoir aux épices,* in which he imaginatively incorporates descriptions of Dutch and Flemish works. A reading of these poems reveals that the treatment of paintings goes beyond the Parnassian tradition of *transpositions d'art* exemplified in Bertrand and Gautier. For Huysmans involves the reader in his own awareness that the paintings he is describing have acted as an escape and have contributed to his confusion between the world of art and the "real" world. As a result of this consciousness Huysmans lost interest in the Dutch and Flemish art and turned to some contemporary artists as a source of inspiration.

This Naturalist period was the time of his most productive art criticism and the time when one can most clearly see the interplay between his views expressed in his articles and those expressed in his creative writing. It is also the moment of greatest confusion for Huysmans because, on the one hand, his official position was one of support for those independent artists who were portraying the contemporary reality of modern-day Paris. On the other hand, Huysmans was growing increasingly despondent and was trying to find a way to escape his immediate environment. It is this ambiguity in Huysmans which explains the way in which he sought in his favorite artists a very subjective viewpoint which corresponded to his own attitude to life.

In Degas, Forain, Rops, and Moreau he thus heralded four great misogynists. In Raffaëlli he only looked at the melancholy aspects of his landscapes, and although his reputation as a great art critic is based to a large extent on his defense of the Impressionists, we have seen that, in fact, Huysmans was critical of many of their fundamental qualities.

The adverbial titles of so many of Huysmans' novels—*A Vau-l'eau, A Rebours, En Rade, Là-Bas, En Route*—are indicative of an effort to move away from the here-and-now and find a meaningful existence elsewhere. In their search for some impossible goal, Huysmans' protagonists such as Léo, André Jayant, des Esseintes, Jaques Marles, and Durtal arrive at moments of happiness, but these are usually illusory and never last. I hope to have shown how art plays an important role in many of the fantasies of these characters and that numerous ideals and views are based on their experience of paintings. As Huysmans proceeds from his Naturalist period to his Decadent stage, in which art is no longer a simple representation of reality but an independent act of creation, he turns to Redon, through whom he can escape into the world of the subconscious. Huysmans' reality becomes increasingly introspective and spiritual to the exclusion of the outside world. So, in *La Cathédrale,* for instance, Huysmans' whole purpose is to decipher the building and its sculpture in order to explicate the mystery of Catholicism. Huysmans' theory of "naturalisme spiritualiste," which the Grünewald *Crucifixion* helped him formulate, concludes a tortuous aesthetic development. He finds an answer in a resolution between his unaltered respect for the documentary approach of the Naturalists and the need to express a meaning beyond and totally apart from the physical world.

From the very outset to the end of his career painters had thus helped Huysmans clarify his views on many topics, both personal and aesthetic. On occasion art misled him but, on balance, it helped to put order and meaning into a world which he largely perceived as chaotic, mediocre, and frightening.

Notes

Introduction

1. "L'Oeuvre et la vie d'Eugène Delacroix," in *Oeuvres complètes de Charles Baudelaire,* ed. Y.-G. Le Dantec (Paris: Gallimard, 1961), pp. 1116–17. All translations are my own except those drawn from Robert Baldick's *Against Nature* (Harmondsworth: Penguin Books, 1959) and Anthony Hartley's *Mallarmé* (Harmondsworth: Penguin Books, 1965).

2. Quoted in Hugh Witemeyer, *George Eliot and the Visual Arts* (New Haven: Yale Univ. Press, 1979), p. 33.

3. J.-K. Huysmans, *Lettres inédites à Edmond de Goncourt,* ed. Pierre Lambert (Paris: Nizet, 1956), p. 57.

4. *En Ménage,* IV, 344. Unless otherwise stated, all references to the works of Huysmans are to *Oeuvres complètes de J.-K. Huysmans,* Vols. I–XXIII (Paris: Crès, 1928–34).

5. Daniel Halévy, *Degas parle* (Paris: La Palatine, 1960), p. 48. Moreover, artists were often sensitive to what they considered a narrow literary approach to their work. Pissarro, for instance, criticized Huysmans on these grounds but nevertheless thought well of his art criticism.

6. It was also conducive to the use of literary elements in painting. See Theodore Reff, "The Artist and the Writer," in *Degas: The Artist's Mind* (New York: Harper and Row, 1976), pp. 147–99.

7. Quoted in H. Van der Tuin, *L'Evolution psychologique, esthétique et littéraire de Théophile Gautier* (Paris: Nizet, 1933), p. 246.

8. Entry of June 7, 1860 in Edmond et Jules de Goncourt, *Journal: mémoires de la vie littéraire 1851–1895* (Paris: Flammarion et Fasquelle, 1935–36), I, 253.

9. The best general study on Huysmans remains Robert Baldick, *The Life of J.-K. Huysmans* (Oxford: Clarendon Press, 1955).

10. Indeed, theater space is more complex than narrative space. In the theater, there appears immediately a dichotomy between scenic space (perceived by the spectator) and extrascenic space (verbally present, not shown). To put it another way, there is in this realm a double space—at once verbal and visual—whereas in the narrative context, spatiality remains purely verbal, referential. Furthermore, in theater the verbal can *refer* to the visual, in the characters' very speeches, which gives rise to a phenomenon of "anchoring."

   There is no equivalent in the realm of the novel, except in the case of an *illustrated* work (in which case, the visual would become the "anchoring" of the verbal . . .) or of a novel that evokes images, *existing* paintings.

En effet, l'espace du théâtre est plus complexe que celui du récit. Au théâtre se manifeste tout d'abord une dichotomie espace scénique (perçu par le spectateur) et espace hors-scène (présenté verbalement, et non montré). Autrement dit, il y a dans ce domaine un espace double, à la fois verbal et visuel, tandis que dans le contexte narratif, la spatialité demeure uniquement verbale, référée. Qui plus est, au théâtre le verbal peut *se référer* au visuel, dans le discours même des personnages, ce qui donne lieu à un phénomène d'"ancrage."

Rien de tel dans le domaine romanesque, à moins qu'il ne s'agisse d'une oeuvre *illustrée* (en ce cas, le visuel deviendrait "l'ancrage" du verbal . . .), ou d'un roman qui évoque des images, des toiles *existantes*. (Michael Issacharoff, *L'Espace et la nouvelle* [Paris: José Corti, 1976], pp. 14–15)

11. Emile Zola, "Céard et Huysmans," *Le Figaro,* April 11, 1881, quoted in Robert Baldick, "Huysmans and the Goncourts," *French Studies,* 6, no. 1 (Jan. 1952), 126.

12. Helen Trudgian, *L'Evolution des idées esthétiques de J.-K. Huysmans* (Paris: Louis Conard, 1934), p. 15.

13. Fernande Zayed, *Huysmans, peintre de son époque* (Paris: Nizet, 1973), p. xv.

14. James Huneker, *Unicorns* (London: T. Werner Laurie, 1918), p. 114.

15. G. R. Turquet-Milnes, *The Influence of Baudelaire in France and England* (London: Constable, 1913), p. 165.

16. A. E. Carter, "J.-K. Huysmans and the Middle Ages," in *Medieval Studies in Honor of Robert White Linker by his Colleagues and Friends,* eds. Brian Dutton, N. Woodrow Hassell Jr. and John E. Keller (Valencia: Ed. Castalia, 1973), p. 53.

17. Arthur Symons, *Studies in Seven Arts* (London: Constable, 1907), p. 54.

18. Anita Brookner, *The Genius of the Future* (London: Phaidon, 1971), p. 1.

19. Marc Eigeldinger, "Huysmans découvreur d'Odilon Redon," *Revue des Sciences Humaines,* 43, nos. 170–171 (April–September 1978), 215.

20. Ruth Antosh, "The Role of Paintings in Three Novels by J.-K. Huysmans," *Nineteenth-Century French Studies,* 12, no. 4, and 13, no. 1 (Summer–Fall 1984), 131–46.

21. Christopher Lehmann-Haupt, review of John Canaday, *What Is Art?,* in *The New York Times,* May 21, 1980, section C, p. 33.

Chapter 1

1. Roger Marx, *Etude sur Huysmans* (Paris, Kleinemann), quoted in Gustave Coquiot, *Le Vrai J.-K. Huysmans* (Paris: Charles Brosse, 1912), pp. 65–66.

2. Arthur Symons, *Figures of Several Centuries* (London: Constable, 1916), p. 280.

3. *Art et Critique,* December 14, 1889, quoted in Félix Fénéon, *Au-delà de l'Impressionnisme* (Paris: Hermann, 1966), p. 141.

4. J.-K. Huysmans, *Lettres inédites à Camille Lemonnier,* ed. Gustave Vanwelkenhuyzen (Genève: Droz; Paris: Minard, 1957), p. 81.

5. Quoted in *Bulletin Huysmans,* no. 39 (1960), p. 108.

6. *Musée des Deux-Mondes,* April 1, 1875. Reprinted in *Bulletin Huysmans,* no. 26 (1953), pp. 1–2.

7. The original article is reprinted in two parts, in *Bulletin Huysmans,* no. 33 (1957), pp. 77–80, and *Bulletin Huysmans,* no. 54 (1968), pp. 69–76.

8. *Musée des Deux-Mondes,* Oct. 1, 1875. Reprinted in *Bulletin Huysmans,* no. 39 (1960), p. 356.

9. "Des Paysagistes contemporains," *La Revue Mensuelle,* Nov. 25, 1867. This article is mentioned in *Marthe.* It has been republished in the 1955 edition of *Marthe* presented by Pierre Cogny (Paris, Cercle du Livre). Cf. Arsène Houssaye in his Salon of 1843:

> The Flemish interiors teach us the personal history of a people, their feelings, character, passions . . . finally, their form and frame . . . historical painting moves [the viewer]. . . . *Genre painting is content* to be true.
>
> Les intérieurs flamands nous apprennent l'histoire intime d'un peuple, ses sentiments, son caractère, ses passions . . . enfin la figure et le cadre . . . la peinture historique meut. . . . La peinture de genre se content d'être vrai. (H. van der Tuin, *Les Vieux Peintres des Pays-Bas et la critique artistique en France de la première moitié du XIX siècle* [Paris: J. Vrin, 1948], p. 111)

10. "Emile Zola et *L'Assommoir,*" II, 161–62.

11. Emile Zola, "Mon Salon," *Oeuvres complètes,* ed. Henri Mitterand (Paris: Cercle du Livre Précieux, 1969), XII, 310.

12. Ibid., p. 797.

13. This brings to mind the line in "Mon Salon" where Zola writes, "if temperament did not exist, all paintings would inevitably be simply photographs" ("si le tempérament n'existait pas, tous les tableaux devraient être forcément de simple photographies") (ibid., p. 797).

14. Marcel Schwob, "Les Portes de l'opium," in *Coeur double,* Vol. VII of *Les Oeuvres complètes* (Paris: François Bernouard, 1927–31), pp. 84–85.

15. Letter of September 1888 in J.-K. Huysmans, *Lettres inédites à Jules Destrée* (Genève: Droz; Paris: Minard, 1967), p. 151.

16. Ibid., pp. 173–74.

17. E.g. Karl Bosch, "The mystical game of a bored pantheist playing with the cult and the dogmas of the Church" ("Das mystische Spiel eines gelangweilten Pantheisten mit Kult und Dogmen der Kirche"), in *J.-K. Huysmans religiöser Entwicklungsgang: ein Beitrag zum sogenannten ästhetischen Katholizismus* (Constance: F. Romer Verlag, 1920), p. 113.

18. T. S. Eliot, "The Place of Pater," in *The Eighteen-Eighties* (Essays by Fellows of the Royal Society), ed. Walter de la Mare (Cambridge: Cambridge Univ. Press, 1930), p. 102.

19. John Ruskin, *La Bible d'Amiens,* translated, annotated and prefaced by Marcel Proust (Paris: Mercure de France, 1947), pp. 55–59.

20. Auguste Rodin, *Les Cathédrales de France* (Paris: Armand Colin, 1925), p. 8.

21. *Le Journal d' "En Route,"* 1965, p. 274.

22. Robert Baldick, *La Vie de J.-K. Huysmans,* trans. Marcel Thomas (Paris: Denoël, 1958), p. 291. The quotation is in the original French.

23. Quoted in Léon Deffoux, *J.-K. Huysmans sous divers aspects* (Paris: Crès, 1927), p. 40.

24. Alphonse James Albert Symons, *The Quest for Corvo* (Harmondsworth: Penguin Books, 1966), p. 187.

25. Ibid., p. 189.

26. Baldick, *Vie,* pp. 278–79.

27. Ibid., p. 319.

Chapter 2

1. This is the first extant article in which Huysmans articulates his attitudes towards women. In "L'Exposition des Indépendants en 1880" Huysmans quotes from an article he claims to have written on Degas in 1876 for *La Gazette des Amateurs.* There is no existing copy of this journal so we must rely on Huysmans' own quotation.

2. A. E. Carter, *The Idea of Decadence in French Literature* (Toronto: Univ. of Toronto Press, 1958), p. 5.

3. In "Le Salon officiel de 1880" in *L'Art moderne* he writes,

    > Manet had neither the stamina nor the backbone to impose his ideas with a strong work . . . he has wandered and groped; he has shown the road to take and has himself stood still . . . struggling with his inarticulate drawing, fighting the freshness of his sketches, which he spoiled by overworking them.

    > Manet n'avait ni les poumons ni les reins assez solides pour imposer ses idées par une oeuvre forte . . . il a erré, tâtonné; il a indiqué la route à suivre et lui-même est demeuré stationnaire . . . se débattant avec les balbuties de son dessin, luttant contre la fraîcheur de ses esquisses qu'il gâtait, en les travaillant. (VI, 177–78)

    and in "Le Salon officiel de 1881" he writes,

    > The year is definitely a bad one, for now Mr. Manet is falling apart, too. Like a wine that is young and a little rough, but whose taste is unusual and pure, this artist's painting was inviting and heady. Now it is adulterated, loaded with fuchsine, stripped of all tannin, all flower.

    > L'année est décidément mauvaise, car voilà M. Manet qui s'effondre, à son tour. Comme un vin vert et un peu rêche, mais d'un goût singulier et franc, la peinture de cet artiste était engageante et capiteuse. La voilà sophistiquée, chargée de fuchsine, dépouillée de tout tanin, de toute fleur. (VI, 201)

4. "La Nana de Manet," *L'Artiste,* May 13, 1877, quoted in *Bulletin Huysmans,* no. 50 (1965), p. 352.

5. "En Hollande, 1887," reprinted in *Bulletin Huysmans,* no. 54 (1968), p. 75.

6. *Croquis parisiens,* VIII, 11.

7. Theodore Reff, in *Degas: The Artist's Mind* (New York: Harper and Row, 1976), p. 243, quotes Paul Mantz, a former Director-General of Fine Arts, as writing of "the instinctive ugliness of a face on which all the vices imprint their detestable promises," and the critic Jules Claretie as writing of "the vicious muzzle of this little, barely adolescent girl, this little flower of the gutter."

8. Theodore Reff believes that the passage in *Marthe* influenced Degas "Not simply because Huysmans singles out the same details in describing the setting and the women's dress, since these are more or less standard in images of the brothel in that period; but rather because he depicts the women themselves in the same positions of total physical abandon, in contrast to

which their attitudes in other works, such as *The Prostitute Elisa* and the drawings of Guys, seem restrained, almost conventional" (ibid., p. 181).

9. *Musée des Deux-Mondes,* October 1, 1875. This article, not included in the *Oeuvres complètes* of Huysmans, has been reprinted in *Bulletin Huysmans,* no. 43 (1962), p. 354.

10. It has been suggested by Theodore Reff that this is a description of Degas' *Chanteuse de café concert.*

11. Henri Mondor, "Paul Valéry et *A Rebours,*" *Revue de Paris,* March 1947.

12. Julius Kaplan, *Gustave Moreau,* Los Angeles County Museum of Art, 1974, p. 41.

13. Paul Valéry, "Degas Danse Dessin," in *Oeuvres* (Paris: Gallimard, 1960), II, 1186.

14. Ibid., 1185–86.

15. André Breton, *L'Art magique,* quoted in *Bulletin Huysmans,* no. 42 (1961), p. 306.

16. Philippe Hamon, "Qu'est-ce qu'une description?," *Poétique; revue de théorie et d'analyse littéraire,* 12 (1972), 474.

17. The similarities between this description and the one of Salome in Flaubert's *Hérodias* lead one to believe that Huysmans had read it and was influenced by it when he wrote *A Rebours.* Flaubert wrote the work at the end of 1876, the year Moreau painted the *Salomé* which features in *A Rebours.* Flaubert begins chapter three with the architectural setting: "The guests filled the banquet hall. It had three naves, like a basilica, divided by columns of algum wood, with bronze capitals covered with sculptures . . ." ("Les convives emplissaient la salle du festin. Elle avait trois nefs, comme une basilique, que séparaient des colonnes en bois d'algumim, avec des chapiteaux de bronze couverts de sculptures . . ."). A long description of all the people present is followed by the entrance of Salome. In the account of her dance Flaubert stresses the same combination of sensuous movement and indifferent expression:

> she twisted at the waist, swayed her belly, *undulating like sea-swells, shook her two breasts,* and *her face remained immobile,* and her feet never stopped.
>   Vitellius compared her to Mnester, the pantomime artist. . . . She fell to every side, like a flower shaken in a tempest. The gems in her ears leapt, the fabric on her back shimmered; from her arms, from her feet, from her garments *flew invisible sparks that set the men afire.*

> elle se tordait la taille, balançait son ventre avec *des ondulations de houle, faisait trembler ses deux seins,* et *son visage demeurait immobile,* et ses pieds n'arrêtaient pas.
>   Vitellius la compara à Mnester, le pantomime. . . . Elle se renversait de tous les côtés, pareille à une fleur que la tempête agite. Les brillants de ses oreilles sautaient, l'étoffe de son dos chatoyait; de ses bras, de ses pieds, de ses vêtements *jaillissaient d'invisibles étincelles qui enflammaient les hommes.* [my italics] (Gustave Flaubert, *Oeuvres complètes* [Paris: Club de l'Honnête Homme, 1972], IV, 269 and 275)

18. Ruth Beharriell Antosh, "Dreams and the Imagination in the Novels of J.-K. Huysmans," (Diss., Indiana Univ., 1978), p. 70.

19. Helen Trudgian, *L'Evolution des idées esthétiques de J.-K. Huysmans* (Paris: Louis Conard, 1934), pp. 272–73.

20. *La Bièvre; Le Quartier Saint-Séverin; Trois Eglises; Trois Primitifs,* XI, 323.

Chapter 3

1. "Cette dernière caractéristique est la plus essentielle: c'est donc improprement que l'on a englobé sous la dénomination d'Impressionnistes des peintres comme M. Degas, M. Forain, M. Raffaëlli,—préoccupés surtout du mouvement, de l'anecdote et du caractère" (*L'Emancipation Sociale* [Narbonne], April 3, 1887, quoted in Félix Fénéon, *Au-delà de l'Impressionnisme,* ed. Françoise Cachin [Paris: Hermann, 1966], p. 83).

2. Helen Trudgian writes:

   What could be more natural than that, having analyzed, as he has, the atmosphere of the moderns and the Impressionists, Huysmans emulates them in his writings? He sometimes borrows the methods of the Independents, M. Monet in particular.

   Quoi de plus naturel si, après avoir analysé comme il l'a fait, l'atmosphère des modernes et des impressionnistes, Huysmans rivalise avec eux dans ses écrits? Il lui arrive d'emprunter aux indépendants leurs méthodes, à Monet en particulier. (*L'Evolution des idées esthétiques de J.-K. Huysmans* [Paris: Louis Conard, 1934], p. 140)

   Robert Baldick writes, for instance, of the "Exposition des Indépendants en 1880" that it is "a brilliant treatise on Impressionist art" (*The Life of J.-K. Huysmans* [Oxford: Clarendon Press, 1955], p. 52).
   Fernande Zayed writes that

   Huysmans' eye is the eye of a first-wave Impressionist—the friend and defender of the painters of the open air, who has introduced into prose the methods particular to painting. There is, too, the fact that he paints, not from imagination, but *de visu.*

   l'oeil de Huysmans est celui . . . d'un impressionniste de la première heure,—ami et défenseur des peintres de plein-air—, qui a acclimaté dans la prose les procédés propres à la peinture. C'est le fait aussi qu'il ne peint pas par imagination mais *de visu.* (*Huysmans, peintre de son époque* [Paris: Nizet, 1973], p. 22)

   Elizabeth Tihany writes that Huysmans' "technique, particularly in *Marthe* and *Les Soeurs Vatard,* corresponds to that of the Impressionists, whose paintings evoke only a static and primarily sensual reorganization of reality" ("Huysmans: The Novel as Compromise," Diss. Yale University 1974, p. 80).

3. Huysmans' preference for Degas, Forain, and Raffaëlli leads the art historian John Rewald, for instance, to write that "Zola's friend, the novelist J.-K. Huysmans, expressed little understanding for the impressionists, especially Berthe Morisot, and instead hailed Degas and his associates, Forain, Raffaëlli and Zandomeneghi" (*History of Impressionism* [New York: Museum of Modern Art, 1973], p. 441).

4. Camille Pissarro, *Lettres à son fils Lucien,* ed. John Rewald (Paris: Albin Michel, 1950), p. 44.

5. Valéry, "Degas Danse Dessin," *Oeuvres,* II, 1179.

6. A fascinating comparison can be made between this analysis and a description in "Autour des fortifications," of an open-air cabaret:

   Theater astonishes when performed in broad daylight, without gas footlights. Gone are the plays of light that caress woman and bring out the graininess of powder and the sauce of makeup. Brutally, the sun deepens lines, shows the skin's grain, tints these epiderms in lilac or orange.

Le théâtre joué en plein jour, sans rampe allumée de gaz, étonne. Les jeux de lumière qui caressent la femme et font valoir le granulé de la poudre et la sauce des fards ne sont plus. Brutalement le soleil fonce les traits, montre le grain de la peau, teint ces épidermes en lilas ou en orange. (I, 118)

7. These cases are discussed in chapter six of Helen Trudgian's *L'Evolution*. In *Les Soeurs Vatard,* for example, we find:

> The sun was resolving to ripen. It was going, gradually deepening the flush of its orb.— The dance of dust in a ray of light began, whirling in spirals from floor to windows.—The light leapt, sprang up, spattered the floor and tables with larger drops, lit up one trembling point on the neck of a carafe and on the belly of a bucket, torched with its red embers the heart of a peony that bloomed, quivering, in its pot of muddy water. . . .

> Le soleil se décidait à mûrir. Il allait, fonçant à mesure la rougeur de son orbe.—La danse de la poussière dans un rayon de jour commença, tournoyant en spirale, du plancher aux vitres.—La lumière sauta, jaillit, éclaboussa de plus large gouttes le plancher et les tables, alluma d'un point tremblant le col d'une carafe et la panse d'un seau, incendia de sa braise rouge le coeur d'une pivoine que s'épanouit, frémissante, dans son pot d'eau trouble. . . . (III, 14–15)

In *En Rade,* to take one other example, we find:

> The sky was drizzling imperceptible filings of palest blue, almost lilac, like those powders that sift the warmed firmaments, in the morning, and whose color deepens in the afternoon.

> le ciel bruinait en une imperceptible limaille d'un bleu très pâle presque lilas comme ces poudres que blutent les firmaments chauffés, le matin, et dont le ton, dans l'après-midi, se fonce. (IX, 145)

8. See Claire Wade, "The Contribution of Color and Light to Differing Levels of Reality in the Novels of Joris-Karl Huysmans," *Symposium,* 28, no. 4 (Winter 1974), 366–81, publ. by Syracuse Univ. Press.

9. Pissarro, *Lettres,* p. 44.

10. John Rewald, *Cézanne et Zola* (Paris: Sedrowski, 1936), p. 112.

11. *La Revue Indépendante,* April 1887.

12. Published in preface of *Marthe,* ed. Pierre Cogny.

13. *Bulletin Huysmans,* no. 33 (1957), p. 78.

14. Huysmans' comment about wallflowers was clearly unorthodox and provoked hostile reactions, to the extent that he incorporates the incident into *Les Soeurs Vatard.* Cyprien, the painter, is shunned by the establishment for having expressed those views:

> Having gone so far as to declare one day that the sadness of wallflowers drying in a pot seemed more interesting to him than the sun-filled laughter of full-blown roses in the earth, he found the doors of honest ateliers closed to him.

> Ayant même déclaré, un jour, que la tristesse des giroflées séchant dans un pot lui paraissait plus intéressante que le rire ensoleillé des roses ouvertes en pleine terre, il s'était fait fermer la porte des ateliers honnêtes. (III, 160)

15. In "Le Salon de 1879" Huysmans writes:

> The architects and engineers who built the Gare du Nord, les Halles, the cattle market of
> La Villette and the new Hippodrome have created a new art, as noble as the old art, an
> entirely contemporary art, appropriate to the needs of our time. . . .
>
> Les architectes et les ingénieurs qui ont bâti la gare du Nord, les Halles, le marché aux
> bestiaux de la Villette et le nouvel Hippodrome, ont créé un art nouveau, aussi élevé que
> l'ancien, un art tout contemporain, approprié aux besoins de notre temps. . . . (VI, 94)

a view reflected in *En Ménage,* where André says,

> Oh! they really aggravate me, all those people who come and praise the apse of Notre-
> Dame and the rood-screen of Saint-Étienne-du-Mont! Oh, so but the Gare du Nord and the
> new Hippodrome, don't *they* exist!
>
> Ah! ils m'enquiquinent à la fin, tous ces gens qui viennent vous vanter l'abside de Notre-
> Dame et le jubé de Saint-Etienne-du-Mont! Ah! ça, bien, et la gare du Nord et le nouvel
> Hippodrome, ils n'existent donc pas! (IV, 128)

Huysmans was impressed by the massive proportions of the metal constructions, as he was
later of the Gothic cathedrals, but he disliked the Eiffel Tower and saw it only as a very negative symbol of a society he disdained. In a letter to a friend of April 27, 1889, he calls it
"the Eiffel Tower's supreme hideousness" ("la hideur suprême de la Tour Eiffel") (*Bulletin
Huysmans,* no. 37 [1959], p. 359), and in a letter to Mallarmé on June 1, 1889, he writes,
"I am deep into the Eiffel Tower; for the moment, I am drawing from its belly a few symbols
that you will like, I hope, when a piece appears on this scrap metal painted in veal drip-
pings . . ." ("Je suis plongé dans la Tour Eiffel; pour l'instant, je lui tire du ventre quelques
emblèmes qui vous plairont, j'espère, lorsqu'un travail sur cette quincaillerie peinte en jus de
veau paraîtra . . .") (H. Mondor, *Vie de Mallarmé* [Paris: Gallimard, 1950], p. 554). The article Huysmans was referring to appeared in *La Revue Indépendante* in August of that year
and was published later that year in *Certains* under the title "Le Fer." Huysmans still believes, theoretically at least, that metal alone can express the particular essence of the times
but he has no kind words for the Eiffel Tower, which he describes as "That look of scaffold-
ing, that broken appearance both assigned to a now-finished building, reveal an absolute lack
of feeling for art" ("Cette allure d'échafaudage, cette attitude interrompue, assignées à un
édifice maintenant complet révèlent un insens absolu de l'art") (X, 156).

16. He dismisses Monet's paintings of La Gare St. Lazare as "ses incertaines abréviations" (VI,
141). As progressive as Huysmans was in his attitude towards industrial scenes, it comes
some twenty years after Baudelaire said of the engraver Méryon in "Le Salon de 1859":

> I have rarely seen represented with more poetry the solemnity of an immense city. The
> Majesty of piled stone . . . the obelisks of industry vomiting their coalition of smoke
> against the firmament. . . .
>
> J'ai rarement vu, représentée avec plus de poésie, la solennité d'une ville immense. Les
> Majestés de la pierre accumulée . . . les obélisques de l'industrie vomissant contre le fir-
> mament leur coalition de fumée. . . . (quoted in A. E. Carter, *The Idea of Decadence in
> French Literature,* p. 10)

17. Raffaëlli naturally responded very kindly to the enthusiastic reviews he was consistently re-
ceiving from Huysmans, and ascribes to him a rather special sensitivity. He sent the following letter to the critic about his Salon of 1879:

Monsieur Huysmans, I read, read again and reread the very fine article that you were kind enough to write about my paintings shown this year. I am very happy about what you think, I am very astonished that you know me as you do without knowing me; thus you speak of the "sorrowful charm of the ramshackle shanties" that my paintings have reawakened in your memory, and those shanties that I have been seeking in Asnières are not yet written into my work, but they have somewhat attracted me in the astonishing [. . .] that I live in. You have therefore foreseen what moves me and stirs me, and one is not used to finding foresight in today's articles on criticism. And feelings of vastness and of brazenness, of power and of sadness, inspired in me by a love of the immense, the gigantic, a contempt for the mob or else the empty sadness of the follies that we are forced to chase after. You unfold all of these feelings with great assurance.—But then, do you feel all that? . . .

Monsieur Huysmans, Je lis, je lis encore et je relis l'article bien beau que vous avez voulu écrire de mes tableaux exposés cette année. Je suis bien heureux de ce que vous pensez, je suis bien étonné que vous me connaissez ainsi sans me connaître; vous parlez ainsi du "charme attristé des cabanes branlantes" que mes toiles ont fait renaître en votre esprit, et ces cabanes que je viens chercher dans l'Asnières ne sont pas écrites encore dans mon oeuvre, mais elles m'ont quelque peu attiré dans l'étonnant [. . .] que j'habite. C'est donc là pressentir ce qui m'émeut et m'agite et l'on n'est pas habitué à trouver des pressentiments dans les articles de critiques qui se font. Et les sentiments d'amplitude et de crânerie, de puissance et de tristesse que m'inspirent un amour de l'immense, du gigantesque, un mépris des uns ou bien la tristesse du néant des folies après lesquelles, forcés, nous courrons. Tour ces sentiments, vous les développez avec une affirmation très grande.—Ah, ça, mais vous sentez tout cela? . . . (*Bulletin Huysmans*, no. 14 [May 1936], pp. 232–33)

18. Trudgian, *L'Evolution,* p. 118.

19. Michael Riffaterre, "The Making of a Literary Sign: miroirs sans tain," *French Forum,* 2, no. 2 (May 1977), 161.

20. Wade, "The Contributions of Color and Light," p. 370.

21. Joyce O. Lowrie, *The Violent Mystique: Thematics of Retribution and Expiation in Balzac, Barbey d'Aurevilly, Bloy, and Huysmans* (Genève: Librairie Droz, 1974), p. 151.

22. In the edition of Huysmans' collected works it is included in *La Bièvre; Le Quartier Saint-Séverin; Trois Églises; Trois Primitifs,* Vol. XI.

23. Cf. "in the plains where an old white horse grazes near a cart sitting sadly . . ." ("dans des plaines où broute un vieux cheval blanc près d'une charrette tristement assise . . .") (VI, 89).

24. Cf. "three ragpickers return to their resting place, accompanied by their dogs. Two drag themselves painfully along, their wicker baskets on their backs and their walking stick in their hands; the third precedes them, bent beneath the load of a sack" ("Trois chiffonniers retournent au gîte, accompagnés de leurs chiens. Deux se traînent péniblement, le cachemire d'osier sur le dos et le 7 en main; le troisième les précède, courbé sous la charge d'un sac") (VI, 52).

25. Michel Lemaire, *Le Dandyisme de Baudelaire à Mallarmé* (Paris: Editions Klincksieck, 1978), p. 166.

26. Wade, "The Contributions of Color and Light," p. 372.

27. To take the most explicit examples: "Some of the plants . . . were dead and the rest . . . seemed, as in cemeteries, to shade graves lost beneath the grass" ("Des plantes . . .

étaient mortes et les autres . . . semblaient, comme dans les cimetières, ombrager des tombes perdues sous l'herbe") (IX, 48); "the lawn was dead, smothered by mosses" ("le gazon était mort, étouffé par les mousses") (IX, 48); "the trees, left to themselves, barricaded it [the road] with their branches" ("les arbres, livrés à eux-mêmes, la barricadaient avec leurs branches") (IX, 49); "soon the road became impassable; low pine branches barred the path, curling along the ground, killing any vegetation beneath them . . ." ("bientôt la route devint impraticable; des branches basses de pins barraient le sentier, couraient en se retroussant par terre, tuant toute végétation sous elles . . .") (IX, 50); "quince trees, pear trees were leafing farther on, but their weakened sap was powerless to beget fruit" ("des cognassiers, des poiriers se feuillaient plus loin, mais leur sève affaiblie était inerte à procréer des fruits") (cf. "Ahasuerus, on the watch for an eroding virility" ["Assuérus, aux écoutes d'une virilité qui s'use"] [IX, 57]); "All the cultivated flowers in the beds were dead" ("Toutes les fleurs cultivées des parterres étaient mortes") (IX, 50).

28. Letter quoted in Robert Baldick, "The Novels of J.-K. Huysmans: A Study of the Author's Craft and the Development of His Thought," Diss. Oxford 1952, Appendix, p. 207.

Chapter 4

1. This role of dream descriptions is similar to that of the fantastic in general. See the definition of Tzvetan Todorov in his *Introduction à la littérature fantastique* (Paris: Editions du Seuil, 1970), p. 98.

   It is appropriate to ask ourselves, what do fantastic elements bring to a work? When we approach the question from this functional point of view, we may arrive at three answers. First, the fantastic produces a particular effect upon the reader—fear, or horror, or simply curiosity—which the other genres or literary forms cannot provoke. Second, the fantastic serves the narration, maintains the suspense: the presence of fantastic elements allows for a particularly tight organization of the plot. Finally, the fantastic has a function that at first appears tautological: it allows a fantastic universe to be described, and this universe, as such, has no reality outside of language; the description and the thing described are not different in essense.

   Il convient de se demander: qu'apportent à une oeuvre ses éléments fantastiques? Une fois placé à ce point de vue fonctionnel, on peut aboutir à trois réponses. Premièrement, le fantastique produit un effet particulier sur le lecteur—peur, ou horreur, ou simplement curiosité—, que les autres genres ou formes littéraires ne peuvent provoquer. Deuxièmement, le fantastique sert la narration, entretient le suspense: la présence d'éléments fantastiques permet une organisation particulièrement serrée de l'intrigue. Enfin, le fantastique a une fonction à première vue tautologique: il permet de décrire un univers fantastique, et cet univers n'a pas pour autant une réalité en dehors du langage; la description et le décrit ne sont pas de nature différente.

2. In a letter to the Belgian poet Camille Lemonnier of 1876, he wrote, for instance, that "I almost never see magazines in France that accept those pretty gems that we adore but that, unfortunately, are meant only for an audience of literary people and painters" ("je ne vois guère de revue en France qui accepte ces jolies orfèvreries dont nous raffolons nous autres mais qui ne s'adressent malheureusement qu'à un public de lettrés et d'artistes") (J.-K. Huysmans, *Lettres inédites à Camille Lemonnier,* p. 5). In another letter to the same poet written in 1877, Huysmans explains that he is trying to please the editor Charpentier with his next novel, *Les Soeurs Vatard:* "I would like to make it a very strongly realistic study—Charpentier seems more or less to like the subject" ("Je voudrais en faire une étude réaliste très poussée—Le sujet a l'air de plaire à peu près à Charpentier") (ibid., p. 15).

3. J.-K. Huysmans, *Lettres inédites à Emile Zola,* publiées et annotées par Pierre Lambert avec une introduction de Pierre Cogny (Genève: Droz; Lille: Giard, 1953), p. 103.

4. J.-K. Huysmans, *Lettres inédites à Jules Destrée,* pp. 66–67.

5. Huysmans, *Lettres inédites à Emile Zola,* p. 116.

6. Quoted in H. Robbers, "Huysmans et Arij Prins," trans. Ch. Gemmeke, *Bulletin Huysmans,* no. 6 (1956–59), pp. 422–23.

7. *Lettres inédites à Emile Zola,* p. 127.

8. Huysmans, *Lettres inédites à Jules Destrée,* p. 65.

9. Odilon Redon, *A Soi-même: Journal 1867–1915* (Paris: José Corti, 1961), p. 26.

10. Quoted in John Rewald. "Quelques notes et documents sur Odilon Redon," *Gazette des Beaux-Arts,* November 1956, p. 82.

11. "Doré, more whimsical, more dramatic, more extravagant; Crane, less dissonant, simpler, following the truth step by step, always introducing an atmosphere of the real even into enchantment . . ." ("Doré, plus fantaisiste, plus dramatique, plus outré; Crane moins dissonant, plus simple, suivant la vérité pas à pas, introduisant toujours une atmosphère de réel même dans la féerie . . .") (VI, 215). According to Todorov's definition of the fantastic, Huysmans is talking more of the marvelous than the fantastic:

    > Let us now cross to the other side [the first being the uncanny] of this median that we have called the fantastic. We are now in the fantastic-marvellous, that is, in the class of narratives that present themselves as fantastic and end with an acceptance of the supernatural. . . . In the case of the marvellous, the supernatural elements provoke no particular reaction either in the characters or in the implicit reader. . . . The genre of the marvellous is generally linked to that of the fairy tale.

    > Passons maintenant de l'autre côté de cette ligne médiane que nous avons appelée le fantastique. Nous sommes dans le fantastique-merveilleux, autrement dit, dans la classe des récits qui se présentent comme fantastiques et qui se terminent par une acceptation du surnaturel. . . . Dans le cas du merveilleux, les éléments surnaturels ne provoquent aucune réaction particulière ni chez les personnages, ni chez le lecteur implicite. . . . On lie généralement le genre du merveilleux à celui du conte de fées. (Todorov, *Introduction à la littérature fantastique,* pp. 57–59)

12. "The fantastic is the hesitation experienced by a being who knows only the laws of nature, confronted by a seemingly supernatural event" ("Le fantastique, c'est l'hésitation éprouvée par un être qui ne connaît que les lois naturelles, face à un événement en apparence surnaturel") (Todorov, ibid., p. 29).

13. *Lettres de Gauguin, Gide, Huysmans, Jammes, Mallarmé, Verhaeren à Redon,* ed. Arï Redon (Paris: José Corti, 1960), p. 97.

14. On a visit to Berlin in 1888 Huysmans took the opportunity to write an article about the aquarium, in which the animals are truly seen through glass. The article was republished under the heading "L'Aquarium" in *De Tout,* Vol. XVI. His view of this "fairyland of animal flowers" ("féerie de fleurs animales") (p. 210) is reminiscent of his descriptions of Redon's ambiguous creatures with human and plant characteristics. Above all it is the frightening beings, born of a sick mind, which impress him:

he also put us in the presence of abominable creatures, which resemble the monsters born in delirium . . . behind glass panels a nightmarish creature stirred, a metallic monster, a sort of crab armor-plated like a man-of-war. . . .

il nous mettait en présence aussi d'abominables créatures, de monstres tels que, seul, le délire des maladies les enfante . . . derrière des cloisons de verre, s'agitait un être de cauchemar, un monstre métallique, une sorte de crabe blindé comme un vaisseau de guerre. . . . (pp. 216–17)

15. André Mellerio, *Odilon Redon* (Paris: Société pour l'Etude de la Gravure française, 1913), p. 10.

16. According to Roseline Bacou, the descriptions in *A Rebours* are based on the two lithographs "Sur la Coupe" and "Le Joueur" from the series *Dans le Rêve* and two charcoal sketches *Le Boulet* and *L'Araignée*. See Roseline Bacou, *Odilon Redon* (Genève: P. Cailler, 1956), I, 232–33.

17. See Angela Nuccitelli, "*A Rebours*'s Symbol of the 'Femme-Fleur': A Key to Des Esseintes's Obsession," *Symposium*, 28, 4 (Winter 1974), 336–45.

18. Huysmans is referring to "another human flower, lately seen in an exhibition" ("une autre fleur humaine naguère vue dans une exposition") (VIII, 162), and with this explicit reference to art, the only one within the poem, Huysmans breaks the suspense of the nightmare.

19. *Bulletin Huysmans*, no. 26 (1953), pp. 1–2.

20. Compare

But the moment at which there took place the irrefutable intervention of the supernatural and the beginning of the anguish, beneath which my once lordly spirit agonizes, was when I saw, raising my eyes, in the street of antique dealers which I had followed instinctively, that I was in front of a lute-maker's shop selling old musical instruments hung on the wall, and, on the ground, some yellow palms and the wings of old birds hidden in the shadow. Like an eccentric I fled, a person probably condemned to wear mourning for the inexplicable Penultimate.

Mais où s'installe l'irrécusable intervention du surnaturel, et le commencement de l'angoisse sous laquelle agonise mon esprit naguère seigneur c'est quand je vis, levant les yeux, dans la rue des antiquaires instinctivement suivie, que j'étais devant la boutique d'un luthier vendeur de vieux instruments pendus au mur, et, à terre, des palmes jaunes et les ailes enfouies en l'ombre, d'oiseaux anciens. Je m'enfuis, bizarre, personne condamnée à porter probablement le deuil de l'inexplicable Pénultième. (Stéphane Mallarmé, "Le Démon de l'analogie," *Oeuvres complètes* [Paris: Gallimard, 1945], p. 273)

21. The obvious source for these dungeons of the castle of Lourps are Huysmans' own nightmares, as he recalls them in his "carnet vert." One entry of 1886 reads: "*Dreams*—last night—going down through the cellar into the sewers; at the approaches of the wastelands—little greenhouses, whited panes—cellar steps—blackness—Black water striking the steps as it runs . . ." ("*Rêves,*—cette nuit—descente par la cave dans les égouts; aux abords sur terrains vagues—petites serres de jardinier, vitres au blanc d'Espagne—des marches de cave—du noir—Eau noire battant les marches en courant . . .") (quoted in J.-K. Huysmans, "Le Carnet secret de Huysmans," ed. Pierre Lambert, *Figaro Littéraire*, 950, July 2, 1964, p. 1). Two of the three dreams in *En Rade* are based on works of art. The few descriptions of peasant life constitute the only truly naturalistic passages in this book which consists, on the one hand, of the surrealistic descriptions of the sinister castle and, on the other hand, of the dream sequences.

22. It was these qualities which appealed to des Esseintes in *A Rebours*.

23. John Rewald, "Quelques Notes et documents sur Odilon Redon," p. 101.

24. *Nouvelles Littéraires*, May 3, 1955.

25. André Mellerio, *Odilon Redon*, p. 98.

26. Rewald, "Quelques Notes et documents sur Odilon Redon," p. 234.

27. Quoted in Gustave Coquiot, *Le Vrai J.-K. Huysmans* (Paris: Charles Bosse, 1912), p. 78. One is reminded here of Huysmans' article "L'Aquarium," discussed in n. 14 above.

Conclusion

1. James D. Merriman, "The Parallel of the Arts: Some Misgivings and a Faint Affirmation," *Journal of Aesthetics and Art Criticism*, 31, no. 2 (Winter 1972), p. 154.

2. Robert Baldick, "Huysmans and the Goncourts," *French Studies*, 6, no. 1 (Jan. 1952), p. 126.

Select Bibliography

The Published Works of J.-K. Huysmans

Huysmans, J.-K. *Le Drageoir à épices*. Paris: Dentu, 1874.
————. *Marthe, histoire d'une fille*. Brussels: Gay, 1876.
————. *Les Soeurs Vatard*. Paris: Charpentier, 1879.
————. *Croquis parisiens*. Paris: Vaton, 1880.
————. *Sac au dos* (in *Les Soirées de Médan*). Paris: Charpentier, 1880.
————. *En Ménage*. Paris: Charpentier, 1881.
————. *Pierrot sceptique*. Paris: Rouveyre, 1881. (In collaboration with Léon Hennique.)
————. *A Vau-l'eau*. Brussels: Kistemaeckers, 1882.
————. *L'Art moderne*. Paris: Charpentier, 1883.
————. *A Rebours*. Paris: Charpentier, 1884.
————. *Croquis parisiens*. Paris: Vanier, 1886.
————. *En Rade*. Paris: Tresse et Stock, 1887.
————. *Un Dilemme*. Paris: Tresse et Stock, 1887.
————. *Certains*. Paris: Tresse et Stock, 1889.
————. *La Bièvre*. Paris: Genonceaux, 1890.
————. *Là-Bas*. Paris: Tresse et Stock, 1891.
————. *En Route*. Paris: Tresse et Stock, 1895.
————. *La Bièvre et Saint-Séverin*. Paris: Stock, 1898.
————. *La Cathédrale*. Paris: Stock, 1898.
————. *La Magie en Poitou: Gilles de Rais*. Paris: Ligugé, 1899.
————. *La Bièvre: Les Gobelins; Saint-Séverin*. Paris: Stock, Société de Propagation des Livres d'Art, 1901.
————. *Sainte Lydwine de Schiedam*. Paris: Stock, 1901.
————. *De Tout*. Paris: Stock, 1902.
————. *Esquisse biographique sur Dom Besse*. Paris, 1902.
————. *L'Oblat*. Paris: Stock, 1903.
————. *Trois Primitifs*. Paris: Librairie Léon Vanier; A. Messein, 1905.
————. *Le Quartier Notre-Dame*. Paris: Librairie de la Collection des Dix, [1905].
————. *Les Foules de Lourdes*. Paris: Stock, 1906.
————. *Trois Eglises et Trois Primitifs*. Paris: Plon-Nourrit, 1908.
————. *Les Oeuvres complètes de J.-K. Huysmans*. Paris: Crès, 1928–34. 23 vols.
————. *Against Nature*. Translated by Robert Baldick. Harmondsworth: Penguin Books, 1959.
————. *La Retraite de Monsieur Bougran*. Paris: Pauvert, 1964.
————. *Là-Haut ou Notre Dame de la Salette*. Texte inédit établi par Pierre Cogny, avec une introduction par Artine Artinian et Pierre Cogny et des notes de Pierre Lambert. Suivi du Journal "d'En Route", établi par Pierre Lambert d'après des documents inédits. Paris: Casterman, 1965.

Correspondence

Huysmans, J.-K. *Correspondance de J.-K. Huysmans et de Mme Cécile Bruyère,* publiée et annotée par René Rancoeur. Paris: Editions du Cèdre, 1950.

————. *Lettres inédites à Emile Zola,* publiées et annotées par Pierre Lambert avec une introduction de Pierre Cogny. Genève: Droz; Lille: Giard, 1953.

————. *Lettres inédites à Edmond de Goncourt,* publiées et annotées par Pierre Lambert et présentées par Pierre Cogny. Paris: Nizet, 1956.

————. *Lettres inédites à Camille Lemonnier,* publiées et annotées par Gustave Vanwelkenhuyzen. Genève: Droz; Paris: Minard, 1957.

————. *Lettres inédites à Jules Destrée,* avant propos d'Albert Guislain, introduction et notes de Gustave Vanwelkenhuyzen. Genève: Droz; Paris: Minard, 1967.

————. *Une Etape de la vie de J.-K. Huysmans; lettres inédites de J.-K. Huysmans à l'abbé Ferret,* présentées et annotées par Elizabeth Bourget-Besnier. Paris: Nizet, 1973.

————. *Lettres inédites à Arij Prins (1885–1907),* ed. Louis Gillet. Genève: Droz, 1975.

Works with Prefaces by J.-K. Huysmans

Bois, Jules. *Le Satanisme et la magie.* Paris: Chailley, 1895.

Broussolle, Abbé J.-C. *La Jeunesse du Pérugin et les origines de l'Ecole ombrienne.* Paris: Lecène-Oudin, 1901.

Cazals, F.-A. *Paul Verlaine, ses portraits.* Paris: Bibliothèque de l'Association, 1896.

Dutilliet, Abbé Henri. *Petit Catéchisme Liturgique.* Paris: J. Bricon, 1895.

Gourmont, Remy de. *Le Latin mystique.* Paris: Mercure de France, 1892.

Hannon, Théodore. *Rimes de joie.* Brussels: Kistemaeckers, 1881.

Verlaine, Paul, *Poésies religieuses.* Paris: Messein, 1904.

Works Consulted

Antosh, Ruth Beharriell. "Dreams and the Imagination in the Novels of J.-K. Huysmans." Diss. Indiana University, 1978.

————. "The Role of Paintings in Three Novels by J.-K. Huysmans." *Nineteenth-Century French Studies,* 12, no. 4, and 13, no. 1 (Summer–Fall 1984), 131–46.

Bachelard, Gaston. *L'Eau et les rêves.* Paris: José Corti, 1942.

————. *La Terre et les rêveries de la volonté.* Paris: José Corti, 1948.

Bacou, Roseline. *Odilon Redon.* Geneva: P. Cailler, 1956. 2 vols.

Baldick, Robert. "Huysmans and the Goncourts." *French Studies,* 6, no. 1 (Jan. 1952), pp. 126–34.

————. *The Life of J.-K. Huysmans.* Oxford: Clarendon Press, 1955.

————. "The Novels of J.-K. Huysmans: A Study of the Author's Craft and the Development of His Thought." Diss. Oxford University, 1952.

————. *La Vie de J.-K. Huysmans.* Trans. Marcel Thomas. Paris: Denoël, 1958.

Baudelaire, Charles Pierre. *Oeuvres complètes de Charles Baudelaire.* Ed. Y.-G. Le Dantec. Paris: Gallimard, 1961.

Bernard, Suzanne. *Le Poème en prose de Baudelaire jusqu'à nos jours.* Paris: Nizet, 1959.

Bilz, Helene. *Die Kunstkritik bei J.-K. Huysmans und ihre Bedeutung für eigene und die allgemeine literarische Entwicklung in Frankreich.* Bottrop: Buch und Kunstdruckerei, 1937.

Bosch, Karl. *J.-K. Huysmans religiöser Entwicklungsgang: ein Beitrag zum sogenannten ästhetischen Katholizismus.* Constance: F. Romer Verlag, 1920.

Bowie, Theodore Robert. *The Painter in French Fiction: A Critical Essay.* Chapel Hill: University of North Carolina, 1950.

Brookner, Anita. *The Genius of the Future.* London: Phaidon, 1971.

Bulletin de la Société J.-K. Huysmans. Paris: Chez Durtal.

Carter, Alfred Edward. *The Idea of Decadence in French Literature*. Toronto: Univ. of Toronto Press, 1958.

————. "J.-K. Huysmans and the Middle Ages." In *Medieval Studies in Honor of Robert White Linker by His Colleagues and Friends*. Eds. Brian Dutton, N. Woodrow Hassell, Jr., and John E. Keller. Valencia: Ed. Castalia, 1973, pp. 17–53.

Cassagne, Albert. *La Théorie de l'art pour l'art en France chez les derniers romantiques et les premiers réalistes*. Paris: Lucien Dorbon, 1959.

Cevasco, George A. "J.-K. Huysmans and the Impressionists." *Journal of Aesthetics and Art Criticism*, 17, no. 2 (Dec. 1958), 201–7.

Champa, Kermit. *Studies in Early Impressionism*. New Haven: Yale Univ. Press, 1973.

Chassé, Charles. *Le Mouvement symboliste dans l'art du XIXe siècle*. Paris: Librairie Floury, 1947.

Chastel, Guy. *J.-K. Huysmans et ses amis*. Paris: Bernard Grasset, 1957.

Chernowitz, Maurice. *Proust and Painting*. New York: International Univ. Press, 1945.

Clark, Kenneth. *The Gothic Revival*. Harmondsworth: Penguin Books, 1962.

Cogny, Pierre. *J.-K. Huysmans à la recherche de l'unité*. Paris: Nizet, 1953.

————. *Le "Huysmans intime" de Henry Céard et Jean de Caldain*, avec de nombreux inédits et une préface de René Dumesnil. Paris: Nizet, 1957.

Colucci, Frank. "Joris-Karl Huysmans' Art Criticism." Diss. Cornell University, 1932.

Coquiot, Gustave. *Le Vrai J.-K. Huysmans*. Paris: Charles Bosse, 1912.

Cressot, Marcel. *La Phrase et le vocabulaire de J.-K. Huysmans*. Paris: Droz, 1938.

Deffoux, Léon. *J.-K. Huysmans sous divers aspects*. Paris: Crès, 1927.

Demolder, Eugène. *Félicien Rops: étude patronymique*. Paris: René Picebourde, 1894.

Denis, Maurice. *Du Symbolisme au classicisme: théories*. Ed. Olivier Revault d'Allonnes. Paris: Hermann, 1964.

Dorbec, Prosper. *Les Lettres françaises dans leurs contacts avec l'atelier de l'artiste*. Paris: Les Universitaires de France, 1929.

Dubois, Jacques. *Romanciers français de l'instantané au XIXe siècle*. Bruxelles: Palais des Académies, 1963.

Dulac, Marie-Charles. *Lettres de Marie-Charles Dulac*. Paris: Blond, 1905.

Duployé, Pie. *Huysmans*. Paris: Desclée de Brouwer, 1968.

Duret, Theodore. *Les Peintres impressionnistes*. Paris: Heymann et Perois, 1878.

————. *Les Peintres impressionnistes*. Paris: Librairie parisienne, 1878.

Eigeldinger, Marc. "Huysmans découvreur d'Odilon Redon." *Revue des Sciences Humaines*, 43, nos. 170–71 (April-Sept. 1978), 207–15.

Eliot, T. S. "The Place of Pater." In *The Eighteen-Eighties: Essays by Fellows of the Royal Society*. Ed. Walter de la Mare. Cambridge: Cambridge Univ. Press, 1930.

Fénéon, Félix. *Au-delà de l'impressionnisme*. Ed. Françoise Cachin. Paris: Hermann, 1966.

Finke, Ulrich, ed. *French Nineteenth Century Painting and Literature*. Manchester: Manchester Univ. Press, 1972.

Flaubert, Gustave. *Oeuvres complètes*. Vol. IV. Paris: Club de l'Honnête Homme, 1972.

Fosca, François. *De Diderot à Valéry: Les Ecrivains et les arts visuels*. Paris: Albin Michel, 1960.

Fouillée, A. *Le Mouvement idéaliste et la réaction contre la science positive*. Paris: Félix Alca, 1896.

Frankl, Paul. *The Gothic: Literary Sources and Interpretations through Eight Centuries*. Princeton: Princeton Univ. Press, 1960.

Gilman, Margaret. *Baudelaire the Critic*. New York: Octagon Books, 1971.

Giovannini, G. "Method in the Study of Literature in Its Relation to Other Fine Arts," *The Journal of Aesthetics and Art Criticism*, 8, no. 3 (March 1950), 185–95.

Gombrich, E. H. *Meditations on a Hobby Horse*. London: Phaidon, 1963.

de Goncourt, Edmond et Jules. *Journal: mémoires de la vie littéraire 1851–1895*. Paris: Flammarion et Fasquelle, 1935–36.

Grassl, Maximilian. *Die Musik in den Werken des J.-K. Huysmans*. Munich: Max Hueber Verlag, 1938.

Griffiths, Richard. *The Reactionary Revolution: The Catholic Revival in French Literature 1870– 1914*. London: Constable, 1966.

Halévy, Daniel. *Degas parle*. Paris: La Palatine, 1960.

Hamon, Philippe. "Qu'est-ce qu'une description?" *Poétique: Revue de Théorie et d'Analyse Littéraire*, 12 (1972), 464–85.

Haskell, F., Levi, A., Shackleton, R. *The Artist and the Writer in France: Essays in Honour of Jean Seznec*. Oxford: Clarendon Press, 1974.

Hatzfield, Helmut, A. *Literature Through Art: A New Approach to French Literature*. New York: Oxford Univ. Press, 1952.

Hautecoeur, Louis. *Littérature et peinture en France du XVII au XX siècle*. Paris: Armand Colin, 1942.

Herbert, Eugenia. *The Artist and Social Reform: France and Belgium 1885–1898*. New Haven: Yale Univ. Press, 1961.

von Holten, Ragnar. *L'Art fantastique de Gustave Moreau*. Paris: Jean-Jacques Pauvert, 1960.

Hourticq, Louis. *L'Art et la littérature*. Paris: Flammarion, 1946.

Huneker, James. *Promenades of an Impressionist*. London: T. Werner Laurie, 1910.

———. *Unicorns*. London: T. Werner Laurie, 1918.

Huret, J. *Enquête sur l'évolution littéraire*. Paris: Charpentier, 1891.

Issacharoff, Michael. *L'Espace et la nouvelle: Flaubert, Huysmans, Ionesco, Sartre, Camus*. Préface de Victor Brombert. Paris: Corti, 1976.

———. *J.-K. Huysmans devant la critique en France 1874–1960*. Paris: Editions Klincksieck, 1970.

Jackson, Holbrook. *The Eighteen-Nineties: A Review of Art and Ideas at the Close of the Nineteenth Century*. London: Jonathan Cape, 1927.

Jouvin, Henri. "Huysmans critique d'art," *Bulletin de la Société Huysmans*, 20 (1947).

Jullian, Philippe. *Dreamers of Decadence*. New York: Praeger Publishers, 1971.

Kaplan, Julius. *Gustave Moreau*. Los Angeles: Los Angeles County Museum of Art, 1974.

Kreitmaier, Josef. *Beuroner Kunst: eine Ausdrucksform der christlichen Mystik*. Freiburg: Herdersche Verlagshandlung, 1914.

Laver, James. *The First Decadent, Being the Strange Life of J.-K. Huysmans*. London: Faber and Faber, 1954.

Lehmann, A. G. *The Symbolist Aesthetic in France 1885–1895*. Oxford: Blackwell, 1950.

Lehmann-Haupt, Christopher. Review of John Canaday, *What Is Art?* In *The New York Times*, May 21, 1980, Section C, 33.

Lemonnier, Camille. *Félicien Rops, l'homme et l'artiste*. Paris: H. Floury, 1908.

Lenz, P. *L'Esthétique de Beuron*. Trans. from the German by Paul Sérusier with an introduction by Maurice Denis. Paris: Bibliothèque de l'Occident, 1905.

Lethève, Jacques. *Impressionnistes et symbolistes devant la presse*. Paris: Armand Colin, 1959.

Lobet, Marcel. "Le Paradis d'art de J.-K. Huysmans," *Revue Générale Belge*, March 1960.

Lowrie, Joyce O. *The Violent Mystique: Thematics of Retribution and Expiation in Balzac, D'Aurevilly, Bloy and Huysmans*. Genève: Droz, 1974.

Mallarmé. Edited with an introduction and prose translations by Anthony Hartley. Harmondsworth: Penguin Books, 1965.

Mallarmé, Stéphane. *Oeuvres complètes*. Paris: Gallimard, 1945.

Martineau, René. *Autour de J.-K. Huysmans*. Paris: Desclée de Brouwer, 1946.

Mélanges Pierre Lambert consacrés à Huysmans. Paris: Nizet, 1975.

Mellerio, André. *Le Mouvement idéaliste en peinture*. Paris: H. Floury, 1896.

———. *Odilon Redon*. Paris: Société pour l'Etude de la Gravure Française, 1913.

Merriman, James D. "The Parallel of the Arts: Some Misgivings and a Faint Affirmation," *Journal of Aesthetics and Art Criticism*, 31, no. 2 (Winter 1972), 153–64, and no. 3 (Spring 1973), 309–21.

Meyers, Jeffrey. "Huysmans and Gustave Moreau," *Apollo*, 99 (Jan. 1974), 39–44.

Michaud, Guy. *Message poétique du symbolisme*. Paris: Nizet, 1961.

Mickelsen, David. "*A Rebours:* Spatial Form," *French Forum*, 3, no. 1 (Jan. 1978), 48–55.

Mitchell, W. J. T., ed. *The Language of Images*. Chicago and London: University of Chicago Press, 1980.

Moore, George. *Confessions of a Young Man*. London: Heinemann, 1926.

———. *Impressions and Opinions*. London: D. Nutt; New York: Scribner's Sons, 1891.

Nochlin, Linda. *Realism*. Harmondsworth: Penguin Books, 1973.

———. *Realism and Tradition in Art 1848–1900*. Englewood Cliffs: Prentice-Hall, 1966.

Nuccitelli, Angela. "*A Rebours's* Symbol of the 'Femme-Fleur': A Key to Des Esseintes's Obsession," *Symposium*, 28, no. 4 (Winter 1974), 336–45.

Paladilhe, Jean. *Gustave Moreau*. Paris: Fernand Hazan, 1971.

Picon, Gaëtan. "Zola's Painters," *Yale French Studies*, no. 42 (1969), pp. 126–42.

Pissarro, Camille. *Lettres à son fils Lucien*. Ed. John Rewald. Paris: Albin Michel, 1950.

Pool, Phoebe. *Impressionism*. New York: Praeger, 1967.

Praz, Mario. *Mnemosyne: The Parallel between Literature and the Visual Arts*. Princeton: Princeton Univ. Press, 1970.

———. *The Romantic Agony*. Trans. Angus Davidson. New York: Meridian Books, 1956.

Proust, Marcel, trans. *La Bible d'Amiens* by John Ruskin. Paris: Mercure de France, 1947.

Raffaëlli, J.-F. *Catalogue illustré des oeuvres de Jean-François Raffaëlli*. Suivi d'une étude des mouvements de l'art moderne et du beau caractéristique. Paris, 1884.

Redon, Arï, ed. *Lettres de Gauguin, Gide, Huysmans, Jammes, Mallarmé, Verhaeren à Redon*. Paris: José Corti, 1960.

Redon, Odilon. *A Soi-même: Journal 1867–1915*. Paris: José Corti, 1961.

Reff, Theodore. *Degas: The Artist's Mind*. New York: Harper and Row, 1976.

Rewald, John. *Cézanne et Zola*. Paris: Sedrowski, 1936.

———. *History of Impressionism*. New York: Museum of Modern Art, 1973.

———. *L'Histoire de l'impressionnisme*. Trans. Nancy Goldet-Bouwens. Paris: Albin Michel, 1955.

———. *Post-Impressionism from Van Gogh to Gauguin*. New York: Museum of Modern Art, 1956.

———. "Quelques notes et documents sur Odilon Redon," *Gazette des Beaux-Arts*, 49 (Nov. 1956), 81–124.

Riffaterre, Michael. "The Making of a Literary Sign: Miroirs sans tain," *French Forum*, 2, no. 2 (May 1977), 160–67.

Rodin, Auguste. *Les Cathédrales de France*. Paris: Armand Colin, 1925.

Rookmaeker, H. R. *Synthetist Art Theories: Genesis and Nature of the Ideas on Art of Gauguin and His Circle*. Amsterdam: Swets and Zeitlinger, 1959.

Sarrazin, Bernard. "A propos de quelques pages de Bachelard: pierres et pierreries: l'expérience symbolique de J.-K. Huysmans," *Revue des Sciences Humaines*, 34, no. 133 (Jan.–March 1969), 99–103.

Schwob, Marcel. *Les Oeuvres complètes*. Paris: François Bernouard, 1927–31.

Seznec, Jean. "Literature and the Visual Arts in Nineteenth Century France," *University of Hull Publications*, 1963.

Shattuck, Roger. *The Banquet Years: The Origins of the Avant-Garde in France 1885 to World War I*. New York: Anchor Books, 1961.

Symons, Alphonse James Albert. *The Quest for Corvo*. Harmondsworth: Penguin Books, 1966.

Symons, Arthur. *Figures of Several Centuries*. London: Constable, 1916.

————. *Studies in Seven Arts.* London: Constable, 1907.

Sypher, Wylie. *Rococo to Cubism in Art and Literature.* New York: Random House, 1960.

Taylor, John. "Joris-Karl Huysmans as Impressionist in Prose," *Papers on Language and Literature; Nicholas Joost,* 8 (Supp.), 67–78.

Tihany, Elizabeth Derricott. "Huysmans: The Novel as Compromise." Diss. Yale 1974.

Todorov, Tzvetan. *Introduction à la littérature fantastique.* Paris: Editions du Seuil, 1970.

Trudgian, Helen. *L'Evolution des idées esthétiques de J.-K. Huysmans.* Paris: Louis Conard, 1934.

van der Tuin, H. *L'Evolution psychologique, esthétique et littéraire de Théophile Gautier.* Paris: Nizet, 1933.

————. *Les Vieux Peintres des Pays-Bas et la littérature en France dans la première moitié du XIX siècle.* Paris: Nizet, 1953.

Turquet-Milnes, G. R. *The Influence of Baudelaire in France and England.* London: Constable, 1913.

Vadé, Yves. "Onirisme et symbolique: d'*En Rade* à *La Cathédrale*," *Revue des Sciences Humaines,* nos. 170–171 (April–Sept. 1978), pp. 244–53.

Valéry, Paul. *Oeuvres.* Paris: Gallimard, 1960. Vol. II.

Vanwelkenhuyzen, Gustave. *J.-K. Huysmans et la Belgique.* Paris: Mercure de France, 1935.

Wade, Claire. "The Contributions of Color and Light to Differing Levels of Reality in the Novels of Joris-Karl Huysmans," *Symposium,* 28, no. 4 (Winter 1974), 366–81.

Ward-Jackson, Philip. "Huysmans," *The Burlington Magazine,* 109 (November 1967), 613–22.

Weinreb, Ruth Plaut. "Structural Techniques in *A Rebours*," *French Review,* 49, no. 2 (Dec. 1975), 222–33.

Wellek, René. "The Parallelism between Literature and the Arts." In *English Institute Annual.* New York: Columbia Univ. Press, 1941.

Wilde, Oscar. *The Picture of Dorian Gray.* Harmondsworth: Penguin Books, 1949.

Witemeyer, Hugh. *George Eliot and the Visual Arts.* New Haven: Yale Univ. Press, 1979.

Zayed, Fernande. *Huysmans, peintre de son époque.* Paris: Nizet, 1973.

Zeldin, Theodore. *France 1848–1945.* Oxford: Clarendon Press, 1973–77. 4 vols.

Zola, Emile. *Oeuvres complètes.* Ed. Henri Mitterand. Paris: Cercle du livre précieux, 1969. Vol. XII.

Index

Angelico, Fra, 61; *Couronnement de la Vierge,* 34, 60, 61, 62
Antosh, Ruth, 9, 60, 62
Art: function of, for Huysmans, as basis for aesthetic discussion, 6, 22, 32; influence of Huysmans, 14, 32, 101; inspiration for Huysmans, 32, 133, 135; and nature, 3, 4, 99; and reality, 1, 3, 4, 7, 14, 17, 32, 68, 94, 98, 103, 134; relation to literature, 1, 2, 4, 6, 11, 15, 71, 133; schools of; Academics, 15, 20, 36, 50, 68, 71; Independents, 15; substitute for life, 14, 32; theory of, 14; *transpositions d'art,* 6, 15, 16, 40, 43, 58, 66, 86, 134; veracity to Realist text, 5
Art, Dutch and Flemish, 15, 17, 18, 19, 36, 76; inspiration to Huysmans, 22; Huysmans' loss of interest in, 134
Art, medieval, 27, 29, 32, 49, 61, 62, 129
Art, modern; defense of, 75; Huysmans' opinion of, 75, 101
Art, religious, 25, 26, 27, 28; role in Huysmans' conversion, 26

Baldick, Robert, 68
Baudelaire, Charles, 18, 19, 104; as art critic, 1, 12, 13
Bernard, Emile, 30, 131; on Redon, 131
Bertrand, Louis Marie Emile, 104, 134
Beuron. *See* Germany
Botticelli, Sandro: *Virgin and Child,* 5
Breton, André, 51
Breughel, Pieter (the Elder), 81; *Wise and Foolish Virgins, The,* 5

Caillebotte, Gustave, 69, 72, 75
Carter, A.E., 8, 34
Catholicism, 4, 8, 14, 22, 61, 62, 66, 118, 131, 135; medieval, 62
Cézanne, Paul, 74; critic of Huysmans, 74
Chartres Cathedral, 4, 14, 34, 60, 96

Confusion, 17, 94–95; between art and reality, 134; in dreams, 105; in Redon, 109; between self and world, 100. *See also* Individual works
Corot, Camille, 73, 75

Decadence, 3, 33–34, 53, 81–82, 135; artificial vs. natural, 92–93, 115; beauty in sordid, 81–82, 87, 91
Degas, Hilaire Germain Edgar: admired by Huysmans, 67, 72; art relating to literature, 2; compared to Moreau, 51, 54; favorite of Huysmans, 13, 14, 19–20, 35–36, 46, 47, 50, 63, 101; importance of subject to, 69; misogynist, 39, 43, 49; position regarding Impressionists, 67, 68; subject of Huysmans article, 33, 38, 39, 41, 43, 48; view on dancers, 55–56; view on prostitutes, 45, 56–57; view on women, 4, 34, 37, 41, 43, 65, 76, 135
Delacroix, Eugène, 27, 30, 69
Destrée, Jules, 22, 106, 108, 110
Dreams and visions, 4, 17–18, 115, 131–32; dual role of, 103; as escape, 103–4, 131; in "Camaïeu rouge", 104; in *En Rade,* 21, 34, 57, 94–95, 96; in *A Rebours,* 53, 105–6; inspiration for writing, 97, 103, 104, 105–6, 107; and Surrealists, 105. *See also* Nightmares
Dulac, Marie-Charles, 31

"L'Exposition des Indépendants en 1880", 36, 38, 72, 77, 121
"L'Exposition des Indépendants en 1881", 39, 47, 57, 80

Fantastic, 100, 101, 104. *See also* Huysmans, works of: fantastic in; Redon, Odilon; Moreau, Gustave
Fantasy, 101, 103, 104. *See also* Huysmans, works of: fantasy in; Redon, Odilon; Moreau, Gustave

Fénéon, Félix, 12, 67
Flaubert, Gustave, 128
Flémalle, Maître de: *Virgin and Child*, 34, 62, 64
Forain, Jean-Louis: diminishing favorite of Huysmans, 47; favorite of Huysmans, 4, 20, 36, 48, 50, 72, 101; misogynist, 34, 39, 40, 41, 49; position regarding Impressionists, 68; subject of Huysmans article, 33, 38, 40, 47, 62, 121; views of prostitutes, 45; views on women, 41, 43, 65, 76, 135

Gautier, Théophile, 3, 134
Germany, Beuron, 29, 30
Goncourt brothers, 4, 104
de Goncourt, Edmond, 2
Goya, Francisco, 117, 120, 128, 131
Greuze, Jean-Baptiste: *La Cruche cassée*, 18, 41
Grünewald, Matthias, 13, 14, 23, 24, 62; *Crucifixion*, 4, 6, 22, 23, 32, 46, 135

Hallucinations, 106, 112. *See also* Huysmans, works of: hallucinations in; Redon, Odilon
Holland: Huysmans' disappointment in, 18; view of, 17. *See also* Huysmans: travels of; Art, Dutch and Flemish
Huysmans, Joris-Karl: aesthetic of melancholy, 76, 77; art critic, 4, 5, 8, 11–12, 13, 14, 17–18, 19, 33, 36, 38, 39, 43, 45, 50, 62, 100, 105, 112, 133, 134; aspects of character, 64; autobiographical elements in works, 134; career, 4, 11, 12–13; conversion to Catholicism, 25, 26, 32, 35; correspondence: with Jules Destrée, 22, 106, 108; with Edmond de Goncourt, 2; with Abbé Moeller, 31; with Gabriel Mourey, 101, 131; with Edmond Picard, 109; with Arij Prins, 106; with Odilon Redon, 110; with Emile Zola, 105, 106, 107; death, 32, 49; depressing view of life, 11, 19, 20, 26, 45, 76, 81–82, 89, 100–101, 118, 124; development as writer, 133; faith in own abilities, 21; health, 22, 32; interest in supernatural, 20, 45, 109; love of painting, 11; painterly descriptions, 7; self criticism, 28; sensual pleasures, 11, 33; stylistic devices, 37–38, 40, 43, 55, 86, 93, 95, 126, 134; metaphor, 37, 40, 84; narrative, 38; simile, 37, 40; travels: as child, 17; as adult, 17–18, 22, 23, 37, 62; works:
—*L'Actualité*, 19, 71, 77
—*L'Art moderne*, 1, 12, 13, 18, 20, 36, 41, 43, 44, 45, 47, 50, 52, 54, 68, 71, 74, 75, 80,

83, 101, 105, 108,110, 112, 113, 114, 115, 129
—"Ballade chlorotique": fantastic in, 104; hallucinations in, 104
—"La Bièvre", 87, 90
—"Le Cabaret des peupliers", 90; nature and poverty, 90
—"Camaïeu rouge", 121, 122; color red, 121; dreams vs. reality, 104; dreams and visions, 104; mirrors, 122
—*La Cathédrale*, 13, 27, 28, 29, 30, 31, 60, 61, 62, 127; confusion, 96; symbolism, 125
—"Cauchemar", 127, 129; as art criticism, 117; as fiction, 117; images in, 117; nightmare in, 106, 117, 118, 119; pessimism in, 118; precursor to *En Rade*, 119; presence of narrator, 118
—*Certains*, 1, 12, 13, 45, 47, 96, 108, 128; criticism of Cézanne, 74
—*Croquis parisiens*, 33, 38, 56, 70, 72, 80, 87, 95, 117, 120; hallucinations, 105; nature, 89; nightmares, 105; presence of narrator, 117; psychological, 117; symbolism, 88
—"Damiens", 106, 120, 121, 132; depression, 124; hallucinations, 120, 123; mirrors, 122; narrator, 120, 121; nightmares, 120; physical suffering, 120; spiritual suffering, 120
—*Le Drageoir aux épices*, 3, 15, 33; dreams, 104; hallucinations, 107
—*Là-Bas*, 6, 20, 21, 23, 45, 56; Madame Chantelouve, 34, 35, 48, 56, 63; Des Hermies, 22, 37; disease imagery, 100; dreams and reality, 107; Durtal, 5, 23, 25, 26, 37, 48, 54, 83, 99, 107; fantastic, 100; hallucinations, 107; landscape contrast with Impressionism, 99; melancholy, 99; nightmares, 98, 107; phallic representation of nature, 100
—*Marthe*, 86, 95; color in, 85, 87–88; fantasy, 6; Naturalism, 19, 33, 72; prostitution, 14, 39, 40, 43, 90, 120, 121
—*En Ménage*, 2, 33, 74, 79, 104
—"Le Monstre", 128; birth of idea for, 129; loss of religious symbolism, 129; purpose of monster, 128
—"L'Oblat", 29, 127
—"Obsession", 106
—"L'Ouverture de Tannhaeuser", 48, 56, 57, 119
—*En Rade*, 16, 21, 34, 39, 57–58, 79, 107; beginnings of, 106; castle, 94; color, 98; confusion, 94, 95; depression, 97, 124; dreams, 94, 97, 107, 123, 125, 126, 127, 128; fantastic, 101, 124; hallucinations, 124, 125, 127; Jacques Marles, 82, 83, 94, 96–97, 98, 124–25, 126, 127, 128; Louise

Marles, 94, 126, 127; moon, 126, 127; Naturalism, 128; nightmares, 98, 119; pessimistic view of nature, 93–94, 95–96, 97, 99, 115; psychological suffering, 94; sexual imagery, 126; subconscious, 97; supernatural, 125; symbolism, 125; witches, 128
—*A Rebours*, 2, 3, 5, 6–7, 16, 17–18, 21, 34, 37, 44, 45, 49, 50, 91, 92–93, 94, 98, 104, 105; art as escape, 112; artificial vs. real, 115; des Esseintes, 2, 3, 6, 13, 14, 34, 42, 45, 49, 52, 53, 54, 56, 58, 59, 82, 89, 92, 93, 97, 99, 103, 104, 105; dreams, 97, 105, 116; image of women, 60, 116; model for des Esseintes, 52; nightmares, 100, 107, 115, 116, 117; preference for suffering, 112; sleep as escape, 116
—"La Rive gauche", 83–84, 85, 87, 93
—*En Route*, 25, 49, 62, 65, 83, 88; Durtal, 49, 88–89; image of woman to Durtal, 60
—"La Rue de Chine", 90
—*Sainte Lydwine de Schiedam*, 14, 31, 49
—*Les Soeurs Vatard*, 33, 41, 72, 86, 95, 104
—*Trois Primitifs*, 1, 13, 24, 34, 62
—*A Vau-l'eau*, 104, 105
—*Vue des remparts du Nord-Paris*, 91; soot, 91

Imagery, 34; animal, 16, 35, 36, 37, 38, 39, 40, 41, 44; death, 76, 79, 83, 104; disease, 84, 100, 115; female, 44, 45; kitchen, 23; machine, 37, 43, 44; medical, 23; mineral, 15; mirrors, 122; musical instruments, 41; nature, 44, 76; physiological, 16; plant, 16, 23; religious, 23, 27, 32, 60; sex, 126; soot, 76, 79, 88, 91, 93; warfare, 38. *See also* Huysmans, works of; Symbolism
Impressionism, 4, 14, 19, 20, 35, 50, 51, 66, 84; abstract form vs. significance, 69; color, use of, 72, 73, 98, 99, 101; contrast with Huysmans' view of life, 70–71; Huysmans' defense of, 101, 105; Huysmans' dissatisfaction with, 70, 75, 135; Huysmans' views on, 72, 103, 135; method, 70; rejection of Academics, 71; substance vs. technique, 69
Industrialization: factories, 79; Huysmans' ambivalence toward, 78–79

Lemaire, Michael, 92
Lenz, Peter, 29, 30
Louvre, Musée du, 4, 14, 26, 61

Mallarmé, Stéphane, 3, 51, 56, 106; *Hérodiade*, 59, 60, 89, 123
Manet, Edouard, 35, 71; *Nana*, 34, 35
Marx, Roger, 12

Millet, Jean François, 77, 81
Misogyny, 11, 103, 135. *See also:* Women; Degas; Forain; Moreau; Rops
Modernity, 4, 18, 19, 78
Monastery, artistic, 4, 29, 30
Moreau, Gustave: *L'Apparition*, 49, 52, 54, 58; and fantastic, 20; favorite of Huysmans, 2, 14, 50, 105; Huysmans critical of, 61; inspiration for Huysmans, 106; in *A Rebours*, 6, 34, 53, 54, 112, 123; precursor to Surrealists, 51; *Salomé*, 5, 23, 49, 52, 54, 55, 56, 59; subject of Huysmans' writing, 13, 15, 20, 62
Morisot, Berthe, 72
Mourey, Gabriel, 101, 131
Mugnier, Abbé, 25, 31, 62
Musée des Deux-Mondes, 41, 122–23
Mysticism, 107; in art, 129–30; in Catholicism, 107; defined by Redon, 130

Narrator: in "Cauchemar", 118, in *Croquis parisiens*, 117, in "Damiens", 120; perceptions of, 120
Naturalism, 5, 13, 19, 21, 71, 81, 104, 107, 134, 135; art compared to photography, 20; end of use in works, 105; and Huysmans, 1, 4, 6, 8, 11, 14, 33, 41, 71, 73, 80, 84, 91, 94
Nature: Huysmans' mournful views on, 4, 45, 77, 84, 85, 87–88, 90, 91, 92, 93, 94, 95–96, 97, 99, 103; phallic representation of, 100; as woman, 91
Nightmares, 106; in *La-Bas*, 98, 107; in *En Rade*, 16, 79; in *A Rebours*, 6, 100, 104
Nineteenth century, 25; artistic environment of, 1, 2

Oblature, 31, 60, 83

Paintings: emulated in literature, 2, 3, 86, 92, 95, 97, 133–34; evoked by text, 6
Picard, Edmond, 109, 110
Pissarro, Camille, 69, 72, 74, 78
Prins, Arij, 22, 28, 106
Proust, Marcel, 27

Raffaëlli, Jean François, 4, 20, 72, 82, 86; favorite of Huysmans, 67, 76, 101, 103; Huysmans' loss of interest in, 79; imagery of factories, 80; imagery of nature, 76, 79, 91, 93, 94, 100–101; imagery of people, 80; minor Impressionist, 67; *Vue de Gennevilliers*, 77, 80; *Vue de Seine*, 86
Reality, escape through: art, 15, 16, 20, 123, 134; dreams, 104; fantastic, 104; literature, 135; religion, 25, 83; sleep, 116

Redon, Odilon, 13, 16, 20, 79, 103, 112–13;
admired by Huysmans, 105, 108, 117;
compared to Moreau, 129; correspondence with André Mellerio, 111; exhibits
of, 109–10, 111, 112; friendship with
Huysmans, 110; influence on Huysmans,
103; influence on Huysmans' works: *A
Rebours*, 116, 117, 131; "Cauchemar", 5;
and subconscious, 135; works of: *A Soi-
même*, 108; confusion in, 109; dreams in,
103–4, 105, 107, 108, 109, 111; dreams as
escape in, 104; fantasy in, 103, 104, 105,
107, 108, 112; hallucinations in, 112;
macabre in, 109; medieval art in, 129;
microscopic plant and animal influence in,
129, 130; nature in, 115; women in, 111
Rembrandt van Rijn, 15, 18, 28, 48; *Flayed
Ox*, 16, 23
Renoir, Pierre Auguste, 72
Riffaterre, Michael, 83
Rops, Félicien, 4, 34, 41, 45, 47, 48, 49;
Huysmans' views on, 62; views on women,
56, 63, 66, 76, 135
Rosicrucians, 29, 30
Rousseau, Henri, 75, 77
Rubens, Peter Paul: *Kermesse de Rubens, La*,
16
Ruysdael, Jacob van: images of nature, 76, 77

Saint-Sulpice, Church of, 27, 30, 83
Schubert, Franz, 93
Schwob, Marcel, 21
Sérusier, Paul, 30
Sex, 37, 42, 45, 49, 51, 100, 103, 126; and evil,
61; and perversity, 34; integrated with
religion, 60

Sisley, Alfred, 72
Spiritual naturalism, 4, 6, 22, 46, 64, 107, 135
Subconscious, 103, 104, 106, 107, 135
Surrealists, 51; and dreams, 105
Symbolism, 73, 80, 89, 94, 101. *See also*
Individual works
Symbolists, 49, 51, 73
Symons, Arthur, 8, 12

Teniers, David, 17, 74
Todorov, Tzvetan, 124
Trudgian, Helen, 7, 62, 68, 81, 133

Valery, Paul, 49, 51, 69, 70
Virtue: and evil, 61; through evil, 46
Visual arts, 1, 2, 3; influence on writing, 134;
integrated with writing, 15

Wade, Clair, 94; light and color in Huysmans,
86
van der Weyden, Roger, 22, 61, 64
Women, 4, 20, 41, 42–43, 49, 86, 103; as
animals, 35; symbols of death, 104;
depiction in works, 33–34; evil, 47–48, 52,
56, 65; as prostitutes, 33, 35, 38–40, 45,
47, 51, 56, 90, 120–21; in Redon, 111. *See
also* Degas; Forain; Imagery; Moreau;
Rops; Symbolism
Working class: Huysmans' fascination with,
81, 84, 86–87

Zayed, Fernande, 7
Zola, Emile, 7, 15, 19, 20, 104, 105;
correspondence with Huysmans, 106;
Naturalism in, 20, 23, 33, 106; rift with
Huysmans, 106